VICTOR HUGO,

novelist, poet and dramatist, was born in Besançon on February 26, 1802. Because Hugo's father was a general in Napoleon's army, his family spent much time in various parts of Europe, moving frequently between Corsica, Spain, Italy and Paris. It was during this early part of his life that Hugo began writing, and by the age of fourteen he had already produced a sizable body of work. In 1819, Victor, with his brother Abel, established the literary journal *Conservateur littérature*, a review associated primarily with the romantic movement. Hugo first gained notoriety for his poetry, receiving a pension from Louis XVIII for his first collection, *Odes et poesies diverses*, published in 1822. Within the next four years, he added two more volumes, *Nouvelle Odes* (1824) and *Odes et ballades* (1826). Hugo's first published prose work appear in 1823 and in 1831 he completed *The Hunchback of Notre Dame*.

Though attributed to his egotism by some, Hugo possessed the grand notion that the poet was to be the one who would lead mankind toward perfection. With this idea, and the influence of Sir Walter Scott, Hugo created works of epic scale. Several of his plays dealt with important historical figures, among them *Lucretia Borgia* (1833) and *Mary Tudor* (1833); this large-scale sensibility is also present in *The Hunchback* and Hugo's most famous novel, *Les Misérables* (1862).

Hugo carried his belief in the importance of the poet's mission into the political arena as well. An outspoken advocate of free compulsory education and universal suffrage, Hugo was elected to the French Academy in 1841 and appointed a seat in Parliament in 1845. He was forced to flee France in 1851 because of his opposition to Prince Louis Napoleon's claim to the title of emperor of France. While in exile Hugo wrote anti-imperial pamphlets and finally returned in 1870 after the empire's fall. Though appointed to the newly formed Senate in 1874, Hugo's political involvement was more limited than it had been previously. In May 1885, Hugo died. His b Triomphe and was then pla in a pauper's bier and borr Panthéon.

Bantam Classics
Ask your bookseller for these other World Classics

CANDIDE by Voltaire
THE PRINCE by Machiavelli
CYRANO DE BERGERAC by Edmond Rostand
THE COUNT OF MONTE CRISTO by Alexandre Dumas
THE HUNCHBACK OF NOTRE DAME by Victor Hugo
MADAME BOVARY by Gustave Flaubert
ANNA KARENINA by Leo Tolstoy
THE DEATH OF IVAN ILYICH by Leo Tolstoy
FATHERS AND SONS by Ivan Turgenev
THE BROTHERS KARAMAZOV by Fyodor Dostoevsky
CRIME AND PUNISHMENT by Fyodor Dostoevsky
THE IDIOT by Fyodor Dostoevsky

The Hunchback of Notre Dame by Victor Hugo

Translated and Abridged by Lowell Bair

BANTAM BOOKS

TORONTO · NEW YORK · LONDON · SYDNEY · AUCKLAND

RL 8, IL 8+

THE HUNCHBACK OF NOTRE DAME
A Bantam Book

PRINTING HISTORY
The Hunchback of Notre Dame *was first published in 1831.*
First Bantam edition / December 1956
Bantam Classic edition / March 1981

Library of Congress Catalog Card Number: 56-11120

Cover photograph by J. Alex Langley
Courtesy of DPI

ISBN 0-553-21032-7

Published simultaneously in the United States and Canada

Bantam Books are published by Bantam Books, Inc. Its trade-
mark, consisting of the words "Bantam Books" and the por-
trayal of a bantam, is Registered in U.S. Patent and Trademark
Office and in other countries. Marca Registrada. Bantam
Books, Inc., 666 Fifth Avenue, New York, New York 10103.

PRINTED IN THE UNITED STATES OF AMERICA

O   0 9 8 7 6 5 4

Table of Contents

BOOK VIII

BOOK IX

THE HUNCHBACK OF NOTRE DAME

Book I

CHAPTER ONE

The Great Hall of the Palace of Justice

ON JANUARY 6, 1482, THE PEOPLE OF PARIS WERE AWAKENED by the tumultuous clanging of all the bells in the city. Yet history has kept no memory of this date, for there was nothing notable about the event which set in motion the bells and the citizens of Paris that morning. It was not an attack by the Picards or the Burgundians, a procession carrying the relics of some saint, an entry of "Our Most Dreaded Lord, Monsieur the King," nor even a good hanging of thieves.

Nor was it the arrival of some foreign ambassador and his train, all decked out in lace and feathers, a common sight in the fifteenth century. It had been scarcely two days since the latest cavalcade of this kind had paraded through the streets: the delegation of Flemish ambassadors sent to conclude the marriage between the Dauphin and Marguerite of Flanders. To his great annoyance, Cardinal de Bourbon, in order to please the king, had been obliged to give a gracious reception to that uncouth band of Flemish burgomasters and entertain them in his mansion.

The cause of all the commotion on the sixth of January was the double holiday of the Epiphany and the Festival of Fools, united since time immemorial. This year the celebration was to include a bonfire at the Place de Grève, a maypole dance at the Chapelle de Braque and the performance of a play in the Palace of Justice, all of which had been announced

1

by public proclamation the day before. All shops were to remain closed for the holiday.

Early in the morning the crowd began streaming toward
the three designated places, each person having decided on
either the bonfire, the maypole or the play. It is a tribute to
the ancient common sense of the people of Paris that the
majority of the crowd went to either the bonfire, which was
quite seasonable, or the play, which was to be performed in
the shelter of the great hall of the palace, leaving the poor
maypole to shiver beneath the January sky in the cemetery of
the Chapelle de Braque.

The avenues leading to the Palace of Justice were particularly crowded because it was known that the Flemish ambassadors, who had arrived two days before, were planning to
attend the play and the election of the Pope of Fools, which
was also to be held in the palace.

It was not easy to get into the great hall that day, even
though it was reputed at the time to be the largest single
room in the world. To the spectators looking out of their
windows, the square in front of the palace, packed solid with
people, presented the appearance of a sea, with five or six
streets flowing into it, constantly disgorging a stream of heads.
The waves of this sea broke against the corners of the houses
jutting out like promontories into the irregular basin of the
square. Shouts, laughter and the shuffling of thousands of
feet blended to produce a mighty uproar.

At the doors and windows and on the rooftops swarmed a
myriad of sober, honest faces, looking at the palace and the
crowd with placid contentment. Many Parisians still find deep
satisfaction in watching people who are watching something;
even a wall behind which something is happening is an object
of great curiosity to them.

Let us now imagine that immense oblong hall inside the
palace, illuminated by the pale light of a January day and
invaded by a motley and noisy crowd pouring in along the
walls and swirling around the seven great pillars. In the middle
of the hall, high up and against one wall, an enclosed gallery
had been erected for the Flemish ambassadors and the other
important personages who had been invited to see the play.
A private entrance opened into it through one of the windows.

At one end of the hall was the famous marble table, so
long, wide and thick that "such a slab of marble has never
been seen before on earth," as an old document puts it. The

play was to be performed on this table, according to custom. It had been set up for that purpose early in the morning. A high wooden platform had been placed on it, the top of which was to serve as the stage. Tapestries hung around the sides formed a sort of dressing room for the actors underneath. A ladder, undisguisedly propped up against the outside of the platform, connected the dressing room and the stage and served for entrances and exits alike. Every actor, no matter how unexpected his appearance in the play, and every stage effect, had to come laboriously up that ladder in full view of the audience.

Four sergeants of the bailiff of the palace, whose duty was to keep order among the people at festivals as well as executions, stood at each corner of the huge marble table.

The play was not scheduled to begin until the great clock of the palace struck noon—quite late for a theatrical performance, but it had been necessary to arrange the hour to suit the convenience of the ambassadors.

Many of the people had been shivering before the steps of the palace since dawn and some declared they had spent the whole night huddled in the great doorway in order to make sure of being among the first to enter. The crowd was growing denser at every moment and, like a river overflowing its banks, it soon began to rise up the walls and spill over onto the cornices, architraves, window ledges and all other projecting features of the architecture. Discomfort, impatience, boredom, the freedom of a day of license, the quarrels constantly breaking out over a sharp elbow or a hobnailed shoe, the fatigue of a long wait—all this gave a tone of bitterness to the clamor of the people as they stood squeezed together, jostled, trampled on and almost smothered. The air was full of complaints and insults against the Flemings, Cardinal de Bourbon, the bailiff of the palace, the sergeants, the cold, the heat, the bad weather, the Bishop of Paris, the Pope of Fools, the pillars, the statues, this closed door, that open window; all to the great amusement of a band of students and lackeys who, scattered throughout the crowd, mixed in their jibes and sarcasm with all that dissatisfaction and thus goaded the general bad humor into becoming even worse.

Some of these merry demons had knocked the glass out of one of the windows and were boldly sitting in it. From there they were able to direct their bantering remarks both inside and outside, toward the crowd in the hall and the crowd in the square. From their mimicking gestures, their loud laugh-

ter and the ribald jokes they exchanged with their comrades
from one end of the hall to the other, it was easy to see that
they did not share the boredom and fatigue of the rest of the
spectators and that they were able to extract enough entertainment from the scene spread out before their eyes to avoid
being impatient for the scheduled performance to begin.

"My God, there's Jehan Frollo!" shouted one of them to
a small blond young man with a handsome, mischievous face
who was clinging to the carved foliage at the top of one of
the pillars. "How long have you been here?"

"More than four hours, by the devil's mercy!" replied
Jehan. "And I hope the time will be taken off my term in
purgatory!"

Just then the clock struck noon.

"Ah!" said the whole crowd with satisfaction. The students
became silent and there ensued a noisy shuffling of feet, a
general craning of necks and a mighty explosion of coughing
as each person stood up and placed himself in the best position to see the stage. Then there was silence. All heads were
thrust forward, all mouths were open and all eyes were turned
toward the great marble table. But nothing appeared on it. The
four sergeants were still there, as stiff and motionless as four
painted statues. The crowd looked up at the gallery reserved
for the Flemish ambassadors. It was empty and the door leading into it remained shut. They had been waiting since morning for three things: noon, the Flemish ambassadors and the
play. Noon was the only one to arrive in time.

This was too much. They waited for one, two, three, five
minutes, a quarter of an hour; nothing happened. The gallery and the stage were still deserted. Impatience began to
turn into anger. An irritated murmur sprang up from one
end of the hall to the other: "The play! The play! The play!"
A storm, which was as yet only rumbling in the distance, began to gather over the crowd. It was Jehan Frollo who made
it burst.

"Let's have the play, and to hell with the Flemings!" he
yelled at the top of his lungs, twisting around his pillar like
a serpent. The crowd applauded.

"The play!" they repeated. "And to hell with Flanders!"

"If they won't show us the play," went on the student, "I
think we ought to hang the bailiff of the palace for entertainment!"

"That's right," shouted the people "and let's start by hanging the sergeants!"

Loud cheers broke out. The poor sergeants turned pale and looked at one another anxiously. They saw the frail wooden balustrade which separated them from the crowd begin to give way as the people pressed forward in a body. It was a critical moment.

At that instant the tapestries forming the dressing room, as we have described above, parted to make way for a man who climbed up on the stage. As if by magic, the sight of him suddenly changed the crowd's anger into curiosity.

"Silence! Silence!"

Quaking with fear, the man walked unsteadily to the front of the stage with profuse bows which almost became genuflections as he came closer. Meanwhile calm had been pretty much restored. There remained only the slight murmur which always rises above the silence of a crowd.

"Ladies and gentlemen," he began, "we have the honor to perform before His Eminence the Cardinal a very fine morality play entitled *The Wise Decision of Our Lady the Virgin*. I shall play the part of Jupiter. His Eminence is at this moment accompanying the honorable ambassadors of the Duke of Austria, who are listening to a speech by the rector of the University. As soon as His Eminence arrives we shall begin."

It is certain that nothing less than the intervention of Jupiter could have saved the four unfortunate sergeants. His costume was superb, which contributed considerably toward calming the crowd by attracting their attention. He was wearing a brigandine covered with black velvet, Greek sandals and a helmet adorned with imitation silver buttons. In his hand he held a roll of gilded cardboard covered with strips of tinsel which the experienced eyes of the audience easily recognized as a thunderbolt.

CHAPTER TWO

Pierre Gringoire

THE UNANIMOUS ADMIRATION AND SATISFACTION PRODUCED by his costume was, however, soon dissipated by his words. When he arrived at the unfortunate conclusion. "As soon as His Eminence arrives, we shall begin," his voice was lost in a thunderous outburst of disapproval.

"Start it right now! The play! The play right now!" shouted the people. Jehan Frollo's voice could be heard piercing the uproar like a fife in a village band. "Start it right now," he screeched.

"Down with Jupiter and Cardinal de Bourbon!" vociferated the other students, perched in the window.

"The play!" repeated the crowd. "Right away! String up the actors and the cardinal!"

Poor Jupiter, terror-stricken, bewildered and pale under his make-up, dropped his thunderbolt, took off his helmet, made a trembling bow and stammered, "His Eminence . . . the ambassadors . . ." He stopped, unable to think of anything else to say. He was afraid he would be hanged by the people if he waited and hanged by the cardinal if he did not. Whichever way he looked he saw the gallows.

Fortunately, someone came forward at this moment to assume responsibility and extricate him from his dilemma. No one had yet noticed a tall, slender young man standing against a pillar between the balustrade and the marble table. He had blond hair, shining eyes, smiling lips and, despite his youth, a number of wrinkles in his forehead and cheeks. His black serge garment was old and threadbare. He stepped up to the marble table and motioned to the wretched actor, but the latter was too panic-stricken to notice him. He stepped closer and said, "Jupiter!" The actor did not hear him. The tall young man shouted almost in his ear, "Michel Giborne!"

"Who is it?" exclaimed Jupiter, starting as if he had been suddenly awakened from a deep sleep.

"It's I."

"Oh," said Jupiter.

"Begin right away. Satisfy the crowd. I'll appease the bailiff and he'll appease the cardinal."

Jupiter heaved a sigh of relief. "Ladies and gentlemen," he shouted to the crowd, who continued to hoot him, "we are going to begin immediately."

There was a deafening outburst of applause which lasted for some time after Jupiter had withdrawn behind the tapestry.

Meanwhile the unknown young man who had so magically calmed the tempest modestly retired to the shadow of his pillar, where he would no doubt have remained as invisible, motionless and silent as before if it had not been for two young ladies who, being in the front rank of the spectators, had overheard his brief conversation with Michel Giborne-Jupiter.

"Master," said one of them, motioning him to come closer.

"Hush, Liénarde," said her companion, a pretty, fresh-looking girl decked out in her Sunday best. "You're not supposed to call a layman 'master'; just call him 'sir.'"

"Sir," said Liénarde.

The stranger stepped up to the balustrade. "What can I do for you, ladies?" he asked eagerly.

"Oh, nothing," said Liénarde, embarrassed. "My friend here, Gisquette la Gencienne, wanted to talk to you."

"I did not!" exclaimed Gisquette, blushing. "Liénarde called you 'master'; I just told her she ought to call you 'sir' instead."

The two girls lowered their eyes. The young man, who would have liked nothing better than to strike up a conversation with them, looked at them with a smile.

"You have nothing to say to me, then?"

"Oh, nothing at all," answered Gisquette.

"Nothing," said Liénarde.

The tall blond man turned to go away. But the two curious girls were not inclined to let him leave so soon.

"Sir," said Gisquette abruptly, with the impetuosity of water bursting through a floodgate or a woman making up her mind, "do you know the soldier who has the part of the Virgin Mary in the play?"

"You mean the part of Jupiter?" asked the stranger.

"Of course," said Liénarde. "She's so stupid! Well, do you know Jupiter?"

"Michel Giborne? Yes, madame."

"He has a fine beard!" said Liénarde.

"Will it be a good play?" asked Gisquette timidly.

"Very good," answered the stranger without the slightest hesitation.

"What's it about?" asked Liénarde.

"It's called *The Wise Decision of Our Lady the Virgin*—a morality play, madame."

"Oh, that's different," said Liénarde.

There was a short silence. The stranger broke it: "This is a brand-new morality play. It's never been performed before."

"Then it's not the same one," said Gisquette, "that was given two years ago for the reception of the legate, the one with three pretty girls playing the parts of . . ."

"Mermaids," finished Liénarde.

"And all naked," added the young man. Liénarde lowered her eyes modestly. Gisquette looked at her and did likewise. He went on, smiling, "It was a very pleasant sight, too. But today it's a morality play written especially for the Princess of Flanders."

"Are you sure it's a good play?" asked Gisquette.

"Of course," he answered. Then he added, with a trace of pompousness, "Ladies, I am the author of the play."

"Really?" said the two young girls, full of wonder.

"Really," answered the poet proudly. "My name is Pierre Gringoire."

The reader has no doubt noticed that a certain amount of time has elapsed between the moment when Jupiter withdrew behind the tapestry and the moment when the author of the new morality play suddenly revealed himself to the naïve admiration of Gisquette and Liénarde. It was remarkable to see how the crowd, who had been so tumultuous a few minutes before, were now waiting quietly and humbly. It was one more proof of that eternal truth which is still being proved every day in our theaters: that the best way to make an audience wait is to announce that the performance is about to begin.

But Jehan Frollo was not asleep at his post. "Hey there, Jupiter! Our Lady the Virgin!" he suddenly cried out in the midst of the peaceful expectation which had succeeded the disturbance. "What are you doing in there, telling each other jokes? Start the play or we'll start again!"

This was enough to set things in motion. An orchestra concealed behind the tapestry began to play and four actors in heavy make-up and brightly colored costumes climbed up the steep ladder to the stage, ranged themselves in a line before the audience and made a deep bow. The music stopped; the play was really about to begin this time.

The four actors, after being amply repaid for their bows by applause, launched into a prologue which we gladly spare the reader. Besides, then as now, the audience was much more interested in examining the actors' costumes than in listening to what they had to say. They wore white and yellow robes which were identical except for the cloth of which they were made: the first was made of gold and silver brocade, the second of silk, the third of wool and the fourth of linen. The first actor held a sword in his hand, the second two golden keys, the third a pair of scales and the fourth a spade. Then, in order to aid those whose minds were so lazy as not to grasp the meaning of these symbols, the words "My name is Nobility" were embroidered in black letters on the bottom of the brocade robe, "My name is Clergy" on the silk one, "My name is Commerce" on the woolen one and "My name is Agriculture" on the linen one. The sex of the two male characters was made obvious to any perceptive spectator by their hats and the relative shortness of their robes, while the two female characters wore hoods and longer robes.

And it would have taken an exceedingly obtuse spectator not to gather from the poetry of the prologue that Agriculture was married to Commerce and Clergy to Nobility, and that these two happy couples possessed in common a magnificent golden dolphin which they intended to present to the most beautiful woman in the world. They were therefore wandering all over the earth in search of this beauty. After successively rejecting the Queen of Golconda, the Princess of Trebizond, the daughter of the Khan of Tartary and many others, they had come to rest on the great marble table of the Palace of Justice to regale the honest audience with a flood of resounding maxims and judgments.

Meanwhile, in all that crowd there was no ear more attentive, no heart more palpitating, no eye more anxious and no neck more oustretched than those of the author, the worthy Pierre Gringoire. He had stepped back behind his pillar, from where he watched, listened to and relished everything going on. The benevolent applause which had welcomed the beginning of his prologue was still ringing in his ears and he was completely lost in that kind of ecstatic absorption with which an author hears his ideas fall one by one from the mouth of an actor into the silence of a vast auditorium.

It is painful to record the fact, but the spell of that first ecstasy was soon broken. A ragged beggar, who had been unable to collect any contributions squeezed in among the crowd and who had no doubt not found sufficient compensation in the pockets of his neighbors, had conceived the idea of placing himself in some conspicuous position in order to attract more attention and alms. During the first verses of the prologue, therefore, he had climbed up one of the columns supporting the reserved gallery and perched himself on the cornice immediately below the balustrade. From there he silently solicited the pity of the crowd with his tattered rags and the hideous sore which covered his right arm.

The prologue was proceeding smoothly and no disaster

would have occurred if misfortune had not decreed that Jehan was to notice the beggar and his grimaces from the top of his pillar. The young student was seized with a fit of wild laughter and, caring nothing about interrupting the performance and disturbing the calm which had settled over the whole audience, he cried out merrily, "Look at that rascal begging up there!"

Anyone who has ever thrown a stone into a pond full of frogs or shot into a flock of birds will be able to imagine the effect which these incongruous words produced amid the general silence and attention. Gringoire started as if he had received an electric shock. The prologue stopped short and all heads turned toward the beggar, who, far from feeling embarrassed, saw the incident as a good opportunity to make a collection and began to say dolefully, with half-closed eyes, "Charity, if you please."

"Well, if it isn't Clopin Trouillefou!" exclaimed Jehan. "Hey there, my friend, I see you've put your sore on your arm—was it uncomfortable on your leg?"

As he said this he tossed a small coin into the greasy hat which the beggar was holding out with his ailing arm. He accepted both the money and the sarcasm without batting an eye and went on wailing piteously, "Charity, if you please."

Gringoire was extremely displeased. As soon as he recovered from his first stupefaction, he yelled angrily to the four actors on the stage, "Go on, for God's sake, go on!" without deigning to cast even a scornful glance at the two men who had caused the interruption.

The actors obeyed his orders, the audience began to listen again and tranquillity was gradually restored. The student kept silent and the beggar counted the coins in his hat; the play was once again the center of attention.

Suddenly, in the midst of an argument between Commerce and Nobility, just as Agriculture was pronouncing this splendid line:

A more triumphant beast was ne'er in forest seen,

the door of the reserved gallery, which had so far remained so unseasonably closed, was even more unseasonably opened and the sonorous voice of the usher abruptly announced,

"His Eminence, Cardinal de Bourbon."

CHAPTER THREE

The Cardinal and the Hosier

POOR GRINGOIRE! HIS WORST FEARS WERE REALIZED. THE cardinal's entrance threw the audience into commotion. All eyes turned toward the gallery. Nothing could be heard except the words, "The cardinal! The cardinal!" repeated on all sides. The ill-starred prologue was cut short a second time.

The cardinal paused for a moment on the threshold of the gallery. The tumult redoubled as he cast a rather indifferent glance over the audience.

He was, to be sure, an extremely distinguished personage, the sight of whom was easily worth as much as any play. He was a handsome man and he had a fine red robe which he wore very gracefully. He greeted the people with a lofty smile and walked slowly to his chair, looking as though his mind were occupied elsewhere. His staff of bishops and abbés followed him into the gallery, which increased the spectators' curiosity. Everyone was eager to point them out, to tell their names, to recognize at least one of them.

As for the students, they swore. It was their day, the Festival of Fools, the annual orgy and saturnalia of clerks and scholars. There was no outrage which was not permitted on that day. Was it not the least they could do to curse a little in the name of God on such a fine day and in the presence of eminent churchmen? They made good use of their license: above the general uproar rose a chorus of horrible blasphemies from the clerks and students.

But the cardinal's expression showed that he was preoccupied with something else, namely the Flemish ambassadors, who arrived in the gallery at almost the same time he did. It was hard for him, Charles de Bourbon, a cardinal, a Frenchman and a connoisseur of good living, to be obliged to welcome a party of ordinary Flemish burgomasters who were given to drinking beer—and in public, too. It was one of the most disagreeable tasks he had ever performed to please the king. Yet when the ushers announced the ambassadors he turned toward the door with the most gracious manner possible, for he had studied his part well. It is needless to add that the entire audience did likewise.

While the cardinal and the leaders of the Flemish delegation were exchanging bows and salutations, a tall, broadshouldered man stepped into the entrance of the gallery. His felt hat and leather jacket were glaringly conspicuous amid all the velvet and silk which surrounded him. Assuming that he was some groom who had wandered into the wrong place, the usher stopped him:

"No admittance here, friend."

The man in the leather jacket pushed him aside with his shoulder. "What's wrong with you, you fool?" he exclaimed in a loud voice which instantly drew the attention of the whole audience. "Can't you see I'm part of the delegation?"

"Your name?" asked the usher.

"Jacques Coppenole."

"Your title?"

"Hosier, at the sign of the Three Chains in Ghent."

The usher was staggered. It was hard enough to have to announce burgomasters, but a hosier—that was going too far. The cardinal, hoping to smooth out the difficulty, said to the usher, "Announce Master Jacques Coppenole, Clerk to the Burgomasters of the City of Ghent."

This was a mistake, for Coppenole overheard the cardinal's instructions. "No, by God!" he thundered. "Jacques Coppenole, hosier! Do you understand, usher? No more, no less. There's nothing wrong with the title of hosier, by God!"

Laughter and cheers rang out from all over the hall. Coppenole was a man of the people and there was an immediate spark of communication between him and the audience. His haughty outburst in the face of a group of noblemen stirred in those plebeian breasts a certain feeling of dignity which was still vague and indistinct in the fifteenth century. This hosier who had just defied a cardinal was their equal—an extremely satisfying reflection to those poor devils who were accustomed to paying respect and obedience to the servants of the sergeants of the bailiff of the Abbot of Saint-Geneviève, the cardinal's train-bearer.

From the moment the cardinal entered, Pierre Gringoire had not ceased his valiant efforts to save his prologue. At first he had urged the actors to speak louder; then, seeing that no one was listening to them, he had ordered them to stop until calm was restored. He now bade them begin again and hoped that at least the remaining part of his masterpiece would be listened to.

It was not long before this hope was disappointed as bitterly as the rest. He had not noticed that the gallery was far from full when the actors resumed their parts. New members of the delegation continued to enter and the intermittent shouts of the usher announcing their names and titles disrupted the prologue in a way which was unbearable to the author. The new arrivals with their varied names, faces and costumes were a continuous diversion to the audience. No one was listening to or looking at the poor forsaken play. All around him Gringoire saw nothing but profiles. And to think that a short while before these same people had been so impatient to see his play that they were on the point of rebelling against the bailiff of the palace and hanging his sergeants! What would he not have given for the return of that delicious moment!

The usher's brutal monologue ceased at least, Gringoire began to breathe again and the actors continued bravely. But suddenly Jacques Coppenole stood up from his seat in the gallery and Gringoire was horrified to hear him make the following speech to the unanimously attentive spectators:

"Citizens of Paris: I don't know what the devil we're doing here! Down there on the stage I see some people who act as if they're about to start a fight. I've been waiting for them to start it for a quarter of an hour now, but nothing happens. They're a bunch of cowards, afraid to do anything except call each other names. I don't know if this is what you call a play, but I do know it's not amusing. You should have brought in some boxers from London or Rotterdam—then, by God, you'd have seen them knock each other around so hard you could hear it from one end of the hall to the other! But these poor fools here are pitiful. This isn't what I was told I'd see. I was told there was going to be a Festival of Fools, with the election of a pope. We have a Pope of Fools in Ghent, too, but this is how we do it: we get a big crowd together, like the one that's here right now, then, one at a time, everybody sticks his head through a hole and makes faces at the others. The one who makes the ugliest face is elected Pope of Fools. It's very amusing. Why don't we elect your pope the way we do in my country? At least it won't be as boring as listening to these actors chatter. If they want to come and make faces through the hole along with everyone else, they'll be welcome. What do you say, citizens? We've got enough ugly faces here to give us some good hearty laughs!"

Gringoire would have liked to answer him, but he was speechless with surprise, rage and indignation. Besides, the popular hosier's suggestion was received with such enthusiasm that any resistance would have been useless. There was nothing left for the poor poet to do but resign himself to being swept along with the tide.

CHAPTER FOUR

Quasimodo

IN THE TWINKLING OF AN EYE EVERYTHING WAS READY TO carry out Coppenole's idea. Townspeople, students and clerks all set to work. The chapel opposite the marble table was chosen for the scene of the election. The glass was knocked out of the small round window over the door and it was agreed that the candidates were to put their heads through it, standing on two barrels placed one on top of the other. Each candidate, man or woman (for it was also permissible to elect a "popess") was to keep his face covered and remain hidden in the chapel until it was time for him to make his appearance. In no time at all the chapel was filled with candidates and the door was closed behind them.

From his seat in the gallery, Coppenole directed and supervised everything. During the uproar, the cardinal, no less disconcerted than Gringoire, withdrew along with his staff on the pretext of urgent business. The crowd, who had been so excited by his arrival, paid hardly any attention to his departure.

The first face which appeared at the window, with its red eyes, gaping mouth and wrinkled forehead, brought forth such inextinguishable laughter that Homer would have taken those simple townspeople for immortal gods. A second face appeared, and a third, and another and another, and each time the laughter and joyous excitement redoubled. The crowd was seized with a kind of frenzied intoxication and fascination which is difficult to conceive of in our own day. Imagine a series of faces successively representing all geometrical forms, from the triangle to the trapezoid, from the cone to the polyhedron; every human expression, from anger to lasciviousness; every animal profile, from the snout to the beak, from the jowl to the muzzle; imagine all those grotesque heads carved on the Pont Neuf, those nightmares petrified under the hand of Germain Pilon, suddenly coming to life and staring at you with flaming eyes; or all the masks of the carnival of Venice passing before you in succession—in short, a human kaleidoscope.

Suddenly there was a thunderous burst of applause mingled with prodigious shouts of acclamation. The Pope of Fools had been elected.

It was indeed a wondrous face which now appeared in the round window. After all those hexagonal, pentagonal and heteroclite faces had passed in review without attaining the ideal of the grotesque which had been built up by the frenzied imagination of the crowd, nothing less than the sublimely monstrous face which now dazzled them could have obtained a unanimous vote of approval. Jacques Coppenole himself applauded and Clopin Trouillefou, who had presented himself as a candidate (and God knows the intensity of ugliness his face was capable of attaining), acknowledged his defeat. We shall do likewise and not attempt to give the reader an idea of that tetrahedron nose, that horseshoe mouth, that small left eye half hidden by a bristly red eyebrow while the right eye disappeared entirely behind an enormous wart, those irregular teeth jagged here and there like the battlements of a fortress, that horny lip over which one of those teeth protruded like an elephant's tusk, that forked chin and especially the expression spread over all this, that expression of mingled malice, amazement and sadness. Let the reader imagine it if he can.

The acclamation was unanimous. The crowd rushed into the chapel and the new Pope of Fools was brought forth in triumph. But it was then that the surprise and admiration reached their height: what had been taken for a twisted grimace was actually his natural expression.

In fact, his whole body might have been described as a twisted grimace: his huge head bristled with stiff red hair; between his shoulders was an enormous hump which had a corresponding projection in front; his legs were so strangely made that they could touch only at the knees, like two sickles with their handles joined; his feet were immense and his hands were monstrous. Yet, with all that deformity, there

was a certain air of formidable vigor, agility and courage—
a strange exception to the classic rule that strength, like
beauty, comes from harmony. The new Pope of Fools looked
like a giant who had been broken into pieces and haphazardly
put back together again.

When this Cyclops-like creature appeared on the threshold of the chapel, motionless, squat, almost as broad as he
was tall and wearing a red and purple coat covered with little
silver bells, the crowd recognized him immediately and cried
out:

"It's Quasimodo the bellringer! Quasimodo, the hunchback
of Notre Dame! One-eyed Quasimodo! Bowlegged Quasimodo! Hurrah! Hurrah!" It was obvious that the poor devil
had a wide choice of nicknames.

"Pregnant women had better look the other way!" shouted
the students.

"And those who want to be pregnant, too!" chimed in
Jehan.

Many of the women present actually did cover their faces.
"What an ugly ape!" exclaimed one.

"And he's as wicked as he is ugly," said another.

"It must be the devil himself!"

"I have the misfortune to live near Notre Dame; every
night I hear him prowling around on the roof."

"With the cats."

"He casts spells on us through the chimney."

"The other night he made a face at me through the window. It scared me half out of my wits."

"I'm sure he goes to the witches' sabbaths. One night he
left a broom on my roof."

"What a hideous hunchback!"

The men, on the other hand, were delighted and applauded
enthusiastically. Quasimodo, the cause of all the tumult, stood
gloomy and grave in the doorway of the chapel and let himself be admired.

A student came too close to him and laughed in his face.
Without a word, Quasimodo seized him by the waist and
threw him ten feet into the crowd.

Jacques Coppenole came up to him, full of wonder. "By
God!" he exclaimed, "you've got the finest ugliness I've
ever seen in my life, Holy Father! You deserve to be elected
pope in Rome as well as in Paris!" He clapped him merrily
on the shoulder as he said this. Quasimodo remained motionless. Coppenole went on: "Now here's a fellow I'd like to go

carousing with some night!" Quasimodo did not answer. "What's the matter with you, are you deaf?" said the hosier.

He actually was deaf. And he was beginning to be annoyed at the way Coppenole was acting with him. He suddenly turned on him with such a formidable snarl that the Flemish giant shrank back in surprise and fear. A circle of terror and respect at least fifteen feet in radius was instantly formed around the strange personage. An old woman explained to Coppenole that Quasimodo was deaf.

"Deaf, too!" cried the hosier, with his lusty Flemish laugh. "He's as fine a pope as anyone could ask for, by God!"

"I know him!" said Jehan, who had climbed down from the top of his pillar in order to get a closer look at Quasimodo. "He's the bellringer for my brother, the archdeacon. Hello, Quasimodo!"

"He can talk when he wants to," remarked the old woman. "He became deaf from ringing the bells, but he's not dumb."

Meanwhile a group of beggars, lackeys, pickpockets and students had brought up the cardboard tiara and the mock robe of Pope of Fools. Quasimodo let himself be decked out in them with a kind of proud docility. He was then made to sit down on a brightly colored litter. Twelve officers of the Brotherhood of Fools lifted it to their shoulders. A bitter and haughty joy spread over the gloomy face of the Cyclops as he saw under his deformed feet the heads of all those handsome, straight and well-made men. Then the ragged, screaming procession began to move, preparing to make the customary tour of the inside galleries of the Palace of Justice before parading through the streets.

CHAPTER FIVE

La Esmeralda

THE READER WILL BE GLAD TO LEARN THAT DURING THIS EN-tire scene Gringoire and his play held their ground. Urged on by him, his actors had not stopped delivering their speeches and he had not stopped listening to them. He had decided to defy the uproar to the end, never giving up hope for a re-turn of the audience's attention. This glimmer of hope became

brighter when he saw Quasimodo, Coppenole and the
tumultuous procession leaving the hall. "Good," he said to
himself, "now we're rid of all those troublemakers." Unfortunately, however, all those troublemakers were his audience.
The great hall was suddenly empty.

To tell the truth, there were still a few spectators left behind, some scattered singly, others clustered in small groups
around the pillars, mostly old people and children who had
had enough of all the noise and confusion. A few students
remained in the windows, from where they were watching the
square outside.

"Well," thought Gringoire, "there are still enough people
here to listen to the end of my play. There aren't many of
them, but they're a select, cultured audience."

Suddenly one of the students in the window began to shout,
"La Esmeralda! La Esmeralda!"

The word had a magic effect on those who were still in the
great hall. They rushed to the windows, climbed up the walls
in order to see and repeated, "La Esmeralda! La Esmeralda!"

At the same time loud applause was heard from outside.

"What does that mean—La Esmeralda?" wondered Gringoire, his hands clasped in despair. He turned back to the
marble table and saw that the performance had been interrupted. It was the very moment when Jupiter was to appear
with his thunderbolt. But Jupiter was standing motionless
beneath the stage.

"Michel Giborne!" cried the poet angrily. "What are you
doing there? Get up on the stage!"

"I can't," said Jupiter. "Some student just took the ladder
away."

Gringoire looked. It was only too true. All communication
with the stage was cut off. "The scoundrel!" he muttered.
"And why did he take away that ladder?"

"So he could climb up to the window and see La Esmeralda," answered Jupiter piteously. "He said, 'Here's a ladder
nobody's using,' and took it."

This was the final blow. Gringoire accepted it with resignation.

"The devil take all of you!" he said to the actors. "You'll
be paid if I am."

He then made his retreat dejectedly, but he waited to be
the last one to leave, like a general who has fought valiantly.
As he was going down the winding staircase of the palace he
muttered to himself, "What a pack of idiots these Parisians

are! They came to hear a play and they don't listen to anything! They're passionately interested in the cardinal, Clopin Trouillefou, Jacques Coppenole, Quasimodo and God knows who else but they pay no attention to the Virgin Mary. I came to see faces and I saw only backs! But I'll be flayed by the devil if I understand what they mean with their La Esmeralda. What kind of a word is that, anyway?"

Book II

CHAPTER ONE

From Charybdis to Scylla

NIGHT FALLS EARLY IN JANUARY. THE CITY WAS ALREADY
wrapped in shadows when Gringoire came out of the Palace of
Justice. This pleased him, for he longed to withdraw to some
dark, deserted street to meditate at leisure and give the philosopher an opportunity to apply the first dressing to the poet's
wounds. Philosophy was his only refuge, as a matter of fact, for
he had no lodging he could go to. After the resounding failure
of his theatrical venture he dared not go back to his tiny room,
having counted on paying his landlord the six months' rent
he owed him with the money the provost was to give him for
the play.

He stood in a doorway for a moment, considering the problem of where to spend the night, having all the pavements of
Paris to choose from. Then he remembered that the week
before he had noticed a footstone for mounting on muleback
in front of the house of a certain counselor of Parliament. He
had remarked to himself at the time that the stone would
make an excellent pillow for a begger or a poet in need.

He thanked Providence for sending him such a good idea
and started out for his chosen resting-place. As he was crossing the square in front of the palace, he saw the procession
of the Pope of Fools again, coming out of the palace with
loud shouts and a great glare of torches. The sight brought
back all the pain of his wounded vanity. He fled.

21

Then he suddenly formed a desperate resolution: since there was no escape from the humiliation the Festival of Fools had brought on him, he would plunge boldly into the heart of the celebration at the Place de Grève. "At least," he thought, "I may be able to get warm at the bonfire."

CHAPTER TWO

Bonfire at the Place de Grève

WHEN PIERRE GRINGOIRE ARRIVED AT THE PLACE DE Grève he was stiff with cold. As he was crossing the Pont-aux-Meuniers to avoid the crowd on the Pont-au-Change, the mills owned by the Bishop of Paris had splashed him as he passed and his coat was soaking wet. He hurried toward the bonfire blazing magnificently in the middle of the square. But it was surrounded by a dense crowd.

"Damned Parisians!" he said to himself, for Gringoire, like a true dramatic poet, was given to soliloquies. "There they are, cutting me off from the fire now! And I really need some heat, too. My shoes leak and all those blasted mills showered water on me. May the devil take the Bishop of Paris and his mills! I'd like to know what a bishop needs a mill for—does he expect to turn miller some day? If all he needs for that is my curse, I give it to him gladly, and to his cathedral and to his mills! No use expecting any of these idle fools to stand aside. What are they doing that's so fascinating, anyway? Warming themselves—what a refined pleasure! Staring at burning logs—what a magnificent sight!"

On looking more closely he saw that the circle of people around the bonfire was too wide to allow them to warm themselves by it and that it was not only the sight of burning logs which had attracted them: a young girl was dancing in the large space left open between the crowd and the fire.

As soon as he saw her Gringoire was so dazzled and entranced by her that for a moment he could not decide whether she was a human being, a fairy or an angel.

She was not tall, although the graceful lines of her slender figure made her seem to be so. Her coloring was dark, but it was easy to see that in the daylight her skin probably had the beautiful golden luster of Andalusian and Roman women. She was dancing and whirling on an old Persian carpet carelessly spread out on the pavement. Her large black eyes flashed fire.

All eyes were fixed on her, all mouths hung open. As she danced to the rhythm of the tambourine which her round, delicate arms held over her head, she seemed to be some sort of supernatural creature, with her billowy, multicolored dress, her bare shoulders, her shapely legs, which her skirt revealed from time to time, her jet-black hair and her fiery eyes.

"She's a nymph, a goddess!" thought Gringoire. Just then a strand of the "goddess's" hair came loose and a brass coin which had been attached to it fell to the pavement. "No, she's not a goddess," he said to himself, "she's a gypsy." The illusion vanished.

She began to dance again. She picked up two swords, balanced them by the point and made them turn in one direction while she turned in the other. No doubt about it, she was a gypsy. But although the spell was broken, the scene was still not without charm and fascination for Gringoire. The bonfire threw a raw, red, flickering light on the faces of the onlookers and, at the edges of the square, cast a dim glow mingled with their wavering shadows against the ancient black façade of the Maison-aux-Piliers on one side and the stone arm of the gibbet on the other.

Among the countless faces tinged scarlet by the light of the flames, there was one which seemed more absorbed in the contemplation of the dancer than all the others. It was a man's face, austere, calm and somber. The crowd surrounding him made it impossible to see what kind of clothes he was wearing. He did not seem to be more than thirty-five years old but he was almost totally bald, with only a few tufts of thin hair, already gray, at the temples. His broad, high forehead was beginning to be furrowed with wrinkles but extraordinary youthfulness and ardor flashed from his deep-set eyes. He followed the nimble young gypsy girl's every movement and as she danced and capered to the pleasure of the crowd his reverie seemed to grow more and more gloomy.

The girl finally stopped, out of breath. The people applauded warmly.

"Come here, Djali," she said. A pretty little white goat,

which had till then been lying on one corner of the carpet watching its mistress dance, stood up and came over to her. It was an alert, glossy animal with gilded horns and hooves and a gilded collar around its neck.

"It's your turn now, Djali," said the girl, sitting down and gracefully holding out her tambourine in front of the goat. "What month is it, Djali?" The goat struck the tambourine once with its hoof. It was, in fact, the first month of the year. The crowd applauded.

"Djali," she said, turning the tambourine a different way, "what day of the month is it?" The goat raised its hoof and tapped the tambourine six times.

"Djali," she went on, with still another movement of the tambourine, "what time is it?" Djali tapped seven times. At the same moment the clock of the Maison-aux-Piliers struck seven.

The people were amazed. "There's witchcraft in that," said a sullen voice from the crowd. It was that of the bald man, who had not taken his eyes off the gypsy girl for an instant. She shuddered and turned away, but a burst of applause covered the sinister remark. She put it out of her mind and continued questioning her goat.

"Djali, how does Master Guichard Grand-Remy, captain of the Paris Pistoleers, walk in the Candlemas procession?" The goat stood up on its hind legs and began to bleat and walk with such comic dignity that the entire circle of spectators burst out laughing at the parody of the captain's hypocritical piety.

"Now, Djali," said the girl, emboldened by her increasing success, "Master Jacques Charmolue, the king's attorney in the Ecclesiastical Court—show us how he preaches." The goat sat down on its rump and began shaking its forefeet in such an odd way that, except for his bad French and worse Latin, it was Jacques Charmolue in the flesh. The people applauded even more enthusiastically.

"Sacrilege! Profanation!" cried out the bald man.

The gypsy girl turned to look at him. "It's that nasty man again!" she said and pushed out her lower lip into a little pout. Then she turned on her heel and began to take up a collection in her tambourine. Coins of all denominations rained into it.

All at once Gringoire saw her passing in front of him. Noticing that he had absent-mindedly put his hand into his pocket, she stopped. "Damnation!" exclaimed the poet as

the hand he had plunged into his pocket touched reality—
nothing. Meanwhile the pretty girl was standing before him,
looking at him with her big eyes, holding out her tambourine and waiting. He began to sweat. If all the gold in Peru
had been in his pcoket, he would have given it to her, but
no gold of any kind was there and, besides, America had not
yet been discovered. Fortunately an unexpected incident
came to his rescue.

"Go away, you gypsy wench!" cried a shrill voice which
came from the darkest corner of the square.

The girl turned around, frightened. It was not the bald
man's voice this time; it was a woman's voice, pious and
malicious.

The exclamation which had frightened the girl delighted
a band of children who were roaming nearby. "There's the
recluse in Roland Tower screeching about something!" they
shouted, laughing. "Maybe she hasn't had any supper!"

Meanwhile Gringoire took advantage of the girl's agitation
to slip away unnoticed. The children's shouted remark reminded him that he had had no supper, either. It is a serious
thing to go to sleep without supper; it is even less amusing
to have no supper and not know where to sleep. This was
Gringoire's situation. He felt necessity pressing in on him
harshly from all sides.

He was absorbed in melancholy reflections on his destiny
when a strange but remarkably sweet song burst into his
reverie. The gypsy girl was singing. Her voice was like her
dancing and her beauty: it had something indefinable and
charming about it, something pure and ethereal. She was
singing in a language which Gringoire did not know and
which she herself seemed not to understand, for the expression with which she sang the words had little relation to
their meaning. Thus she sang these words with wild gaiety:

> Un cofre de gran rigueza
> Hallaron dentro un pilar,
> Dentro del, nuevas banderas
> Con figuras de espantar.

And an instant later the way she sang the following lines made
tears came into Gringoire's eyes:

> Alarabes de cavallo
> Sin poderse menear,

Con espadas, y los cuellos,
Ballestas de buen echar.

But her voice exuded joy above all; she seemed to sing, like a bird, from sheer light-heartedness.

Gringoire listened, spellbound. It was the first time in several hours that he had been able to forget his suffering.

But the moment was short. The same woman's voice which had interrupted the girl's dancing now interrupted her singing:

"Stop your chirping, cricket from hell!"

The "cricket" stopped short. Gringoire put his hands over his ears. "Silence, you blasted screech owl!" he cried out angrily. The crowd began to mutter their agreement and the invisible interrupter might have had cause to regret her attacks on the gypsy girl if their attention had not been diverted at that moment by the procession of the Pope of Fools, which, after parading through a number of the streets of the city, had just entered the Place de Grève with all its torches and tumult. From the time it had left the Palace of Justice, it had been joined along the way by all the vagabonds and unemployed thieves of Paris, so that it had swelled to impressive size by the time it reached the Place de Grève.

At the head of the procession marched the Egyptians, as the gypsies were called in those days. First came the Duke of Egypt on horseback, with his counts walking beside him; behind him were all the other gypsies, men and women, carrying their bawling children over their shoulders. All of them, including the duke and the counts, were in rags and tatters. Next came the Kingdom of Slang—all the thieves and robbers of France. The King of Slang, surrounded by his unruly subjects, rode crouched in a small cart drawn by two enormous dogs. After the Kingdom of Slang came the Empire of Galilee. The Emperor of Galilee marched majestically in his purple robe stained with wine, preceded by his court jesters and surrounded by his mace bearers and subordinate officials. Lastly came the clerks, carrying flower-decked maypoles and large yellow candles, wearing their black robes and marching to music that was worthy of a witches' sabbath. In the center of this crowd the high officers of the Brotherhood of Fools carried a litter adorned with more candles than the shrine of St. Geneviève in time of plague. On the litter, decked out with all the symbols of his office, was the new Pope of Fools, the bellringer of Notre Dame, Quasimodo the hunchback.

It is difficult to give an idea of the look of proud self-satisfaction which had come over Quasimodo's sad and hideous face during the journey from the Palace of Justice to the Place de Grève. It was the first feeling of pride he had ever known. Until then he had known only humiliation, scorn for his condition and disgust for his person. Now, therefore, despite his deafness, he enjoyed like a real pope the cheers of that crowd whom he hated in order to feel himself hated by them. He took seriously all their ironic applause and mock respect, in which, however, it must be added, there was also a certain amount of genuine fear. For, although a hunchback, he was strong; although bowlegged, he was agile; although deaf, he was malicious—three qualities which temper ridicule.

But it is doubtful that the new Pope of Fools had any clear awareness of either his own feelings or those he aroused in the people around him. The mind which was lodged in that blighted body necessarily had a certain incompleteness and deafness also. What he felt at that moment was, therefore, vague and confused. Joy and pride alone penetrated his consciousness and shone in his dark, misshapen face.

It was therefore not without surprise and alarm that, just as he was passing before the Maison-aux-Piliers in that state of semi-intoxication, the crowd saw a man rush up to him and angrily snatch away from him the gilded wooden crosier, the symbol of his mock papacy. It was the bald man who, a short while before, had chilled the poor gypsy girl's blood with his words of menace and hatred. He was wearing an ecclesiastical robe. Just as he came out from among the crowd, Gringoire, who had not noticed him till then, recognized him.

"Why, it's Dom Claude Frollo, the archdeacon!" he exclaimed. "What the devil is he doing to that one-eyed monster? He'll get himself eaten up!"

The crowd shrieked with terror as the formidable Quasimodo leaped down from the litter and the women hid their eyes in order not to see the archdeacon torn to pieces. But Quasimodo came up to the priest, looked at him and fell to his knees. The priest broke his crosier, pulled off his tiara and ripped his tinsel-covered robe. Quasimodo remained on his knees, lowered his head and clasped his hands together.

They then began a strange dialogue of signs and gestures, neither one of them speaking; the priest standing, angry, threatening and imperious; Quasimodo kneeling, humble and supplicating. Yet there was no doubt that Quasimodo could have crushed the priest with his thumb.

The archdeacon finally shook Quasimodo's powerful shoulder and motioned him to stand up and follow him. Quasimodo stood up. The Brotherhood of Fools, recovered from their first stupefaction, now moved forward to defend their pope, who had been so abruptly dethroned. Quasimodo placed himself before the priest, clenched his mighty fists, glared at them and snarled like an angry tiger. The priest resumed his somber gravity, made a sign to Quasimodo and withdrew in silence. Quasimodo walked in front of him, scattering the people from his path.

When they had gone through the crowd and across the square, a number of curious people decided to follow them. Quasimodo then took up the rear guard and walked backward behind the archdeacon, squat, massive, monstrous, shaggy, growling like a wild beast and producing large waves in the crowd with a gesture or a look.

They both disappeared down a dark, narrow street. No one dared follow them into it; the mere thought of Quasimodo's threatening snarls was enough to keep everyone back.

"An amazing incident," said Gringoire to himself, "but where the devil am I going to get something to eat?"

CHAPTER THREE

The Hazards of Following a Pretty Girl through the Streets at Night

FOR NO PARTICULAR REASON, GRINGOIRE DECIDED TO FOLLOW the gypsy girl. When he saw her turn into the Rue de la Coutellerie, he did likewise. "Why not?" he asked himself. A practical philosopher of the streets of Paris, he had already discovered that nothing is so conducive to reverie as following a pretty girl without knowing where she is going. Furthermore, nothing produces a tendency to follow people in the street like having nowhere to sleep. He therefore walked along thoughtfully behind the girl, who quickened her step and made her goat trot as she saw all the townspeople going home and all the taverns closing, the only shops which had been open that day.

"After all," he thought, "she must live somewhere. Gypsies are good-hearted . . . Who knows . . . ?" The uncertainty of this "Who knows?" included some very pleasant possibilities.

Meanwhile the streets were becoming darker and more deserted every minute. Curfew had long since sounded and it was only at rare intervals that a passer-by was to be seen in the street or a light in a window. Following the gypsy girl, Gringoire was soon lost in a tangled maze of narrow streets and blind alleys but she seemed to be quite sure of her way. She never hesitated and continually quickened her pace. As for Gringoire, he would not have had the slightest idea of where he was if he had not perceived the octagonal mass of the pillory at Les Halles as he turned a corner.

The girl finally became aware of his presence. Several times she turned around and looked at him uneasily and once she stopped short, taking advantage of a ray of light coming from the half-open door of a bakery to examine him thoroughly from head to toe. She then made the little pout which he had noticed and continued on her way.

That little pout set Gringoire to thinking. It seemed to him to contain a great deal of scorn and mockery. He was beginning to walk with his head down, counting the paving stones, and to follow her from a greater distance when, having momentarily lost her from sight around a corner, he suddenly heard her scream.

He ran toward her. The street was full of shadows but a wick soaked in oil burning in an iron cage at the foot of a statue of the Virgin Mary on the corner enabled him to see the girl struggling with two men who were trying to stifle her cries. The terrified little goat was bleating with its head down and its horns thrust forward.

Gringoire hurried bravely to the rescue. Then one of the men turned around and he found himself looking into the face of the formidable Quasimodo. Gringoire did not run away but neither did he come any closer. Quasimodo came up to him, gave him a backhanded blow which sent him sprawling on the pavement several yards away, then plunged swiftly into the shadows, carrying the girl under one arm. His companion followed him and the poor goat ran after them, bleating plaintively.

"Murder! Murder!" screamed the unfortunate girl.

"Halt, you scoundrels!" suddenly roared a horseman who came dashing up from a side street. It was a captain of the

King's Archers with his sword drawn. He snatched the girl
from the arms of the stupefied Quasimodo and threw her
across his saddle. Just as the redoubtable hunchback recovered
from his surprise and rushed at him to snatch back his prey,
fifteen or sixteen soldiers, who had been following their captain, appeared on the scene armed with broadswords. They
were a detachment assigned to the watch by the Keeper of
the Provostry of Paris.

Quasimodo was surrounded, seized and bound. He bellowed, foamed, kicked and bit; and if it had been daylight,
his face alone, made still more hideous by rage, might well
have been enough to put the whole detachment to rout. As
it was, however, darkness deprived him of his most formidable
weapon: his ugliness. Meanwhile his companion had managed
to escape in the confusion.

The gypsy girl sat up gracefully on the young officer's
saddle. Placing her hands on his shoulders, she looked at him
intently for a few moments, as if delighted with his handsome
face as well as the way he had come to her rescue. Then,
breaking the silence, she said to him, making her sweet voice
even sweeter, "What's your name, sir?"

"Captain Phoebus de Châteaupers, at your service," replied
the officer, drawing himself up proudly.

"Thank you," she said. Then, as Captain Phoebus was
stroking his mustache, she slid down from his horse and
vanished into the darkness with the speed of lighting.

CHAPTER FOUR

More Hazards

GRINGOIRE, STUNNED BY HIS FALL, HAD REMAINED STRETCHED
out on the pavement in front of the statue of the Virgin Mary.
Little by little he came back to his senses. At first he floated
for several minutes in a kind of dreamy reverie in which the
airy figures of the gypsy girl and her goat were mingled with
the heaviness of Quasimodo's fist. This state ended when he
abruptly became aware of a vivid sensation of cold in the parts
of his body which were in contact with the pavement.

"Where's this cold coming from?" he exclaimed. Then he noticed that he was lying in the middle of the gutter.

"Damn that hunchbacked Cyclops!" he muttered and tried to stand up. But he was still so dazed and bruised that he had to stay where he was. He held his nose and resigned himself to his plight.

"The mud of Paris," he thought (for he felt sure that the gutter was to be his bed that night), "has an extremely foul odor. It must contain large amounts of volatile and nitrous salts. At least that's the opinion of Nicolas Flamel and the alchemists . . ."

The word "alchemists" suddenly reminded him of the archdeacon, Claude Frollo. He remembered that, in the violent scene he had just witnessed, the gypsy girl had been struggling with two men, that Quasimodo had had a companion; and the archdeacon's sullen, haughty face floated confusedly in his memory. "That would be strange!" he thought and on that foundation he began to erect a fantastic edifice of hypotheses, the card house of a philosopher. Then suddenly coming back to reality again, he exclaimed, "My God, I'm freezing!"

His position was, in fact, becoming more and more untenable. Each particle of water in the gutter carried away a particle of heat from him and the equilibrium between the temperature of his body and the temperature of the gutter was beginning to establish itself in a merciless way.

Then he was assailed by a completely different kind of annoyance. A group of children, of those little savages who have in all ages roamed the streets of Paris under the name of gamins, came running up to the street corner where Gringoire was lying. Their shouts and laughter showed little concern for the sleep of the people of the neighborhood. They were dragging along some sort of shapeless bag and the noise of their wooden shoes alone would have been enough to wake up the dead. Gringoire, who was not yet entirely dead, raised himself a little.

"Hey, Hennequin Dandèche! Jehan Pincebourde!" they yelled at the top of their lungs, "old Eustache Moubon, the ironmonger, just died and we've got his straw mattress. We're going to make a bonfire out of it!"

So saying, they dropped the mattress right on top of Gringoire, whom they had not noticed in the darkness. At the same time one of them took a handful of straw and lit it at the wick burning beneath the statue of the Virgin Mary.

"My God!" grumbled Gringoire. "Now I'm about to be too hot for a change!" Making a superhuman effort, he stood up, threw the mattress over the children and fled.

"Holy Virgin!" cried the children. "It's the ironmonger's ghost!" And they too ran away.

The mattress was left in undisputed possession of the field. Belleforêt, Father Le Juge and Corrozet assure us that the next morning it was picked up with great pomp by the clergy of the neighborhood and carried to the treasury of the Church of Saint-Opportune, where until 1789 the sacristan derived a rather large income from the statue of the Virgin on the corner of the Rue Mauconseil which had, by its sole presence on the memorable night of January 6, 1482, exorcized the soul of Eustache Moubon, which, in order to trick the devil, had hidden itself in his mattress when he died.

CHAPTER FIVE

The Broken Jug

AFTER RUNNING THROUGH THE WINDING STREETS FOR SOME time without knowing where he was going, our poet stopped short, first because he was out of breath, but also because he was in the grip of a dilemma which had just presented itself to his mind. "It seems to me, Master Pierre Gringoire," he said to himself, placing his finger on the side of his nose, "that you're running around like a brainless idiot. Those little rascals were just as much afraid of you as you were of them. It seems to me you heard their wooden shoes clattering off southward while you were headed northward. Now, either they have run away or they have not. If they have, then they must have left the mattress behind in their terror and that mattress is precisely the hospitable bed which you've been wandering around in search of since morning and which the Virgin Mary has miraculously sent you to reward you for having written such a fine morality play in her honor. If they have not, then they've set the mattress on fire, and that fire is exactly what you need to make you warm and dry again and cheer you up. In either case, whether it's a bed or a fire right now, that mattress is a gift from heaven. It may well be that the blessed Virgin Mary on the corner of the Rue Mauconseil made Eustache Moubon die for that very reason. It's silly of you to run away like this, leaving behind what you've been looking for; and you're a fool!"

He turned around and, sniffing the air and keeping his ears cocked, tried to find his way back to the mattress. But in vain. He was constantly finding himself at the end of some blind alley or standing undecided at some complicated crossroads. He finally lost patience and cried out solemnly, "Curse these crossroads! The devil must have made them in the image of his pitchfork!"

This exclamation relieved him a little. Just then he perceived a reddish glow at the end of a long and narrow street. This brought back his good spirits completely. "God be praised!" he said. "There it is! That's my mattress burning!" Then, comparing himself to a sailor whose ship is sinking in the night, he added piously, "*Salve, Maris Stella!*" We cannot say for sure whether he addressed this fragment of a litany to the Holy Virgin or to the straw mattress.

He had not gone far along the street, which was unpaved, uphill and extremely muddy, when he noticed something rather strange: the street was not deserted. All along it were vague, shapeless masses crawling toward the fire.

There is nothing like an empty stomach to make a man adventurous, so Gringoire continued to walk forward and soon caught up with one indistinct figure which was lagging behind the others. Looking closely, he saw that it was a wretched legless cripple who was hopping along on his hands. The lower part of his body rested in a large metal bowl. As Gringoire drew alongside this spiderlike creature with a human face it looked up at him and said piteously, "*La buona mancia, signor! La buona mancia!*"

"The devil take you," said Gringiore, "and me along with you, if I understand a word you're saying." He went on ahead of him.

He overtook another of those moving masses and examined it. This one was partially paralyzed and had only one arm. The complicated system of crutches which supported him gave him the appearance of a walking scaffold. Gringoire, who was fond of noble and classic comparisons, compared him in his mind to the living tripod of Vulcan.

The living tripod took off its hat to him as he passed, then thrust it under his chin like a barber's basin and bawled in his ear, "Señor caballero, para comprar un pedaso de pan!"

"This one talks too," said Gringoire, "but it sounds like a barbarous language and he's more gifted than I am if he can understand it."

He quickened his pace but for the third time something barred his way. This something, or rather someone, was a blind man, a small blind man with a bearded Semitic face who, rowing in the space around him with a stick and being pulled along by a large dog, whined at him in a Hungarian accent, "Facitote caritatem!"

"At last!" said Gringoire. "Here's one that talks a Christian language. I must have a very kind face to be asked for charity when my purse is empty." Turning to the blind man he said, "My friend, a week ago I sold my last shirt; in other words, since you understand only the language of Cicero, Vendidi hebdomade nuper transita meam ultimam chemisam."

Having said this, he turned his back on the blind man and went on. But the blind man also began to walk faster and the two cripples hurried up beside him with a great clatter from the metal bowl and the crutches. Then the three of them, bumping into one another as they followed along at Gringoire's heels, took up their respective chants:

"Caritatem!" whined the blind man.

"La buona mancia!" wailed the legless man.

"Un pedaso de pan!" chimed in the cripple with the crutches.

Gringoire stopped up his ears. "A real Tower of Babel!" he cried and began to run. The blind man and the two cripples also began to run.

As he went further along the street he passed swarms of blind men, cripples, one-armed men, one-eyed men and lepers with open sores. Some came from houses, others from cellars, still others from side streets, and all were howling, bellowing and yelping, all hobbling toward the fire. Gringoire, still followed by his three persecutors and no longer knowing what to expect, went on bewildered, stepping around the cripples on crutches and over those in bowls, bogged down in that limping, shuffling mass like the English captain who was overwhelmed by a legion of crabs.

It occurred to him to try to turn back. But it was too late. The whole crowd had closed in behind him and his three beggars seized him by the arms. He therefore went on, pushed forward by that irresistible tide, by fear and by a dizziness which made it all seem like a horrible dream.

He finally arrived at the end of the street. It led into an enormous square in which a thousand lights were flickering in the darkness. He broke away from the three infirm specters who were holding him and plunged forward, expecting to outrun them.

"Ondè vas, hombre!" cried the one-armed cripple, throwing away his crutches and running after him on two of the best legs that ever strode over the pavements of Paris. A moment later the legless cripple, standing on his own two feet, had clapped his heavy metal bowl over Gringoire's head and the blind man was glaring at him with fiery eyes.

"Where am I?" asked the poet, terrified.

"In the Court of Miracles," answered a fourth specter which had come up to them.

"Well, it's true that the lame walk and the blind see here but where's the Saviour?" A sinister laugh was the only reply.

The poor poet looked around him. He was really in the dreaded Court of Miracles, which no honest man ever entered at such an hour: a magic circle where the officers of the Châtelet and the sergeants of the watch who ventured into it always vanished without a trace; a city of robbers, a hideous wart on the face of Paris; a sewer which disgorged every morning and received every night that foul stream of vice, mendicity and crime which always overflows into the streets of a great city; a false hospital in which gypsies, unfrocked priests, ruined students and scoundrels of all nations and religions, covered with sores and begging during the daytime, transformed themselves into bandits at night; an immense dressing room, in short, for all the actors of that everlasting drama which robbery, prostitution and murder have always enacted in the streets of Paris.

It was an enormous square, irregular and badly paved, like all the squares of Paris in those days. Fires, around which strange groups were gathered, were blazing here and there. Movement, confusion and uproar were everywhere; the air was filled with shrill laughter, the crying of children and the voices of women. The hands and feet of this crowd, black against the luminous background, made a thousand fantastic gestures. From time to time a dog which looked like a man or a man who looked like a dog could be seen passing near one of the fires. The boundaries between races and species seemed to have been obliterated in this city as in a pandemonium: men,

women, animals, age, sex, sickness, health, everything seemed
to be in common among these people; everything went together, mingled, confused, superimposed; everyone participated in
everything.

The dim, flickering light of the fires enabled Gringoire, despite his agitation, to distinguish all around the immense
square a hideous border of ancient houses whose cracked,
crumbling, shrunken façades, each pierced by one or two small
lighted windows, appeared in the darkness to be so many enormous heads of old women ranged in a circle, monstrous and
sullen, watching the witches' sabbath with blinking eyes.

It was like a new world, unknown, unheard-of, deformed,
reptilian, swarming and fantastic.

Growing more and more frightened, tightly gripped by the
three beggars, deafened by a crowd of other faces bleating and
barking around him, the unfortunate Gringoire strove to rally
his presence of mind. But his efforts were vain: his mind and
memory were hopelessly confused and, doubting everything,
floating between what he saw and what he felt, he posed himself this insoluble problem: "If I exist, does this? Or if this
exists, do I?"

At this moment a distinct shout rose from the buzzing
crowd surrounding him: "Take him to the king! Take him to
the king!"

"Holy Virgin!" muttered Gringoire. "The king of this place
must be a goat!"

"To the king! To the king!" repeated every voice.

They dragged him along, each striving to lay hands on him.
But the three beggars held fast to him, pulling him away from
the others and bellowing, "He's ours!"

As he crossed the horrible square his dizziness was dispelled.
The feeling of reality returned to him after he had taken a few
steps and he began to adapt himself to the atmosphere of the
place. In the first few moments there had risen from his poetic
brain (or perhaps, more prosaically, from his empty stomach)
a kind of vapor which, spreading itself between him and the
objects around him, had made him see them through the incoherent mists of a nightmare, through those dream-shadows
which make all outlines waver, all forms grimace, all objects
cluster together in disproportionate conglomerations, chang-
ing things into chimeras and men into phantoms. Little by
little this hallucination gave way to a less bewildered and exaggerated perception. Reality began to break through to his
consciousness again, assailing his eyes, treading on his feet and

demolishing bit by bit the macabre poetry with which he had at first imagined himself to be surrounded. He was forced to recognize that he was not walking in the Styx but in the mud; that he was not being elbowed by demons but by robbers; that his soul was not in danger but merely his life (for he lacked that efficient mediator between the honest man and the robber: a full purse).

In short, on examining the scene more closely and calmly, he fell from the witches' sabbath into the tavern. The Court of Miracles was, in fact, nothing but a vast tavern; but a tavern of bandits who were stained as much with blood as with wine.

The spectacle which presented itself to him when his ragged escort had finally brought him to his destination was not suited to bring him back to poetry, even the poetry of the Inferno. It was more than ever the prosaic and brutal reality of the tavern.

Around a great fire which was burning on a large round flagstone, a number of tables had been set up at random. On them were mugs full of wine and beer, around which were grouped a host of bacchanalian faces, reddened by the fire and the wine. A man with a huge paunch and a jovial face was noisily kissing a plump, husky harlot. A false soldier was whistling merrily as he unwrapped the bandages of his false wound and limbered up his sound, vigorous knee, which had been swathed in ligatures since morning. A man in a complete pilgrim's costume was practicing a hymn. Two tables away, a young rascal was taking lessons in epilepsy from an old expert in the art of foaming at the mouth by chewing on a piece of soap. Beside them, four or five women thieves were quarreling over a child who had been stolen that evening.

Coarse laughter burst forth everywhere and obscene songs. Everyone swore and made his own comments without listening to his neighbor. Mugs bumped against each other, which led to quarrels, which led to the tearing of already tattered clothing.

Several children were mingled in with the orgy. The stolen child was weeping and screaming. Another, a big four-year-old boy, was sitting silently on a bench. A third was gravely spreading over the table with his finger the melted tallow dripping from a candle. A fourth, a little boy, was crouching in the mud, almost lost inside a huge iron pot which he was scraping with a piece of tile, drawing sounds from it which would have made Stradivarius faint in agony.

A large barrel was standing on end near the fire. On it sat a beggar. It was the king on his throne.

Gringoire's three captors led him before this barrel and for a moment the whole bacchanalia was silent, except for the pot inhabited by the boy. Gringoire dared not raise his eyes or even breathe.

"*Hombre, quita tu sombrero,*" said one of the three men holding him and, before he could understand what was meant, another of them had snatched off his hat—a shabby hat, it is true, but still good for protection against the sun and the rain.

"Who's this rascal?" asked the king.

Gringoire started. Although it was now accentuated by a tone of menace, that voice reminded him of another one which that very morning had struck the first blow at his play by whining in the middle of the audience: "Charity, if you please." He looked up and saw Clopin Trouillefou.

Except for the insignia of his royalty, Trouillefou wore exactly the same ragged clothes he had worn that morning. The sore on his right arm had disappeared. In his hand he held one of the whips with white leather thongs which were used by the sergeants of the watch in those days to keep back the crowds. On his head was a kind of round hat fastened together at the top, but it was impossible to tell whether it was a nightcap or a royal crown.

Gringoire, without knowing exactly why, regained some hope when he recognized the King of the Court of Miracles as his cursed beggar of the Palace of Justice.

"Master . . ." he stammered, "my lord . . . sire . . . What should I call you?" he asked finally, arriving at the culminating point of his crescendo and knowing neither how to go higher nor come down lower.

"My lord, your majesty or comrade, call me whatever you like, but hurry up! What do you have to say in your defense?"

(" 'In your defense,' " thought Gringoire. "I don't like the sound of that.") "I'm . . ." he went on stammering, "I'm the one who . . . this morning . . ."

"Just give your name, you scoundrel, and nothing else!" broke in Trouillefou. "Listen: you're standing in the presence of three mighty sovereigns. First, there's me, King Clopin Trouillefou, Supreme Ruler of the Kingdom of Slang; that yellowish old man with the rag around his head is Mathias Hungadi Spicali, Duke of Egypt and Bohemia; then there's Guillaume Rousseau, Emperor of Galilee— he's the fat fellow over there who's too busy caressing his wench to listen to us. We're your judges. You're a foreigner in our kingdom. You've violated the privileges of our city. You must be punished unless you're a thief, a beggar or a tramp. Are you anything like that?"

"Alas," replied Gringoire, "I haven't the honor to be any of those things. I'm the author of . . ."

"That will do!" interrupted Trouillefou. "You're going to be hanged. It's very simple—when one of you honest citizens is in our territory, we treat him the way you treat us in your territory. We apply the same law to you that you apply to us. If it's a harsh law, it's your own fault. It's only fair that the grimace of an honest man should be seen above a collar of hemp from time to time. Come on, my friend, divide your rags graciously among these young ladies here. I'm going to have you hanged to amuse my subjects and you'll give them what's in your purse to buy drinks with. If you've got any rigmarole you want to go through first, there's a fine stone crucifix we stole from Saint-Pierre-aux-Boeufs. You have four minutes to throw your soul at it."

"Well said, by God!" cried the Emperor of Galilee. "Clopin Trouillefou preaches like the pope himself!"

"Your majesties, emperors and kings," said Gringoire coolly, having somehow recovered his self-control, "you cannot mean what you say. My name is Pierre Gringoire. I am the poet whose morality play was performed this morning in the great hall of the Palace of Justice."

"Ah, so you're the one!" said Trouillefou. "I was there too. But, comrade, because you bored us this morning, is that any reason why we shouldn't hang you tonight?"

Gringoire made one more attempt: "I can't understand why you don't consider a poet one of you. Aesop was a tramp; Homer was a beggar; Mercury was a thief . . ."

"You're just trying to mix us up with all that gibberish!" exclaimed Trouillefou. "For God's sake, let yourself be hanged and don't make such a fuss about it!"

"Excuse me, your majesty," said Gringoire, "but this is worth making a fuss about . . . Wait a minute! Listen to me! You can't sentence me to death without letting me speak!"

His voice was drowned out by the uproar around him. The little boy was scraping his pot more energetically than ever and, to climax everything, an old woman had just put on the fire a frying pan full of grease, which yelped and squealed like a gang of children at a carnival.

Meanwhile Clopin Trouillefou appeared to be conferring for a moment with the Duke of Egypt and the Emperor of Galilee, who was dead drunk. Then he shouted irritably,

"Quiet!" Since the pot and the frying pan paid no attention and continued their duet, he jumped down from his barrel and gave one kick to the pot, which rolled for ten feet with the boy inside it, and another to the frying pan, which spilled out all its grease into the fire. He then gravely remounted his throne, ignoring the stifled crying of the child and the grumbling of the old woman, whose supper was going up in fine white flames.

Trouillefou made a sign to the duke, the emperor and all the other high officials of his kingdom. They stepped forward and ranged themselves around him in a semicircle. It was a semicircle of rags, tatters, pitchforks, axes, unsteady legs, bare brawny arms and sordid, dull faces. Clopin Trouillefou stood out in this Round Table of the gutter and dominated the others, first because of the height of his barrel, but also because of a certain fierce, haughty and formidable look which flashed from his eyes. He was like a wild boar among ordinary swine.

"Listen," he said to Gringoire, stroking his deformed chin with his calloused hand, "I see no reason why you shouldn't be hanged. It seems to upset you but that's only natural— you honest citizens aren't used to the idea. You give it too much importance. After all, we have nothing against you, so here's a way you can get out of it for a while: would you like to become one of us?"

It can easily be imagined what effect this proposal had on Gringoire, who had been helplessly watching his life slip away from him. He clutched at the chance eagerly:

"Of course I would!"

"Do you agree," said Trouillefou, "to become a subject of our kingdom?"

"Yes, a subject! Of course!"

"To become an outlaw?"

"Yes, an outlaw!"

"In your soul?"

"In my soul."

"Let me point out to you," said the king, "that you'll be hanged just the same."

The poet swore loudly.

"The only difference," went on Trouillefou imperturbably, "is that you'll be hanged later, with more ceremony, at the expense of the good city of Paris, on a fine stone gibbet and by honest men. That's some consolation."

"That's true," agreed Gringoire.

"There are other advantages. For example, you won't have to pay any taxes."

"So be it," said the poet. "I'm an outlaw, a thief, a tramp or anything else you want me to be."

"So, you scoundrel," said Trouillefou, "you really want to become one of us, do you?"

"I certainly do."

"Well, there's more to it than just wanting. Good intentions never put another onion in the soup. The only thing they're good for is to get you into heaven and our kingdom has nothing to do with heaven. If you want to be admitted into it, you'll have to pick the dummy's pocket."

"Anything you say."

The king made a sign. A few of his subjects went away and came back a moment later carrying two long posts with a flat base attached to one end so that they could stand upright on the ground. A crossbar was fitted between the tops of the posts and Gringoire had the satisfaction of seeing a portable scaffold erected before him in the twinkling of an eye. Nothing was lacking, not even the rope, which dangled gracefully from the crossbar.

"What are they up to now?" he wondered uneasily. A jingling sound put an end to his anxiety: it was only a dummy they were hanging with a rope, a sort of scarecrow dressed in red and covered with enough little bells to equip the harnesses of thirty Castilian mules. They jingled for a while, then died down as the dummy stopped swinging.

Trouillefou pointed to a rickety old stool placed under the dummy. "Stand on it," he ordered.

"But I'll break my neck!" protested Gringoire. "Your stool is crippled!"

"Stand on it," repeated Trouillefou.

Gringoire climbed up on the stool and managed to balance himself on it after flailing his arms awhile.

"Now," said the king, "cross your right foot behind your left leg and stand on the tip of your left foot."

"Your majesty," said Gringoire, "are you dead set on having me break an arm or a leg?"

Trouillefou shook his head. "Listen, my friend," he said, "you talk too much. Here's what you do: stand on tiptoe like I told you; that way you'll be able to reach the dummy's pocket. Put your hand in it and take out the purse that's inside. If you do all that without making any of the bells jingle, you've passed the test."

"What if I fail?"

"You'll be hanged."

"And what happens if I pass the test?"

"In that case you'll become one of us and we'll beat you steadily for a week. Understand?"

"Not very well, your majesty. What's the advantage? I'll be hanged in one case and beaten in the other."

"But what about being one of us?" exclaimed Trouillefou. "I suppose that's not worth anything! We'll beat you for your own good, so you'll be used to it later."

"Thank you very much."

"All right, hurry up!" said the king, kicking against his barrel, which resounded like a bass drum. "Pick the dummy's pocket and get it over with. I warn you one last time that if I hear the slightest sound you'll take the dummy's place at the end of the rope."

The crowd applauded his words and ranged themselves around the scaffold with raucous laughter. Gringoire saw that he amused them too much to be able to expect anything but the worst from them. His only hope was the slim chance of succeeding in the ticklish task imposed on him. He addressed a fervent prayer to the dummy, whose heart would have been easier to soften than those of the people watching him. The myriad of bells, with their little copper tongues, seemed like the gaping jaws of serpents ready to hiss and strike. He made one last appeal to Trouillefou: "What if there should be a gust of wind?"

"You'll be hanged," was the unhesitating answer.

Seeing that there was no possibility of reprieve or escape, he bravely set about carrying out the operation. He crossed his right leg behind his left, stood on one toe and stretched up his arm. But just as he touched the dummy, his body, which had only one leg, tottered on the stool, which had only three. He unthinkingly clutched at the dummy, lost his balance and fell heavily to the ground, his ears filled with the fateful jingling of a thousand bells.

He uttered an oath as he fell, then lay like a dead man with his face against the ground. He heard the horrible chiming above his head, the diabolical laughter of the crowd and Trouillefou's voice saying, "Pick the rascal up and hang him right away!"

He stood up. The dummy had already been taken down to make room for him. He was made to climb up on the stool again. Trouillefou came over to him, put the rope around his neck and said, patting him on the shoulder, "Farewell, friend. You couldn't escape now if you were the pope!"

The word "Mercy!" died away on Gringoire's lips. He looked around him. No hope: everyone was laughing.

"Bellevigne de l'Etoile," said the king to a husky scoundrel who stepped out of the crowd, "climb up to the crossbar." A moment later the terrified Gringoire saw him crouching above his head.

"Now," went on Trouillefou, "when I clap my hands, you, Andry-le-Rouge, kick the stool out from under him; you, François Chante-Prune, pull down on his legs; and you, Bellevigne, jump onto his shoulders. And all three of you at the same time, understand?"

Gringoire shuddered. "All set?" said Trouillefou to the three men ready to pounce on him like three spiders on a fly. The poor prisoner had a moment of horrible suspense while the king leisurely kicked into the fire a few twigs which the flames had missed. "All set?" he repeated and prepared to clap his hands.

Then he stopped, as if an idea had suddenly occurred to him. "Wait," he said, "I was forgetting something—it's our custom not to hang a man without first asking if there's any woman who wants him. My friend, this is your last chance."

Gringoire breathed again. It was the second time he had come back to life in the last half-hour. This time he was afraid to let his hopes rise too high.

"Step up, ladies, women, females!" shouted Trouillefou, standing on his barrel again. "Do any of you want this miserable rascal? Come take a look at him! A man for nothing! Who wants him?"

In his wretched state, Gringoire must not have looked very appealing, for the women showed little interest in the offer. The poor poet heard them answer, "No! No! Hang him, that will amuse all of us!" Three of them, however, did step up to take a look at him.

The first was a fat, square-faced girl. She carefully examined his tattered clothes with an expression of disgust. "What rags!" she remarked. Then she said to him, "Let me see your coat."

"I lost it," he replied.

"What about your hat?"

"They took it away from me."

"And your shoes?"

"The soles are almost worn through."

"Your purse?"

"Alas, it's empty."

"Hang, then, and be thankful!" said the wench and turned her back on him.

The second woman, old, dark, wrinkled and so ugly that she stood out even in the Court of Miracles, walked around him several times. He was almost trembling for fear she would take him. But she finally muttered, "Too thin," and went away.

The third was a young girl, rather fresh-looking and not too ugly. "Save me!" the poor man whispered to her imploringly. She gazed at him for a moment with a look of pity, then lowered her eyes and stood undecided for a while, toying with her skirt. His eyes followed all her movements; she was his last glimmer of hope. "No," she said finally, "Guillaume would beat me." She stepped back into the crowd.

"My friend," said Trouillefou, "you're unlucky." Then, standing up on his barrel, he shouted, imitating an auctioneer to everyone's amusement, "Nobody wants him? Going once! Going twice!" Then, nodding toward the gallows, "Gone!"

Bellevigne de l'Etoile, Andry-le-Rouge and François Chante-Prune approached Gringoire. Just then a shout went up from the crowd: "La Esmeralda! La Esmeralda!"

Startled, Gringoire turned his head in the direction from which the clamor was coming. The crowd opened and made way for a graceful and dazzling figure. It was the gypsy girl. Her extraordinary charm and beauty seemed to dominate even the Court of Miracles. The people respectfully drew back to let her pass and their brutal faces softened at the sight of her.

She walked lightly up to the condemned man, followed by Djali, her pretty little goat. Poor Gringoire was more dead than alive. She looked at him for a moment in silence.

"Are you going to hang this man?" she asked Trouillefou gravely.

"Yes, sister," he answered, "unless you should take him for your husband."

She made her delicate little pout and said, "I'll take him."

Gringoire was by now convinced that he had been in a dream since morning and that this abrupt change of fortune was only part of it. The noose was removed from his neck and he was taken down off the stool. His emotions were so violent that he had to sit down.

Without a word, the Duke of Egypt brought a clay jug.

The gypsy girl handed it to Gringoire. "Throw it on the ground," she told him. It broke into four pieces.

"Brother," said the Duke of Egypt, placing a hand on the forehead of each of them, "she is your wife. Sister, he is your husband. For four years. Go."

CHAPTER SIX

A Wedding Night

A SHORT WHILE LATER, OUR POET FOUND HIMSELF IN A WARM, cozy little room with a vaulted ceiling, seated before a table, having a good bed in prospect and all alone with a pretty girl. The adventure had something magic about it. He was beginning to believe seriously that he was the hero of some fairy tale. From time to time he looked steadfastly at the holes in his coat in order to keep his grip on reality. His reason, tossed to and fro in imaginary space, was hanging by a thread.

The girl seemed to take no notice of him. She was bustling back and forth, shifting things around, talking to her goat, making her little pout here and there. She finally sat down near the table and Gringoire was able to contemplate her at leisure.

"So this is what they meant by La Esmeralda!" he thought. "A celestial creature! A street dancer! So much and so little! She's the one who gave the finishing stroke to my play this morning and she's the one who saved my life tonight. My evil genius, my guardian angel! A very pretty girl, too. . . . She must be madly in love with me to have taken me that way. That reminds me—I don't know exactly how it happened but I'm her husband!"

With this idea in mind and in his eyes, he suddenly stood up and approached the girl in such a bold and gallant way that she shrank back.

"What do you want with me?" she asked.

"How can you ask such a question, adorable La Esmeralda?" he answered in such a passionate tone that he himself was startled when he heard himself speak.

The gypsy girl opened her large eyes. "I don't know what you mean."

"What!" exclaimed Gringoire, growing more and more heated and thinking that, after all, he was dealing only with the false virtue of the Court of Miracles. "Am I not yours, sweet friend? Are you not mine?" With this, he confidently put his arm around her waist.

She slipped through his hands like an eel, sprang to the other side of the room, bent down and straightened up again with a small dagger in her hand before Gringoire had time to see where it came from. She stood facing him, angry and proud, her lips puffed out, her nostrils distended, her cheeks scarlet and her eyes flashing lightning. At the same time her white goat placed itself in front of her and lowered its head, aiming its gilded and sharply pointed horns threateningly at Gringoire. It was all done in the twinkling of an eye.

Our philosopher stood speechless, casting bewildered glances first at the goat, then at the girl.

"Holy Virgin!" he exclaimed when he had recovered a little from his surprise. "You two certainly aren't very friendly!"

"And you're certainly very impudent!" said the girl.

"Excuse me," said Gringoire, smiling. "But then why did you take me for a husband?"

"Should I have let you be hanged?"

"So," said the poet disappointedly, "your only reason for marrying me was to save me from the gallows?"

"What other reason did you expect me to have?"

Gringoire bit his lip. "I see I'm not such a triumphant lover as I thought," he said to himself. "But then what was the use of breaking that poor jug?"

Meanwhile La Esmeralda's dagger and her goat's horns were still on the defensive.

"Mademoiselle La Esmeralda," said the poet, "let's come to terms. I'm not a clerk of the Châtelet, so I won't quarrel with you about carrying a dagger in Paris in direct violation of the provost's prohibition, although I'm sure you know that only a week ago Noël Lescripvain was fined heavily for carrying a short sword. But that's not my affair and I'll come to the point: I swear to you by my chance of salvation that I will never come near you without your permission; but please give me something to eat."

The truth is that Gringoire did not have a very passionate temperament. He was not of that romantic and military breed who take young ladies by storm. In amorous matters, as in all others, he was quite ready to temporize and steer a middle course and a good supper with a pleasant companion seemed to him an excellent intermission between the prologue and the climax of an amorous adventure.

The gypsy girl did not answer. She made her disdainful little pout and burst out laughing. The dagger vanished as quickly as it had appeared; Gringoire was unable to discover where the wasp hid its sting.

A moment later, a loaf of rye bread, a slice of bacon, some wrinkled apples and a pitcher of beer had been set on the table. Gringoire fell to avidly. Listening to the furious chatter of his iron fork on the earthenware plate, one might have thought that all his passion had been transformed into appetite.

The girl, seated before him, watched him in silence. She was evidently preoccupied by other thoughts, which occasionally brought a smile to her lips as her soft hand stroked the head of the intelligent goat between her knees.

When the first cravings of his stomach had been appeased, Gringoire felt a twinge of shame at seeing that one apple was all that remained of the food. "Aren't you going to eat, Mademoiselle La Esmeralda?" he asked.

She shook her head and looked thoughtfully up at the ceiling.

"What the devil can she be thinking about?" wondered Gringoire, turning his eyes in the same direction as hers. "It surely can't be that grinning dwarf carved on the keystone that's absorbing her attention. At least I'm not that ugly!"

He raised his voice: "Mademoiselle!"

She did not seem to have heard him.

He said still louder, "Mademoiselle La Esmeralda!"

His efforts were vain. The girl's mind was elsewhere and his voice did not have the power to call it back. Fortunately the goat intervened and began to pull its mistress gently by the sleeve. "What do you want, Djali?" she asked sharply, as if she had been suddenly awakened.

"She's hungry," said Gringoire, delighted at the chance of opening the conversation.

La Esmeralda began to crumble some bread, which Djali ate gracefully out of the palm of her hand. Gringoire did not give her time to go back to her reverie. He decided to risk a delicate question: "So you won't have anything to do with me as your husband?"

She looked him in the eyes and said, "No."

"As your lover, then?"

She made her little pout and said, "No."

"As your friend?"

She continued to look him in the eyes and said, after a moment of reflection, "Perhaps."

This "perhaps," so dear to a philosopher's heart, emboldened him. "Do you know what friendship is?" he asked.

"Yes," she replied. "It's being brother and sister, two souls which touch without mingling, like two fingers of a hand."

"And what about love?"

"Oh, love!" she said. Her voice trembled and her eyes sparkled. "It's being two and yet being only one. A man and a woman fused into an angel. It's heaven!"

As she said this she shone with a beauty which struck Gringoire powerfully and seemed to him in perfect harmony with the almost Oriental exaltation of her words. Her pure, rosy lips were half smiling; her candid, serene forehead was clouded now and then by her thoughts, like a mirror which is momentarily breathed upon; and from her long, lowered eyelashes emanated a kind of ineffable light which gave her profile that ideal sweetness which Raphael was later to find at the mystic point of intersection of virginity, maternity and divinity.

Gringoire went on nevertheless: "What must a man do, then, to please you?"

"He must be a man."

"What am I, then?"

"A man has a helmet on his head, a sword in his hand and spurs on his heels."

"I see—the horse makes the man. Are you in love with anyone?"

She was thoughtful for a moment, then she said with an odd expression, "I'll know soon."

"Why not tonight?" asked the poet tenderly. "Why not me?"

She looked at him gravely. "I could love only a man who can protect me."

Gringoire blushed, feeling that this was aimed directly at him. It was obvious that she was alluding to the feeble assistance he had given her in the critical situation she had been in two hours earlier. This memory, effaced by his other adventures that night, came back to him. He struck his forehead.

"That reminds me," he said, "I should have asked you about

that in the beginning. Excuse me; I've been very upset. How did you manage to escape from the clutches of Quasimodo?"

The question made her shudder. "Oh! That horrible hunchback!" she said, hiding her face in her hands and shivering as though she were freezing cold.

"Horrible is right!" said Gringoire. "But how did you escape from him?"

She smiled, sighed and kept silent.

"Do you know why he followed you?" asked Gringoire, hoping to return to his question by way of a detour.

"I don't know," she said. Then she added sharply, "But you were following me too! Why were you?"

"I honestly don't know either."

There was a silence. Gringoire whittled on the table with his knife. The girl smiled and seemed to be looking through the wall at something. All at once she began to sing almost inaudibly:

> Quando las pintadas aves
> Mudas están, y la tierra . . .

She broke off abruptly and began to caress Djali.

"That's a pretty little animal you have there," remarked Gringoire.

"She's my sister."

"Why do they call you 'La Esmeralda'?"

"I have no idea."

"How can that be?"

She drew from her bosom a small oblong bag attached to a necklace she wore around her neck. It gave off a strong odor of camphor. It was covered with green silk and in the center of it was a large glass imitation emerald.

"Maybe it's because of this," she said.

Gringoire put out his hand toward the little bag. She stepped back. "Don't touch it! It's an amulet; you'd either injure the charm or it would injure you."

The poet's curiosity was more and more aroused. "Who gave it to you?" he asked.

She put a finger to her lips and hid the amulet in her bosom. He questioned her further but she hardly answered him.

"What does 'La Esmeralda' mean?"

"I don't know."

"What language is it?"

"I think it's a gypsy word."

"I thought so. You're not French, are you?"

"I don't know."

"Are your parents living?"

She began to sing an old song:

> *My father's a bird*
> *And so is my mother . . .*

"All right," said Gringoire. "How old were you when you came to France?"

"I was a little girl."

"And when did you come to Paris?"

"Last year. Just as we were entering the city I saw a linnet fly through the air. It was at the end of August and I said, 'We'll have a hard winter.'"

"You were certainly right!" said Gringoire, delighted to have this topic of conversation. "I've spent this whole winter blowing on my fingers. . . . So, you have the gift of prophecy?"

"No," she said, becoming laconic again.

"That man they call the Duke of Egypt, is he the chief of your tribe?"

"Yes."

"Yet he's the one that married us," timidly observed the poet.

She made her customary pout and said, "I don't even know your name."

"My name? If you want it, here it is: Pierre Gringoire."

"I know a prettier name than that."

"That's an unkind thing to say! But I don't mind; I won't let you irritate me. Maybe you'll love me when you know me better. Also, you've told me your story with such confidence that I owe you an account of myself.

"To begin with, my name is Pierre Gringoire, as I said. I am the son of a notary at Gonesse. My father was hanged by the Burgundians and my mother was ripped open by the Picards during the siege of Paris twenty years ago. At the age of six, therefore, I was an orphan, with no other sole to my foot than the pavement of Paris.

"I really can't say how I managed to live between the ages of six and sixteen; sometimes a fruit-seller would give me a plum, sometimes a baker would toss me a crust and at night I would get myself picked up by the watch, who would throw me in jail, where I at least had a bundle of straw to sleep on. In spite of all this I grew up, tall and thin, as you can see. In winter I warmed myself in the sun under the porch of the Hôtel de Sens and it seemed ridiculous to me that the bonfire of Saint John came in the middle of summer.

"At sixteen I decided it was time to take up a profession and I tried my hand at just about everything. I became a soldier but I wasn't brave enough. I became a monk but I wasn't pious enough; and besides, I'm a bad drinker. In despair I became a carpenter's apprentice but I wasn't strong enough. I finally realized that I was unfit for everything, so I became a poet. It's a profession a man can always practice while he's a vagabond and it's better than stealing, as some of my dishonest friends advised me to do. One day I was lucky enough to meet Dom Claude Frollo, the Reverend Archdeacon of Notre Dame. He took an interest in me and I owe it to him that today I am a learned man. I know Latin, from Cicero's Offices to the Mortuology of the Celestine Fathers, and I am not barbarous in scholastics, poetics, rhythmics or even in alchemy, the greatest science of them all.

"I am the author of the play which was triumphantly performed today in the Palace of Justice before an enormous audience. I have also written a book, which will be six hundred pages long, on the prodigious comet of 1465 which caused a man to go mad. I have had other successes, too. For example, having some skill as an artillery carpenter, I worked on that huge cannon which, as you know, blew up at the Pont de Charenton the day it was tried out and killed twenty-four curious bystanders. As you can see, I'm not at all a bad match. I know a number of good tricks which I'll teach to your goat. For one thing, I can teach it to imitate the Bishop of Paris, that cursed Pharisee whose mills splash water on people all along the Pont-aux-Meuniers. Also, my play will bring in a lot of money—if they pay me for it. In conclusion, let me say that I am at your service, Mademoiselle, I and my intelligence, my learning and my literary talent, ready to live with you in whatever way you like: chastely or joyfully; as husband and wife if it suits you, or as brother and sister if that suits you better."

Gringoire paused, waiting to see what effect his speech would have on the girl. She was looking at the floor.

"Phoebus," she said softly. Then, turning toward the poet: "What does that mean?"

Gringoire, without understanding very well what connection this had with what he had been saying, was not displeased to have an opportunity to display his erudition. "It's a Latin word which means 'sun,'" he replied.

"Sun!" she repeated.

"It's the name of a certain handsome archer, who was a god," added Gringoire.

"A god!" she exclaimed. There was something pensive and passionate in her tone.

Just then one of her bracelets came loose and fell to the floor. Gringoire quickly bent down to pick it up. When he straightened up, she and her goat had vanished. He heard the sound of a bolt on the other side of the door, which no doubt led into another room.

"Did she at least leave me a bed?" wondered our philosopher. He explored the room. There was nothing in it fit to sleep on except a rather long wooden chest, but it had a carved lid which, when he lay down on it, gave him a sensation like that which Micromegas must have felt when he lay down full length on the Alps.

"Well," he said, making himself as comfortable as he could, "there's no use complaining. But I must say this is a very strange wedding night!"

Book III

CHAPTER ONE

The Kindly Souls

SIXTEEN YEARS BEFORE THE EVENTS WE HAVE BEEN RELATING, on Quasimodo Sunday just after morning mass, a living creature was deposited on the wooden shelf set into one wall of the Cathedral of Notre Dame, where it was customary to expose foundlings to public charity. Anyone who cared to adopt them could do so. Under the wooden shelf was a copper basin to receive alms.

The living creature which lay on this shelf on Quasimodo Sunday of the Year of Our Lord 1467 appeared to arouse great curiosity among the rather large group of people who gathered around it. Nearly all of them were old women.

In the front row were four whose gray cassocks gave the impression they might belong to some sort of religious order. I see no reason why history should not transmit to posterity the names of these four venerable ladies. They were Agnès la Herme, Jehanne de la Tarme, Henriette la Gaultière and Gauchère la Violette, all widows and all sisters of the Chapelle Etienne-Haudry, who had come to Notre Dame to hear the sermon with the permission of their superior.

"What's that, sister?" said Agnès to Gauchère, watching the little creature screaming and writhing on its wooden bed, terrified by all the strange faces.

"What's to become of us if that's how they're making children nowadays?" said Jehanne.

"I don't know much about children," said Agnès, "but it must be a sin just to look at this one."

"That's not a child, Agnès."

"It's a misshapen ape," observed Gauchère.

"It's a miracle!" said Henriette.

"It's a real monster of abomination, not a foundling," said Jehanne.

"It's screaming loud enough to deafen a choirmaster."

"I think it must be some kind of diabolical animal," said Agnès, "something that isn't Christian and should be drowned or burned."

"I hope nobody will adopt it!" said Henriette.

"Good heavens!" exclaimed Agnès, "those poor nurses in the foundling home! What if they're given this monster to suckle? I'd rather suckle a vampire!"

"Poor Agnès, you're so ignorant!" rejoined Jehanne. "Can't you see this little monster is at least four years old and would much rather have a piece of roast beef than your breast?"

She was quite right: the little "monster" (it would be difficult to find another word to describe it) was not a newborn baby. It was a small, angular, writhing mass imprisoned in a canvas bag with only a head showing. This head was deformed and exhibited a forest of red hair, one eye, a mouth and some teeth. The eye was weeping, the mouth was screaming and the teeth seemed anxious to bite something.

Dame Aloïse de Gondelaurier, a rich and noble lady with a long veil hanging from the peak of her bonnet, passed by at this moment leading her pretty little girl, about six years old. She stopped and looked at the unfortunate creature for a short time while her daughter, Fleur-de-Lys de Gondelaurier, spelled out the letters of the sign hanging from the wooden shelf: FOUNDLINGS.

"I always thought," said the lady, turning away in disgust, "that only children were allowed to be left here."

A moment later the grave and learned Robert Mistricolle, king's notary, passed by with his wife, Guillemette.

"A foundling!" he said after examining the object. "It looks to me as if it had been found on the banks of the River Phlegethon."

"It has only one eye," observed Guillemette. "There's a big wart over the other one."

"That's not a wart," said her husband. "It's an egg which contains another demon just like this one, which has another egg containing another little devil, and so on."

"How do you know?" asked Guillemette.

"I know it for certain," he replied.

"Sir," said Gauchère, "what do you predict will happen because of this foundling?"

"Great disasters."

"Good heavens!" exclaimed an old woman standing nearby. "We already had such a terrible plague last year and this year they say the English are going to land a big army at Harfleur."

"Maybe that will keep the queen from coming to Paris in September," said another old woman, "and business is already very bad."

"In my opinion," said Jehanne, "it would be better for the people of Paris if this little sorcerer were lying on a fagot instead of a shelf!"

"A fine flaming fagot!" added an old woman.

"That would be more prudent," said Mistricolle.

A young priest had been listening to this discussion for some time. He had a severe face with a wide forehead and piercing eyes. He silently pushed his way through the crowd, examined the "little sorcerer" and stretched out his hand over him. It was high time, too, for the pious bystanders were beginning to look forward to the "fine flaming fagot."

"I adopt this child," said the priest.

He wrapped him in his cassock and carried him away. The bystanders looked after him in bewilderment. A moment later he had vanished through the door leading from the church to the cloister. When they had recovered from their first surprise, Jehanne leaned near Henriette's ear and said, "Didn't I tell you that young priest, Claude Frollo, was a sorcerer?"

CHAPTER TWO

Claude Frollo

AS A MATTER OF FACT, CLAUDE FROLLO WAS NOT AN ORDINARY person. He belonged to one of those families which in the last century were indifferently called either *haute bourgeoisie* or *petite noblesse*. This family had inherited from the Paclet brothers the fief of Tirechappe, which was held under the

Bishop of Paris and included twenty-one houses. As the owner of this fief, Claude Frollo was one of the one hundred and forty-one lords claiming manorial rights in Paris and its suburbs.

From his earliest childhood, his parents had destined him for the Church. Latin was the first language he was taught to read. He was taught to lower his eyes and speak softly. His father placed him in Torchi College in the university at an early age and he grew up there on the missal and the lexicon.

He was a melancholy, solemn boy who studied ardently and learned quickly. His recreations were sober, he had little to do with the bacchanalia of the Rue de Fouarre and he took no part in the student rebellion of 1463.

When the Abbot of Saint-Pierre de Val began his lectures on canon law, the first scholar he perceived was always Claude Frollo, equipped with his inkhorn, chewing on his pen, scribbling on his knee and, in winter, blowing on his fingers. The first student to enter the School of Chef-Saint-Denis when the doors were opened on Monday morning was always Claude Frollo, all out of breath. At the age of sixteen the young cleric was a match for a Father of the Church in mystic theology, for a Father of the Council in canonical theology, and for a Doctor of the Sorbonne in scholastic theology.

When he had mastered theology, he plunged into the study of the decretals. With his passionate appetite for knowledge he devoured decretal after decretal until he had made himself thoroughly familiar with that vast and tumultuous period, begun by Bishop Theodore in 618 and ended by Pope Gregory in 1227, in which civil law and canon law were struggling and laboring amid the chaos of the Middle Ages.

Having digested the decretals, he went on to medicine and the liberal arts. He studied the science of herbs and unguents. He became such an expert on fevers, contusions, wounds and abscesses that he could easily have qualified as either a physician or a surgeon. He also passed through every degree in the Faculty of Arts. He studied languages: Latin, Greek and Hebrew, a triple sanctuary which was seldom frequented in those days. He had a veritable fever for acquiring and storing up knowledge. It seemed to the young man that life had only one goal: to know.

It was about this time that the intense heat of the summer of 1466 generated that great plague which swept away more than forty thousand souls in the Viscounty of Paris. A rumor reached the university that the Rue Tirechappe was especially hard-hit by the disease. This was the street where Claude's parents lived, in the middle of their fief. The young student ran to their house in great alarm. When he entered, he found that both his parents had died the night before. A baby brother was still alive, crying, abandoned in his cradle. He was all that remained of Claude's family. The young man took the baby in his arms and walked out thoughtfully. Until then he had lived only in his studies; he was now beginning to live in life.

This disaster was a crisis in his existence. An orphan and head of a family at the age of nineteen, he felt himself harshly awakened from the reveries of the school to the realities of the world. Moved by pity, he became passionately devoted to his baby brother. This human affection was both strange and sweet to the young scholar, who had never loved anything but books before.

His devotion developed to an extraordinary degree. To such an inexperienced soul it was like a first love. Separated since childhood from his parents, whom he had hardly known, cloistered and completely absorbed in his books, avid above all for study and knowledge, the poor scholar had not yet had time to feel where his heart was. His young brother, that little child which had suddenly fallen from the sky into his arms, made a new man of him. For the first time he became aware that there were other things in the world than the speculations of the Sorbonne and the verses of Homer. He discovered that a man needs affection and that a life without tenderness and love is a dry, creaking wheel. Being at an age when illusions are replaced only by other illusions, however, he assumed that the affections of blood and family would be sufficient and that a little brother to love would be enough to fill an entire life.

He therefore threw himself into the love of his little Jehan with all the passion of a character which was already profound, ardent and concentrated. That frail, blond, curly-headed little creature, that orphan whose only support was an orphan, moved him to the depths of his being and, serious thinker as he was, he began to reflect on Jehan with infinite compassion. He took care of him like something exceedingly fragile and precious. He was more than a brother to the child: he became a mother to him.

Little Jehan's real mother had died before he was weaned, so Claude put him out to nurse. Besides the fief of Tirechappe, he had inherited from his father a mill standing on a hill near the Château de Bicêtre. The miller's wife there was already suckling a child. Claude carried his little Jehan to her himself.

From then on the weight of his responsibility made him take life very seriously. The thought of his little brother became not only his recreation but the goal of his studies. He resolved to devote himself entirely to Jehan's future, for which he felt himself answerable before God, and never to have any other wife or child but the happiness and prosperity of his brother. He therefore attached himself even more strongly to his ecclesiastical vocation. His merit, his learning and the fact that he was an immediate vassal of the Bishop of Paris threw the doors of the Church wide open to him. He became a priest at the age of twenty by a special dispensation of the Holy See. As the youngest of the chaplains of Notre Dame, he performed the service at the *altare pigrorum* ("altar of the lazy"), so called because of the lateness of the Mass which was said there.

There, more than ever immersed in his beloved books, which he left only to run over to the mill for an hour or so from time to time, that mixture of knowledge and austerity, so rare at his age, quickly gained him the respect and admiration of the cloister. From the cloister, his renown as a learned man spread among the people, where it was to a certain extent converted into the reputation of being a sorcerer, as happened rather frequently in those days.

It was as he was returning from saying Mass for the lazy at their altar on Quasimodo Sunday that his attention was attracted by the group of old women cackling around the bed of the foundling. It was then that he approached the unfortunate little creature, the object of so much hatred and so many threats. The sight of that distress, that deformity and that abandonment; the thought of his little brother; the painful idea which suddenly crossed his mind that if he were to die, his dear little Jehan might also be mercilessly abandoned there—all this rushed into his heart at once and filled him with profound pity. He picked up the child and carried him away.

When he took him out of the bag he found that the foundling was even more deformed than he had thought. The poor little devil had a wart over his left eye, his head was sunk down between his shoulders, his back was arched, his breastbone protruded and his legs were twisted. But he appeared to be quite lively and, although it was impossible to tell what language he was stammering, his cries gave evidence of considerable strength and health.

His extreme ugliness only increased Claude's compassion and he vowed in his heart to raise this child out of love for his brother so that, whatever faults little Jehan might have in the future, he would always have to his credit this piece of charity performed on his account. It was a sort of investment of good works which he was making in his brother's name, a stock of good deeds which he wished to lay up for him in advance in case the little rascal should some day run short of that kind of coin, the only one accepted at the toll-gate of heaven.

He baptized his adopted child and named him Quasimodo, either in order to commemorate the day on which he found him or because he wished to express by this name the degree to which the poor little creature was incomplete and imperfectly molded. Indeed, Quasimodo, one-eyed, hunchbacked and bow-legged, was only an approximation of a human being.

CHAPTER THREE

The Bellringer of Notre Dame

By 1482 QUASIMODO HAD GROWN UP. HE HAD BEEN BELL-ringer of the Cathedral of Notre Dame for several years, thanks to his foster-father, Claude Frollo, who had become the Archdeacon of Josas.

In the course of time a certain intimate bond developed between the bellringer and the church. Cut off forever from society by the double fatality of his deformity and his unknown parentage, the unfortunate Quasimodo became accustomed to seeing nothing in the world beyond the religious walls which had given him shelter in their shadows. Notre Dame had been for him, according to the stage of his growth and development, his egg, his nest, his home, his country and his universe.

And there can be no doubt that there was a kind of mysterious pre-existent harmony between him and the edifice.

When, while still a small child, he crawled tortuously around beneath its gloomy arches, he seemed to be, with his human face and his bestial members, the native reptile of that damp, dark floor, on which the shadows of the capitals of the Roman pillars projected so many other grotesque forms.

Later, the first time he mechanically grasped the rope in the tower, hung on it and set the bells in motion, his foster-father felt like a parent hearing his child beginning to learn to speak.

Thus, little by little, developing in harmony with the cathedral, living and sleeping in it, almost never leaving it, continuously undergoing its mysterious influence, he came to resemble it, to be molded by it and form an integral part of it. His salient angles dovetailed, if we may be allowed the expression, into the receding angles of the edifice and he seemed to be not only its inhabitant but its natural contents. There was such a deep, instinctive sympathy between him and the old church, so many magnetic and material affinities, that he adhered to it like a tortoise to its shell.

It is hardly necessary to describe how familiar the entire cathedral became to him as the result of such long and intimate contact with it. It had no depths into which he had not penetrated, no heights which he had not scaled. He often climbed up the façade assisted only by the projections of its sculpture. He was frequently seen crawling along the outside of the towers like a lizard on a vertical wall; those twin giants, so high, so threatening and so formidable, held no terror for him and produced no giddiness in him. Seeing them so gentle under his hands, so easy to climb, one would have said that he had tamed them. All his jumping, climbing and playing amid the abysses of the gigantic cathedral had turned him into something between a monkey and a mountain goat, just as the children of Calabria swim before they can walk and play with the sea while they are still babies.

Moreover, not only did Quasimodo's body seem to be molded by the cathedral, but also his mind. It would be difficult to determine the state of that soul and what form it had assumed, under its twisted envelope, in that savage life. Quasimodo was born one-eyed, hunchbacked and lame; it was only with great difficulty and great patience that Claude Frollo succeeded in teaching him to speak. But an evil fate pursued the poor foundling. Having become the bellringer of the cathedral at the age of fourteen, a new infirmity came to complete his misfortune: the sound of the bells broke his eardrums and he became deaf. The only door which nature had left wide open between him and the world was suddenly closed forever.

In closing, it cut off the only ray of joy and light that had still been able to penetrate into Quasimodo's soul, which was now plunged into profound darkness. The wretched creature's melancholy became as incurable and complete as his deformity. And, to a certain extent, his deafness made him dumb, for, in order not to be laughed at by others, he resolutely maintained a silence which he hardly ever broke except when he was alone. He voluntarily tied up that tongue which Claude Frollo had taken such pains to loosen. Thus it happened that when necessity occasionally forced him to speak, his tongue was stiff and awkward, like a door whose hinges have grown rusty.

If we were to attempt to penetrate into Quasimodo's soul through its thick, hard outer shell, if we could sound the depths of that twisted mind, explore the shadowy interior of that opaque creature, illuminate its obscure corners and absurd blind alleys and suddenly throw a clear light on the spirit enchained at the bottom of that cavern, we would no doubt find it stunted and rickety, like those prisoners in the dungeons of Venice who grew old bent double in a stone box too low to stand in and too short to lie in.

Quasimodo scarcely felt within himself the blind stirrings of a soul made in his own image. The impressions of external objects underwent considerable refraction before they reached his understanding. His brain twisted all the ideas which passed through it. He was therefore the victim of endless optical illusions and aberrations of judgment; his thoughts wandered aimlessly, sometimes mad, sometimes idiotic.

The first effect of his deformity was to confuse the view he took of things. He received almost no immediate preceptions. The external world seemed further away to him than it does to us. The second effect was to make him malicious. He was malicious because he was savage; he was savage because he was ugly. His nature had its logic the same as ours. His extraordinary strength was a further cause of his maliciousness. *Malus puer robustus*, as Hobbes says.

But we must do him the justice of stating that his maliciousness was perhaps not innate. From his earliest contact with mankind he was mocked, insulted and rejected. Human speech for him was always either a jeer or a curse. As he grew up he found nothing but hatred around him; in becoming malicious he only picked up the weapon with which he had been wounded.

He therefore turned to mankind only with regret. His cathedral was enough for him. It was peopled with marble figures of kings, saints and bishops who at least did not laugh in his face and looked at him with only tranquillity and benevolence. The other statues, those of monsters and demons, had no hatred for him—he resembled them too closely for that. It was rather the rest of mankind that they jeered at. The saints were his friends and blessed him; the monsters were his friends and kept watch over him. He would sometimes spend whole hours crouched before one of the statues in solitary conversation with it. If anyone came upon him then he would run away like a lover surprised during a serenade.

The cathedral was not only society to him; it was also the world and all of nature. He dreamed of no other trees than the stained glass windows which were always in bloom, of no other shade than that of the stone foliage at the top of the pillars, of no other mountains than the colossal towers of the church, and of no other ocean than the city of Paris which swirled at their feet.

But the bells were what he loved above all else. They alone awakened his soul and allowed it to spread its wings; they sometimes even gave him a feeling of happiness. He loved them, caressed them, spoke to them and understood them. The two towers and the belfry of the transept were for him like three great cages whose birds sang for him alone. These were the same bells which had made him deaf, but mothers are often fondest of the child which has caused them the greatest pain.

Their voices were the only ones he could still hear. On this account the great bell, named Marie, was his favorite. She and her sister Jacqueline, a bell of lesser size, were alone in the southern tower. The northern tower contained six other bells and six smaller ones dwelt in the belfry of the transept along with the wooden bell which was rung only between the afternoon of Holy Thursday and the morning of Easter Eve. Quasimodo therefore had fourteen bells in his seraglio besides his favorite, big Marie.

It is difficult to conceive of his joy on days when the bells were to ring in full peal. The instant the archdeacon gave him the signal he would run up the winding staircase of the tower faster than anyone else could have run down it and enter big Marie's lofty chamber out of breath. He would gaze on her lovingly for a moment, then speak to her and stroke her as if she were a good horse ready to set out on a long and difficult journey, pitying her for the pain she was about to undergo. After these first caresses, he would shout an order to his assistants stationed in a lower story of the tower.

They seized the ropes, the windlass creaked and the ponderous mass of metal slowly began to move. Quasimodo, quivering with excitement, followed it with his eyes. The first blow of the clapper against the bronze wall surrounding it shook the wooden platform on which he was standing. "Vah!" he shouted with a burst of senseless laughter. Meanwhile the movement of the bell was accelerating and as it covered a wider angle Quasimodo's eye also opened wider and shone more brightly. Finally the great peal began, causing the whole tower to tremble; rafters, roof, stones, everything groaned at once, from the piles of the foundation to the ornamental foliation at the summit. Quasimodo boiled over with savage glee, running to and fro, trembling in unison with the tower from head to toe. As the great bell turned its bronze throat first to one wall, then to another, there burst forth from it a thunderous roar which could be heard four leagues away. Quasimodo placed himself before that gaping throat, alternately crouching and standing as the bell swung toward him and away from him, inhaling its furious breath, looking down at the square swarming with people two hundred feet below him and up at the enormous copper tongue which bellowed in his ear every few seconds. It was the only speech he understood, the only sound that troubled the universal silence in which he lived. He basked in it, like a bird in the sunshine.

All at once he would be seized by the frenzy around him. A wild look would come into his eyes and he would watch the swinging bell like a spider lying in wait for a fly, then suddenly leap on it with all his might. Suspended high in the air, soaring in breathtaking sweeps, he would cling to the bronze monster, grip it with his knees, spur it on with his heels and increase the fury of the peal with all the weight and strength of his body. He would shriek and gnash his teeth, his red hair bristling, his chest heaving like the bellows of a forge and his eyes flashing fire as the monstrous bell neighed and panted under him. It was then no longer the great bell of Notre Dame and Quasimodo; it was a dream, a whirlwind, a tempest; frenzy riding on uproar; a strange centaur, half man and half bell; a sort of horrible Astolpho carried along on a prodigious hippogriff of living bronze.

The presence of this extraordinary being seemed to breathe life into the whole cathedral. There seemed to come from him, at least according to the exaggerated superstitions of the people, a mysterious emanation which animated all the stones of Notre Dame and made the old church quiver to its very entrails. Knowing that he was there was enough to make the hundreds of statues along the galleries and over the doorways seem to live and move. Indeed, the cathedral seemed to be a docile and obedient creature under his hand, permeated through with his presence and awaiting only his bidding to raise its mighty voice. Sometimes, in fact, he seemed to be all over it at once, multiplying himself at all points of the edifice. A spectator in the square below might be stricken with fright on seeing at the top of one of the towers a strange dwarf climbing, twisting, crawling on all fours, coming down the wall high overhead, hopping from one projection to another, then thrusting his hand down the throat of some sculptured Gorgon—it was Quasimodo clearing out crows' nests. Sometimes a visitor to the church would come across a sort of living chimera squatting and scowling in some dark corner —it was Quasimodo meditating. Sometimes an enormous head and a bundle of disorderly limbs could be seen swinging furiously at the end of a rope in one of the towers—it was Quasimodo ringing vespers or the Angelus. Often at night a hideous form was seen prowling along the delicate openwork balustrade of the apse—it was again the hunchback of Notre Dame. At those times, said the neighbors, the whole cathedral took on a fantastic, supernatural and frightening aspect; eyes and mouths would open here and there; strange noises could he heard coming from the stone dogs, serpents and monsters which day and night kept watch around the edifice with outstretched necks and gaping jaws. On Christmas Eve the great bell seemed to be groaning as it summoned the faithful to midnight mass and the gloomy façade wore such a strange and sinister air that the huge doorway appeared to be devouring the crowd while the great round window stared down at them from above. And all this was due to Quasimodo. Ancient Egypt would have taken him for the god of the temple; the Middle Ages took him for its demon; he was its soul.

Today, for those who know that Quasimodo once existed, Notre Dame is deserted and lifeless. That immense body is empty, nothing but a skeleton; the spirit has vanished. It is like a skull in which there are still two sockets, but no eyes.

CHAPTER FOUR

The Dog and His Master

THERE WAS ONE PERSON WHOM QUASIMODO EXEMPTED FROM his malice and hatred and whom he loved as much as, or perhaps more than, his cathedral. That person was Claude Frollo.

It was only natural: Claude Frollo had taken him in, adopted him, nourished him and raised him. As a little child it was between Claude Frollo's legs that he took refuge when dogs or children came yelping after him. Claude Frollo taught him to speak, to read and to write. It was Claude Frollo, finally, who had made him bellringer of Notre Dame—and giving the great bell to Quasimodo was like giving Juliet to Romeo.

Quasimodo's gratitude was therefore deep, passionate and unbounded; and although his foster-father's face was often dark and severe and his words were usually curt, harsh and imperious, this gratitude had never wavered for a single instant. The archdeacon had in Quasimodo the most submissive of slaves, the most docile of servants and the most vigilant of watchdogs. When the poor bellringer became deaf the two men developed a mysterious language of signs and gestures which was understood by them alone. Thus the archdeacon was the only person with whom Quasimodo maintained communication. There were only two things in the world with which he felt any connection: Notre Dame and Claude Frollo.

Nothing could be compared to the archdeacon's dominion over the bellringer or the bellringer's devotion to the archdeacon. A sign from Claude Frollo and the idea of pleasing him would have been enough to make Quasimodo jump from the top of the towers of Notre Dame. It was remarkable to see all that physical strength, developed to such an extraordinary degree in Quasimodo, placed blindly at the disposal of another person. It was a question not only of filial devotion but also of the fascination exerted by one mind on another. It was a poor, dull, awkward creature standing with lowered head and supplicating eye before a high, profound, powerful and superior intellect. But above all it was gratitude; gratitude pushed so far toward its extreme limit that we have nothing with which to compare it. This is not a virtue whose most striking examples are to be found among men; we will therefore say that Quasimodo loved the archdeacon as no dog, horse or elephant ever loved its master.

CHAPTER FIVE

More about Claude Frollo

IN 1482 QUASIMODO WAS ABOUT TWENTY YEARS OLD, THE archdeacon about thirty-six. Claude Frollo was no longer the simple student of Torchi College, the fond protector of a little child or the young, dreaming philosopher who knew many things and was ignorant of many others. He was now a solemn, austere and morose priest laden with the care of souls, Archdeacon of Josas, second acolyte of the bishop, in charge of two deanships and one hundred and seventy-four parish priests. He was a somber and awe-inspiring personage who made the choirboys and inferior priests tremble as he walked slowly along beneath the lofty arches of the choir, majestic, thoughtful, his arms crossed and his head bowed so low that no part of his face was visible except his bald, broad forehead.

Dom Claude Frollo had abandoned neither the pursuit of knowledge nor the education of his young brother, which had always been the two main preoccupations of his life, but a touch of bitterness had become mingled with them in the course of time. Young Jehan Frollo had not developed in the direction in which Claude tried to guide him. His elder brother had counted on a pious, docile, studious and honorable pupil; but, like those young trees which frustrate the efforts of the gardener by stubbornly turning in the direction from which air and sunshine come to them, his little brother would grow only in the direction of laziness, ignorance and debauch. He was a veritable devil, extremely dissolute, which made Dom Claude frown, but also extremely clever and witty, which made him smile. Claude enrolled him in that same Torchi College in which he himself had spent his first years of study

and meditation and it was a great sorrow to him that this
sanctuary which had formerly been edified by the name of
Frollo was now scandalized by it. He sometimes delivered long
and severe sermons on the subject to Jehan, who listened to
them bravely, then returned to his scandalous ways as soon
as the sermon was over. Sometimes it was a newly arrived
student at the university whom he had welcomed with a sound
thrashing—a precious tradition which has been preserved
down to our own time. Sometimes he had incited a band of
students to make a raid on a tavern, assault its owner and
merrily pillage it down to the casks of wine in the cellar. Furthermore—and this was the culminating disgrace for a six-
teen-year-old student—it was reported that his debauches
sometimes led him into the infamous Rue de Glatigny.

Saddened and discouraged by all this, Dom Claude threw
himself even more ardently into the arms of science, that sister who at least never laughs in a man's face and always repays,
if sometimes in a rather hollow coin, the attention he devotes
to her. He therefore became more and more learned and, as a
natural consequence, more and more rigid as a priest and more
and more melancholy as a man.

Since Claude Frollo had in his youth gone through nearly
the entire range of positive, lawful human knowledge, he was
obliged to seek other food for the insatiable appetite of his understanding. The ancient symbol of a serpent biting its own
tail is particularly appropriate to science. It was said by a number of serious persons that, after tasting all the fruit on the
tree of knowledge, Claude Frollo had finally bitten into the
forbidden fruit; that, perhaps at the risk of his eternal soul,
he had sat down at that mysterious table of alchemy and astrology, one end of which was occupied in the Middle Ages by
Averroës, William of Paris and Nicolas Flamel, while the
other extends into the Orient and is occupied by Solomon,
Pythagoras and Zoroaster.

Whether these conjectures were right or wrong, it is in any
case true that when the archdeacon paid his frequent visits
to the Saints-Innocents Cemetery where his parents were
buried along with the other victims of the plague of 1466, he
seemed to devote much less attention to the cross over their
graves than to the strange figures inscribed on the nearby
tomb of Nicolas Flamel and Claude Pernelle.

It is also true that he was often seen furtively entering the
small house on the corner of the Rue Marivault and the Rue
des Ecrivains. This was the house which Nicolas Flamel built

and in which he died in 1417. Deserted since then, it was already beginning to fall into ruin because so many alchemists and occultists from all over the world had scratched their names on the walls that they were almost worn through. Some of the neighbors even claimed that they had once peeked in and seen the archdeacon digging and turning over the earth in the two cellars of the house, the buttresses of which had been covered with innumerable verses and hieroglyphics by Nicolas Flamel himself. It was believed that Flamel had buried the philosopher's stone in one of these cellars and for two centuries the alchemists, from Magistri to Father Pacifique, never stopped digging in them until the house, undermined and weakened, finally collapsed around their ears.

It is true, moreover, that the archdeacon was seized with a singular passion for the symbolical doorway of Notre Dame, that occult page written in stone by Bishop William of Paris, who has no doubt been damned for attaching such an infernal frontispiece to the sacred poem which is eternally chanted by the rest of the edifice. The archdeacon was believed to have discovered the meaning of the colossal statue of Saint Christopher and of that tall enigmatic statue which in those days stood at the entrance to the square in front of the church and which the people derisively called "Monsieur Legris." Everyone was able to observe the endless hours he spent contemplating the sculpture of the doorway, sometimes examining the Foolish Virgins with their lamps upside down, sometimes the Wise Virgins with their lamps right side up, and sometimes calculating the angle of vision of the raven on the left-hand side of the doorway looking at some mysterious point inside the church, where the philosopher's stone must certainly be hidden if it is not in Nicolas Flamel's cellar. It was, let us remark in passing, a strange fate for the Cathedral of Notre Dame to be loved at that time in two such different manners and by two men so dissimilar as Claude Frollo and Quasimodo; loved by one, a sort of instinctive and savage half-man, for its beauty, stature and the harmony of the magnificent whole; loved by the other, a learned, passionate and imaginative man, for its hidden meaning, for its myth, for the symbols concealed beneath the sculpture of the façade like the first text under the second one on a palimpsest; in short, for the riddle which it constantly proposes to the understanding.

It is also true, finally, that the archdeacon had set up for himself, in the top of the tower nearest the Place de Grève, a small secret room which no one—not even the bishop, it was said—ever entered without his permission. It had originally been made by Bishop Hugo of Besançon, who practiced black magic in it. No one knew what it contained, but through its small window in the back of the tower people often saw a strange red glow appear and disappear at regular intervals, apparently governed by the blast of a pair of bellows and coming from a fire rather than a lamp or candle. It made a singular impression in the darkness and at that height. When the good women of the neighborhood saw it they would say, "There's the archdeacon puffing again; hell is crackling up there!"

There was, after all, no great proof of sorcery in all this but there was nevertheless enough smoke to lead to the conclusion that there was also fire, and the archdeacon had a rather formidable reputation. It must be noted, however, that necromancy, the sciences of Egypt and magic, even the whitest and most innocent, had no more determined enemy and no more merciless accuser before the officials of Notre Dame than Dom Claude Frollo. But whether his horror was sincere or whether it was merely the trick played by the criminal who shouts, "Stop thief!" it did not prevent the archdeacon from being considered by the learned heads of the chapter as a soul who had already ventured upon the threshold of hell, lost in the caverns of the cabala and groping in the shadows of the occult sciences. The people had no doubts on the subject, either; anyone who had any sagacity at all regarded Quasimodo as a demon and Claude Frollo as a sorcerer. It was obvious that the bellringer was to serve the archdeacon for a certain length of time, at the end of which he would carry off his soul as payment. Thus the archdeacon, despite the extreme austerity of his life, was in bad odor with all good Christians and there was not a pious nose among them which could not smell out the magician in him.

If, as he grew older, his knowledge had reached certain abysses, it was also true that abysses had been formed in his heart; at least there was good reason to believe so when one examined that face in which the workings of his mind could be seen only through a dark cloud. Whence came that bald forehead, that head always bent down, that chest always heaving with sighs? What secret thoughts made his lips smile with such bitterness at the very moment when his frowning eyebrows approached each other like two bulls about to fight? Why was his remaining hair already gray? What was that inner fire which sometimes flashed in his eyes, making them seem like two holes in the wall of a furnace?

These symptoms of a violent moral preoccupation had reached an especially high degree of intensity by the time at which our story takes place. More than one choirboy had fled in terror on meeting him alone in the church, so strange and fiery was his look. More than once during services in the choir those next to him had heard him mingle unintelligible parentheses with the chants. More than once the laundress who washed for the members of the chapter had noticed with horror the marks of claws and clenched fingers on the surplice of the Archdeacon of Josas.

Meanwhile he redoubled his austerity and led a more exemplary life than ever. By character as well as by calling, he had always remained strictly aloof from women; he now seemed to hate them even more than ever. The mere rustle of a silk petticoat made him pull his hood down over his eyes.

His horror of gypsy women had become especially marked of late. He had requested the bishop to issue an edict expressly forbidding them to dance in the square in front of the cathedral. At the same time he had begun searching through the musty archives to gather cases of witches and sorcerers who had been burned or hanged for practicing black magic with the aid of goats or swine.

The archdeacon and Quasimodo, as we have already noted, were held in no great affection by the people living in the neighborhood of the cathedral. When they went out together, as they frequently did, they were always assailed by insults, sinister innuendo and mockery, except on the rare occasions when Claude Frollo walked along with his head erect and overawed the scoffers with his stern and imperious countenance.

Sometimes a mischievous urchin would risk his neck for the ineffable pleasure of sticking a pin into Quasimodo's hump; sometimes a pretty young girl, somewhat bolder than she should have been, would rub against the priest's black robe and sarcastically sing under his very nose, "Hide, hide, the devil's caught!" Sometimes a group of squalid old women squatting on the steps of a porch would curse them as they passed and fling them such gracious remarks as, "There they go—one's soul is as twisted as the other's body!"

But these friendly greetings usually went unheeded. Quasimodo was too deaf to hear them and Claude Frollo was too deeply absorbed in his thoughts.

Book IV

CHAPTER ONE

Medieval Justice

THE NOBLE ROBERT D'ESTOUTEVILLE, PROVOST OF PARIS IN the Year of Our Lord 1482, was a lucky man. Not only did he hold his own court sessions as Provost and Viscount of Paris, but he also had a share in the justice meted out by the king himself. There was no head of any respectable rank which did not pass through his hands before being delivered up to the executioner.

Here, surely, was more than enough to make a happy and illustrious life. Yet when Messire Robert d'Estouteville awoke on the morning of January 7, 1482, he was in a murderously bad humor. He himself would have been at a loss to explain it. Was it because the sky was gray? Was it because his old sword belt was too tight and squeezed his portly figure in an unseemly way? Was it the band of worthless scoundrels who had jeered at him as they passed beneath his window? Or was it a vague presentiment of the drastic cut in the revenue of the provostry which the future King Charles VIII was to make the following year? The reader may decide for himself; as for us, we are inclined to believe that he was in a bad humor simply because he was in a bad humor.

Besides, it was the day after a public festival, an annoying day for everyone, but especially for the magistrate whose duty was to clear away all the filth, in both the literal and the figura-

71

tive sense of the word, which a Paris holiday always leaves behind. Then, too, he had to hold a court session in the Grand-Châtelet. Now it is our observation that judges usually manage to hold their sessions on days when they are in a bad humor, in order to have someone to take it out on conveniently in the name of law and justice.

Meanwhile the session had begun without him. His deputies were handling his duties for him, according to custom, and since eight o'clock in the morning a crowd of several dozen citizens jammed in between the wall and a strong oaken barrier had been blissfully taking in the varied and edified spectacle of civil and criminal justice being administered confusedly and at random by Master Florian Barbedienne, Auditor of the Châtelet and Deputy Provost of Paris.

The room was small, low and vaulted. At one end was a table decorated with fleurs-de-lis, a large carved oaken chair which was reserved for the provost and was as yet empty, and a stool for the auditor, Master Florian. Below sat the court clerk, busily scribbling. In front were the people and near the door and the table were a number of sergeants of the provostry wearing purple uniforms with white crosses on them. Two sergeants of the Parloir-aux-Bourgeois, dressed in their red and blue uniforms, stood sentry before a low closed door behind the table. A pale ray of January sunlight came in through the single small pointed window set in the thick wall.

Picture to yourself the auditor, Master Florian Barbedienne, seated at the provost's table between two stacks of legal documents, leaning on his elbows, his foot on the hem of his plain brown robe, and his round red face, with its majestic jowls and double chin, buried in his white fur-trimmed collar.

Now this auditor was deaf, which is no doubt only a minor defect in a judge. It did not prevent Master Florian from passing competent judgments without appeal. It is sufficient for a judge to appear to listen and the venerable auditor was able to fulfill this condition even better than most because his attention was never diverted by any sound.

Among the spectators, however, there was one merciless critic of all the auditor's words and actions: our friend Jehan Frollo, who was sure to be seen everywhere in Paris except at his professors' lectures.

"Look," he said to his companion, Robin Poussepain, who sat beside him snickering at his comments on the scene before them, "there's that pretty Jehanneton du Buisson . . .

What! He's fining her for wearing two strings of beads! His eyes must be as bad as his ears! . . . Here come two gentlemen who've been shooting dice . . . He's fining them a hundred livres! But I hope to be my brother the archdeacon if that will stop me from gambling day and night and betting my soul if I lose my last shirt! . . . Holy Virgin! Look at all the girls! Ambroise Lécuyère, Isabeau la Paynette, Bérarde Gironin—I know them all, by God! . . . Accused of wearing gilded belts. . . . Go ahead, fine them, you deaf imbecile! . . . Here's another amorous lady . . . accused of leaving the Rue Glatigny without permission. He'll fine her, of course! . . . Look over there, Robin! Who's being brought in? See all those sergeants? All the hounds of the pack are there, by God! They must have made some sensational catch, a wild boar at least! . . . Look! It is a wild boar! It's yesterday's Pope of Fools! It's our hunchback, Quasimodo!"

It was indeed Quasimodo, tightly bound and well guarded. The detachment of sergeants surrounding him were accompanied by the captain of the watch in person. There was, however, nothing about Quasimodo to justify such a formidable array of weapons and guards. He was somber, silent and calm. Only rarely did his single eye cast a look of sullen anger at the bonds which held him fast. He cast the same look around him, but it seemed so dull and sleepy that the women pointed at him only in laughter.

Meanwhile Master Florian was attentively reading over the document containing the charges against Quasimodo. Thanks to this precaution he always knew the prisoner's name, occupation and crime in advance. This enabled him to make the expected replies to the expected answers and thus get through the routine of the interrogatory without revealing his deafness too clearly. When his infirmity occasionally betrayed itself in some incoherent remark or unintelligible question it was taken for profundity by some of his listeners and stupidity by others. In either case the honor of the magistracy remained unstained, for it is better for a judge to be considered profound or stupid than deaf. He therefore took great pains to conceal his deafness from everyone and he succeeded so well that he finally deceived even himself, which is easier to do than one might think. He believed himself to be slightly hard of hearing and this was the only concession he would make to public opinion on this point in his moments of frankness and self-examination.

Having thoroughly read over the charges against Quasimodo, he threw back his head and half closed his eyes in order to appear more majestic and impartial, then began the interrogatory:

"Your name?"

Now here was a case which the law had not provided for: one deaf man questioning another. Quasimodo, unaware of the question which had been addressed to him, continued to look steadfastly at the judge without answering. The judge, unaware of the prisoner's deafness, believed he had answered the question like any other prisoner and pursued the interrogatory with his mechanical and stupid self-assurance:

"Very well. And what is your age?"

Quasimodo did not answer this question either. The judge went on:

"Now, what is your occupation?"

Still the same silence on the part of Quasimodo. The spectators, however, began to whisper and look at each other.

"That will do," said the imperturbable auditor when he presumed that the prisoner had finished giving his third answer. "You have been brought before us accused, first, of making a nocturnal disturbance; second, of making an unlawful assault upon the person of a lewd woman; and, third, of resistance and disloyalty to the Archers of the Guard of Our Lord the King. You will now explain yourself with regard to these three accusations." Then, turning to the court clerk, he said, "Clerk, have you written down everything the prisoner has said so far?"

This unfortunate question brought forth such a violent, contagious burst of laughter from everyone in the courtroom, officials as well as spectators, that neither of the two deaf men could help noticing it. Quasimodo turned around and shrugged scornfully, while Master Florian, equally surprised and assuming that the laughter had been provoked by some disrespectful answer from the prisoner, made visible for him by his shrug, reprimanded him indignantly:

"You deserve to be hanged for that answer, you wretched scoundrel! Do you know to whom you're speaking?"

These remarks were not suited to check the general outburst of merriment. They seemed to everyone so incongruous and ridiculous that the wild laughter spread even to the sergeants of the Parloir-aux-Bourgeois, whose stupidity was proverbial. Quasimodo alone kept a straight face, for the good reason that he did not have the slightest idea of what was happening. The judge, more and more outraged, thought it best to continue in the same tone, hoping to strike terror into the prisoner, which would also affect the spectators and bring them back to a properly respectful attitude.

"How dare you show such disrespect for the Auditor of the Châtelet, the magistrate in charge of the police of Paris, appointed to inquire into crimes and misdemeanors, to control all trades and prevent monopolies and unfair practices, to keep the pavements in good repair, to cleanse the city of filth and the air of contagious diseases; in short, to keep continuous watch over the public welfare and all without salary or hope of reward! Do you realize that I am Florian Barbedienne, not only Deputy Provost of Paris, but also a commissioner, an examiner . . ."

There is no reason why a deaf man talking to a deaf man should ever stop. God only knows where and when Master Florian would have finally dropped anchor in this sea of eloquence if the low door behind the table had not suddenly opened and admitted the Provost of Paris in person. Master Florian abruptly turned around and directed toward the provost the harangue with which he had been blasting Quasimodo a moment before. "Sir," he said, "I request such punishment as you may see fit to inflict upon this prisoner for deliberate and flagrant contempt of court."

He sat down out of breath and began to wipe away the perspiration which trickled down his forehead and fell like tears on the parchments spread out before him. Messire Robert d'Estouteville frowned and commanded Quasimodo's attention with such an expressive and imperious gesture that the deaf bellringer clearly understood his meaning.

"What have you done to be brought here, scoundrel?" asked the provost sternly.

The poor devil, supposing that the provost had asked him his name, broke his habitual silence and answered in a hoarse, guttural voice, "Quasimodo."

The spectators once again burst into laughter and the provost cried out, scarlet with rage, "What! You have the impertinence to mock me too!"

"Bellringer of Notre Dame," replied Quasimodo, thinking the judge had asked him his occupation.

"Bellringer!" retorted the provost, who, as we have already noted, had awakened that morning in such a bad humor that his fury had no need to be stirred up by such perverse answers. "Bellringer! I'll have a peal of rods rung on your back through all the streets of Paris!"

"If it's my age you want to know," said Quasimodo, "I think I'll be twenty next Martinmas."

This was too much. The provost was beside himself with rage. "I'll teach you to make fun of the Provost of Paris!" he roared. "Sergeants, take this scoundrel to the pillory at the Place de Grève. Have him flogged and then turned for one hour. And have a public proclamation of this sentence made with four trumpeters."

A few moments later the clerk had drawn up the sentence. It was simple and brief. The procedures of the provostry and the Viscounty of Paris had not yet been reconstructed by President Thibaut Baillet and King's Advocate Roger Barmne; they were not yet overgrown with that dense forest of hair-splitting quibbles and stilted formalities which these two jurists planted at the beginning of the sixteenth century. Everything was clear, explicit and quick. Justice went straight to the point in those days and at the end of every path, without underbrush or detours, the prisoner immediately perceived the gallows, the wheel or the pillory. At least he knew where he was going.

The clerk handed the sentence to the provost, who affixed his seal to it, then left to continue his tour of the other court-rooms, in a frame of mind which must have filled all the jails of Paris that day. Jehan Frollo and Robin Poussepain laughed up their sleeves and Quasimodo looked on with an air of detached astonishment.

As Master Florian was reading over the sentence before signing it, the clerk felt a surge of pity for the wretched prisoner and, in the hope of obtaining some mitigation of his punishment, approached as closely as he could to the auditor's ear and said, pointing to Quasimodo, "This man is deaf!"

He hoped that this mutual infirmity might arouse the auditor's sympathy but we have already observed that Master Florian did not care to have his deafness known. Besides, he did not hear a word of what the clerk said to him. Pretending to have understood, he replied, "Oh, I didn't know that. In that case, have him kept on the pillory for an extra hour." And he signed the sentence with this modification.

CHAPTER TWO

The Rat Hole

LET US NOW RETURN TO THE PLACE DE GRÈVE, WHICH WE left yesterday with Gringoire in order to follow La Esmeralda.

It is ten o'clock in the morning. Everything indicates the day after a festival. The pavement is strewn with debris: ribbons, rags, feathers, drops of wax from the torches and scraps from the public feast. A good many citizens are strolling around here and there, kicking the embers of the bonfire, standing before the Maison-aux-Piliers enraptured by the memory of the beautiful hangings with which it was draped the day before and taking a residual pleasure in looking at the nails with which they had been attached. Beer and wine vendors roll their casks through the crowd. A few industrious-looking individuals hurry along, apparently on business errands. The merchants gossip and call to one another from the doorways of their shops. Everyone is speaking of the festival, the Flemish ambassadors, Jacques Coppenole and the Pope of Fools, each trying to make the wittiest comment and laugh the loudest. Meanwhile four sergeants on horseback who have just stationed themselves on the four sides of the pillory have already concentrated around them a good part of the scattered populace in the square, who willingly condemn themselves to immobility and boredom in the hope of seeing a small execution.

If, after contemplating the lively and clamorous scene which is being enacted all over the square, the reader will now turn his eyes toward that ancient half-Gothic, half-Roman building known as Roland Tower which stands on the western side of the square near the Seine, he will notice at one corner of it a public breviary, richly illuminated, sheltered from the weather by a small roof and protected against thieves by a metal grill which, however, does not prevent its pages from being turned. Beside this breviary is a narrow pointed window opening onto the square and guarded by two iron bars placed before it in the shape of a cross. It is the only opening through which air and light can reach a small doorless cell built into one wall of the old building. Its peace and silence are made even more profound and melancholy by the fact that a public square, the noisiest and most populous in Paris, is swarming and clamoring just outside it.

This cell had been famous in Paris for nearly three centuries, ever since Madame Rolande de la Tour-Roland, in mourning for her father, who had been killed in the Crusades, had it cut into the wall of her own house and shut herself up in it for the rest of her life. This small room, whose door was walled up and whose window remained open winter and summer alike, was the only part of her mansion she kept for herself; she gave the rest of her possessions to the poor and to God. The heartbroken lady awaited death for twenty years in her anticipated tomb, praying night and day for her father's soul, sleeping in ashes without even a stone on which to lay her head, dressed in black sackcloth and living only on the bread and water which the passers-by left on her windowsill out of pity, thus receiving charity after she had given it.

Before she died she bequeathed her cell forever to afflicted women who might have strong reasons to pray for themselves or for others, or who might wish to bury themselves alive because of some great sorrow or penitence. The poor people of her time honored her funeral with their tears and blessings, but to their great regret the pious lady was not canonized as a saint for lack of sufficient patronage. Those who were slightly impious hoped that her canonization could be brought about more easily in heaven than in Rome and addressed their prayers to God rather than to the pope. Most of them were content to keep her memory sacred and make relics of her rags. The City of Paris founded in her honor a public breviary which was attached to the wall near the window of her cell in order that passers-by might stop there from time to time, if only to pray, that prayer might make them think of charity and that the poor recluses who would inherit Madame Rolande's cell might therefore not die altogether from hunger and neglect.

Following the custom of the time, a Latin inscription on the wall indicated to the literate passer-by the pious purpose of the cell. Until the middle of the sixteenth century it was customary to explain a building by a brief motto above the door. Thus in France we may still read over the wicket of the prison of the seignorial mansion of Tourville: "*Sileto et spera*"; in Ireland, under the coat of arms over the grand entrance to Fortescue Castle: "*Forte scutum, salus ducum*"; in England, above the main entrance of the hospitable manor of Earl Cowper: "*Tuum est.*" In those days every building was a thought.

Since there was no door to the walled-up cell of Roland Tower, these two words were engraved in large letters above the window: "*Tu, ora.*" It was not long before the people had transformed this into *Trou-aux-Rats* (pronounced "troo-o-rah" and meaning "rat hole"), which became the common name of the gloomy and squalid cell. A translation less sublime than the original, perhaps, but more picturesque.

CHAPTER THREE

The Story of a Cake

AT THE TIME OF OUR STORY THE CELL IN ROLAND TOWER WAS occupied. If the reader wishes to know who the occupant was, he has only to listen to the conversation of three worthy ladies who, at the moment when we directed his attention to the Trou-aux-Rats, were walking along the river toward that very place.

Two of these ladies were dressed like respectable Parisians. Their fine white collars, linsey-woolsey skirts with red and blue stripes, white knitted stockings pulled tightly over their legs, square-toed shoes of brown leather with black soles, and especially their hats—a sort of horn laden with tinsel, ribbons and lace which is still worn by the women of Champagne, in common with the grenadiers of the Russian Imperial Guard —all this announced that they belonged to that class of rich merchants' wives midway between what lackeys called women and what they called ladies. They wore no rings or gold crosses but it was easy to see that this was not on account of poverty but simply out of fear of being fined.

Their companion was attired in nearly the same fashion but there was something about her dress and bearing which made her stand out as a provincial. The way her belt was above her hips showed that she had not been in Paris long. Furthermore, she had a pleated collar, bows of ribbons on her shoes, a skirt whose stripes were horizontal rather than vertical and countless other enormities repugnant to good taste.

The first two walked with that step peculiar to Parisian women who are showing the city to their provincial friends. The provincial friend held a big, chubby boy by one hand while he carried a large cake in the other. We regret that we are obliged to add that, due to the harshness of the weather, he was using his tongue as a handkerchief.

The child made his mother drag him along, stumbling at every step, to her great annoyance. It is true that he looked more at the cake than at the pavement. He must have had some serious reason for not biting into it (the cake), for he contented himself with gazing at it tenderly.

Meanwhile the three ladies were all talking at once.

"Let's hurry, Mahiette," said the youngest, who was also the fattest, to the provincial. "I'm afraid we'll get there too late. In the Châtelet they said they were going to take him to the pillory right away."

"What are you talking about, Oudarde?" retorted the other Parisian. "He'll be on the pillory for two hours. We have plenty of time . . . Have you ever seen anyone pilloried, Mahiette?"

"Yes," said the provincial, "in Reims."

"Do you call that a pillory? In Reims it's only a wretched little cage where they turn nothing but peasants."

"Peasants!" exclaimed Mahiette. "I'll have you know we've had some fine criminals in Reims. Some of them killed both their parents. Peasants! What do you think we are, Gervaise?"

She was on the point of becoming angry for the honor of her pillory but fortunately the tactful Oudarde changed the subject in time:

"By the way, Mahiette, what did you think of our Flemish ambassadors? Do you have such fine ones in Reims?"

"I admit," replied Mahiette, "that Paris is the only place to see Flemings like those."

"Did you see that great ambassador who's a hosier?" asked Oudarde.

"Yes."

"And that fat one whose face looked like a naked belly?" said Gervaise. "And that short one with little eyes and red eyelids?"

"Look at those people gathered there at the end of the bridge!" suddenly cried Mahiette. "They're all looking at something."

"And I hear a tambourine," said Gervaise. "It must be little Esmeralda with her goat. Come on, Mahiette, walk faster and pull your boy along. You came here to see the sights of Paris. Yesterday you saw the Flemings; today you must see the gypsy girl."

"The gypsy girl!" exclaimed Mahiette, abruptly turning around and taking a firm grip on her son's arm. "God preserve me from her! She'd steal my child! Come on, Eustache!" She began to run along the river toward the Place de Grève until she had left the bridge far behind her. Her child, whom she had been dragging along, finally fell to his knees from exhaustion. She stopped to catch her breath and the two other ladies caught up with her.

"What makes you think the gypsy girl would steal your child?" asked Gervaise. "What a strange idea!"

Mahiette nodded thoughtfully.

"What's strange," remarked Oudarde, "is that Sister Gudule has the same idea about gypsies."

"Who's Sister Gudule?" asked Mahiette.

"It's easy to see you're from Reims if you don't know that!" answered Oudarde. "She's the recluse in the Trou-aux-Rats."

"Do you mean that poor woman we're taking this cake to?" asked Mahiette.

Oudarde nodded. "Precisely," she said. "You'll see her soon through her little window overlooking the Place de Grève. She has the same opinion as you about those vagabond gypsy women who dance in public and tell fortunes. Nobody knows why she has such a horror of them. But you, Mahiette, why does merely the sight of one of them make you run away like that?"

"Oh!" said Mahiette, taking her son's round head between her hands, "I don't want the same thing to happen to him as happened to Paquette la Chantefleurie's child!"

"You must tell us the story, Mahiette," said Gervaise, taking her by the arm.

"I'm perfectly willing," replied Mahiette, "but it's easy to see you're from Paris if you don't know it already. Well, to begin with—but we can keep walking while I tell you the story—Paquette la Chantefleurie was a pretty girl of eighteen at the same time I was, in other words, eighteen years ago, and it's her own fault if she's not now, as I am, a plump, handsome mother of thirty-six with a husband and a son. From the time she was fourteen, though, it was already too late! She was the daughter of Guybertaut, the boat minstrel of Reims, the one who played before King Charles the Seventh during his coronation ceremony when he went down our Vesle River from Sillery to Muison. He died while Paquette was still a child, so she had only her mother, who was a sister of Monsieur Mathieu Pradon, a master coppersmith and brazier here in Paris. You can see she came from a good family. Her mother was a kind, good-natured woman but unfortunately she taught her nothing but a little needlework, which wasn't enough to keep her from always being poor. They both lived in Reims, near the river on the Rue Folle-Peine. Now pay attention to this, because I think it's what caused all Paquette's troubles: in 1461, the year of the coronation of Louis the Eleventh, God bless his soul, she was so pretty and gay that no one called her anything except La Chantefleurie. Poor girl! She had pretty teeth and she liked to laugh to show them off and 'a girl who likes to laugh is on the way to weeping.'

"She and her mother had a hard time making a living. Things had been growing worse and worse for them ever since the minstrel's death. Their needlework never brought in more than six deniers a week. Gone were the days when Guybertaut used to earn twelve sols at a coronation with one single song. One winter—it was the winter of 1461—they had no wood to burn and it was very cold, which gave Paquette such a beautiful color that men began to notice her more than ever and she was ruined. Eustache! Leave that cake alone! We saw she was ruined one Sunday when she came to church wearing a gold cross around her neck. Only fourteen years old! Can you imagine that?

"First it was the young Viscount of Cormontreuil, whose castle is about three quarters of a mile from Reims. Then it was Henri de Triancourt, the king's horsemaster; then, lower than that, Chiart de Beaulion, a sergeant-at-arms; then, still lower, Guery Aubergeon, the king's carver; and so on, always with men of lower and lower rank until finally she came to Thierry de Mer, who was only a lampmaker. By then all men were the same to her. And it all happened in one year! Poor Paquette!"

Mahiette sighed and wiped a tear from her eye.

"That's not a very unusual story," said Gervaise, "and I don't see what it has to do with gypsies and children."

"Be patient," said Mahiette. "I haven't come to the part about the child yet. In 1466 Paquette gave birth to a little girl, which made her very happy, poor woman. She'd been wanting a child for a long time. Her mother, a good woman who always closed her eyes to her daughter's shortcomings, was dead. Paquette had no one left in the world to love and no one to love her. In the five years since her downfall, she'd been leading a miserable life. She was all alone in her shame, pointed at in public, jeered at in the streets, beaten by the sergeants of the watch and mocked by little boys. Also, she was twenty by then, which is old for women like that. Her sin began to bring in less than her needlework had before; every wrinkle that came into her face took a little more off her income. The winter became hard for her again; soon there was very little wood in her fireplace and very little bread in her cupboard. She couldn't work any more because when she became voluptuous she also became lazy, and she suffered more because when she became lazy she became even more voluptuous. At least that's how our priest explains why women like that are colder and hungrier than other poor women when they grow old."

"Yes," remarked Gervaise, "but what about the gypsies?"

"Just wait a minute, Gervaise!" said Oudarde, who was less impatient by nature. "What would be left for the end of a story if everything were at the beginning? Please go on, Mahiette. That poor Paquette!"

Mahiette continued: "Well, she was very sad and very poor and she wore furrows in her cheeks with her tears. But even in her shame and sin, it seemed to her she would be less shameful and less sinful if she had something or someone in the world she could love. It would have to be a child, because only a child could be innocent enough for that. She discovered this after trying to love a robber, the only kind of man who would have anything to do with her, but after a while she saw that even the robber despised her. Women like that have to have either a lover or a child to fill their hearts, otherwise they're terribly unhappy. It was impossible for her to have a lover, so she set her whole heart on having a child, and since she hadn't stopped being religious, she constantly prayed to God to let her have one. God took pity on her and gave her a little girl.

"I can't tell you how happy she was. How she wept and hugged and caressed her child! She suckled it herself and made its clothes out of her only blanket, but she no longer felt cold or hunger. She became beautiful again; 'an old maid makes a young mother,' as the saying goes. Men began to come to her again and with the money she earned by her sin she bought clothes, blankets, lace and little satin bonnets for her baby, without even thinking of buying a new blanket for herself. Eustache! How many times have I told you to keep away from that cake?

"Little Agnès—that was the baby's name—wore more ribbons and embroidery than a princess. Among other things she had a pair of little shoes which I'm sure were finer than anything King Louis ever wore. Paquette sewed and embroidered them herself and she was still a very skillful needleworker. They were the prettiest little pink shoes you ever saw. They were no longer than my thumb and you had to see the baby's little feet come out of them to believe they could fit into them. When you have children, Oudarde, you'll know that nothing is as pretty as a baby's little hands and feet."

"I'd like nothing better," said Oudarde, sighing, "but I'm still waiting for my husband to make up his mind to it."

"Paquette's baby had more than pretty feet," went on Mahiette. "I saw her when she was only four months old. She was absolutely adorable! Her eyes were bigger than her mouth and she had beautiful fine black hair which was already curly. What a lovely brunette she would have made at sixteen! Her mother loved her more every day. She hugged her, kissed her, played with her, washed her and dressed her every minute she could spare. She was almost wild with joy and never stopped thanking God for her. Those pink little feet, especially, were an endless wonder to her. She was always kissing them and was always amazed at how tiny they were. She would spend whole hours putting the little shoes on them and taking them off again."

"That's a fine story so far," said Gervaise in an undertone, "but we still haven't heard anything about gypsies."

"I'm just about to come to them," replied Mahiette. "One day some very strange-looking people came to Reims on horseback. They were beggars and vagabonds roaming across the country led by their dukes and counts. They were dark, had curly hair and wore silver rings in their ears. The women were even uglier and darker than the men. They always went bareheaded and wore ragged clothes, with an old piece of sackcloth tied around their shoulders. Their hair was tied in back like a horse's tail. The children running around between their legs would have frightened a monkey. The whole excommunicated band of them came to Reims straight from Egypt by way of Poland. They say the pope confessed them and ordered them as a penance to wander for seven years without ever sleeping in a bed. It seems they were Saracens before that, which means they believed in Jupiter. When they came to Reims they were naturally forbidden to enter the city, so they camped on a hill outside, near the old chalk pits.

"Everyone in Reims went out to see them. They would look in your hand and prophesy all sorts of wonderful things. If Judas had come to them they'd have predicted he'd be pope some day. But there were also rumors that they stole children, cut purses and ate human flesh. Wise people told foolish people not to go near them, then went out to see them in secret. The fact is they predicted things that would have amazed a cardinal. Mothers were full of pride for their children after the gypsies had read all sorts of miracles in their hands. One was going to be an emperor, another the pope, another a great captain, and so on. Poor Paquette was also curious. She wanted to know if her pretty little Agnès was going to be Empress of Armenia or something like that, so she took her to the gypsies. They caressed her, admired her, kissed her with their black mouths and wondered at her tiny hands, which, alas, made Paquette very happy. They were especially fascinated by her pretty little feet and shoes. The child was still less than one year old. She was plump and round, laughed at her mother, babbled and had more charming little ways than an angel of paradise. She was afraid of the gypsies and cried, but her mother kissed her and took her away delighted with the things they had predicted for her. She was to be a beautiful and virtuous queen. When Paquette returned to her attic room on the Rue Folle-Peine she was proud to be bringing back a queen.

"The next day while the child was asleep she left the door ajar and ran off to tell one of her neighbors that a day would come when her daughter Agnès would be served at table by the King of England and the Archduke of Ethiopia and a dozen other surprising things like that. When she came back and heard no crying as she came up the stairs, she said to herself, 'Good, she's still asleep.' But she noticed that the door was open wider than she had left it. When she came in, poor mother, and ran over to the bed—her baby wasn't there! Nothing was left except one of her pretty little shoes.

"Paquette ran out of the room and down into the street. She began to beat her head against the walls and scream, 'My baby! Who took my baby?' But the street was deserted and no one could tell her anything. She went all over town, searching every street, running back and forth all day long, furious and bewildered, sniffing at every door and glaring into every window like a wild animal that has lost its young. She was panting, disheveled and frightening to look at and she had a fire in her eyes that dried up all her tears. She stopped people in the street and cried, 'My daughter! My daughter! My pretty little baby! If anyone gives her back to me I'll be his servant, his dog's servant! He can eat my heart if he wants to!' It was heart-rending, Oudarde. I know one very hardhearted man who actually wept when he saw her. Oh, the poor mother!

"She came back home that night. While she was away, one of her neighbors had seen two gypsy women go furtively up to her room carrying a bundle in their arms, then come down and run away. Since then, the crying of a child had been heard coming from her room. When she heard this she laughed wildly, ran up the stairs as if she had wings, threw open the door—and saw something horrible. Instead of her lovely little Agnès, so pink and fresh, a real gift of God, she saw a kind of little monster, hideous, lame, one-eyed, crawling on the floor and squalling. She put her hands over her eyes in horror. 'Oh!' she said, 'have those witches changed my baby into this terrible animal?' The neighbors took it away immediately; the sight of it would have driven her mad. It was the monstrous child of some gypsy woman who had given herself to the devil. It seemed to be about four years old and babbled something that wasn't like any human language.

"Paquette clutched the little shoe, all that was left of everything she had loved. She lay still and breathless so long that the neighbors thought she might be dead. Suddenly she trembled all over, covered the shoe with passionate kisses and burst out sobbing as if her heart were broken in two. And we all cried too. She said, 'Oh, my little girl! My pretty little girl! Where are you?' It was enough to tear your heart out. It still makes me cry just to think of it. A mother loves her child more than her own life. . . . My Eustache is so handsome! If you only knew how nice he is! Only yesterday he said to me, 'I want to be a gendarme when I grow up.' Oh, my Eustache! If I ever lost you . . .

"Well, after a while Paquette jumped up all at once and started running through the streets shouting, 'To the gypsy camp! To the gypsy camp! Send sergeants to burn the witches!' But the gypsies were gone. It was a dark night and the sergeants couldn't follow them. The next day, on a heath a few miles outside of Reims, they found the ashes of a big fire, a few ribbons which had belonged to Paquette's baby, several drops of blood and some goat dung. The night before was a Saturday; it was obvious that the gypsies had held a witches' sabbath on that heath and eaten the child in the company of Beelzebub. When Paquette heard about these horrible things she stopped crying and moved her lips as if she were trying to speak; but she couldn't say a word. The next day her hair had turned gray; the day after that she disappeared."

"What a terrible story!" said Oudarde. "It would make a Burgundian weep!"

"No wonder you're scared to death of gypsies!" added Gervaise.

"And you were right to run away with your Eustache just now," said Oudarde, "especially since the gypsies are from Poland too."

"No, they're not," said Gervaise. "They're supposed to have come from Spain and Catalonia."

"Catalonia?" said Oudarde. "Maybe so; anyway I'm sure of one thing: they're real gypsies."

"And I'm sure their teeth are long enough to eat children," remarked Gervaise. "In fact, I wouldn't be surprised if Esmeralda took a little bite now and then. And her white goat knows so many malicious tricks that I'm sure there's something unholy at the bottom of it."

Mahiette walked on in silence, absorbed in that reverie which is a sort of prolongation of a sad story and which does not stop until it has communicated its shock by successive vibrations to the innermost fibers of the heart. "Did anyone ever find out what became of Paquette?" asked Gervaise. Mahiette did not answer. Gervaise repeated the question, shaking her arm and calling her by name. Mahiette seemed to awaken from her thoughts.

"What became of Paquette?" she said, mechanically repeating the words, whose impression was still fresh in her ears. Then, making an effort to focus her attention on their meaning, she said, "No, no one ever knew." After a pause she added, "Some people say they saw her leave Reims at twilight by the Fléchembault Gate, others say it was at dawn by the old Basée Gate. Her gold cross was found hanging on the stone cross in the field where the fair was held. That was the gift that led to her ruin in 1461; it was given to her by the Viscount of Cormontreuil, her first lover. It was very precious to her and she'd always refused to sell it, no matter how poor she was, so when we saw it we thought she must be dead. Yet some people say they saw her on the road to Paris, walking barefooted on the stones. But in that case she'd have had to leave Reims by the Vesle Gate, so none of the stories agree. For my part, I think she went out the Vesle Gate all right, but into the next world."

"I don't understand," said Gervaise.

"The Vesle," explained Mahiette with a melancholy smile, "is the name of our river."

"Poor Paquette!" said Oudarde, shuddering. "Drowned!"

"Drowned!" rejoined Mahiette. "And who could have told her father, Guybertaut, when he used to float down that river singing in his boat, that one day his dear little Paquette would also float down it, but without either a boat or a song."

"What became of the little shoe?" asked Gervaise.

"It vanished along with Paquette," answered Mahiette.

"Poor little shoe!" said Oudarde.

Oudarde, a plump, sensitive woman, would have been satisfied to sigh in company with Mahiette, but Gervaise, who was more curious, had not yet run out of questions.

"And what about the monster?" she asked suddenly.

"What monster?"

"The little monster the gypsies left in Paquette's room in exchange for her daughter. What did the neighbors do with it? I hope they drowned it too. Did they?"

"No," replied Mahiette.

"What! Well, did they burn it, then? Come to think of it, that's a better thing to do with a witch's child."

"It was neither drowned nor burned, Gervaise. The archbishop took an interest in it, exorcised it, blessed it and, after making very sure it was no longer possessed by the devil, he sent it to Paris to be exposed in front of Notre Dame as a foundling."

"Those bishops!" muttered Gervaise. "Just because they're so learned, they think they can't do anything like other people. Can you imagine exposing the devil as a foundling! And I'm sure the little monster really was a devil. Well, Mahiette, what happened to it in Paris? I'm sure no charitable person would have anything to do with it."

"I don't know," replied Mahiette. "Not long after that my husband bought a place in Beru, which is several miles outside of Reims, and we never heard anything more about the story."

As they were carrying on this conversation, the three worthy ladies had arrived at the Place de Grève. They were so preoccupied that they passed in front of the public breviary at Roland Tower without stopping and mechanically directed their steps toward the pillory, around which the crowd was growing larger at every moment. It is probable that the spectacle which was then attracting everyone's attention would have made them completely forget about the Trou-aux-Rats and the stop they had intended to make there if the fat six-year-old Eustache had not abruptly reminded them of it. "Mother," he said, as if some instinct had told him that the Trou-aux-Rats was behind him, "now can I eat the cake?"

If Eustache had been cleverer, or less greedy, he would have waited until they were much farther away before asking this question.

"That reminds me," said Mahiette, "we're forgetting the recluse! Show me where the Trou-aux-Rats is so I can bring her the cake."

"It's right over there," said Oudarde.

This did not suit Eustache at all. "I want my cake," he said, alternately striking each ear against a shoulder, which in such cases is a sign of supreme dissatisfaction.

The three ladies turned back. When they were near Roland Tower, Oudarde said to the two others, "We mustn't all three look into the cell at the same time—that might frighten her. You two pretend to be reading the breviary when I put my head up to the window. She knows me a little. I'll let you know when it's all right for you to come."

She went up to the window alone. As soon as she looked into it a look of deep pity came over all her features and her gay and candid face changed expression and color as abruptly as if it had passed from sunlight into moonlight. Her eyes became moist and her mouth contracted as if she were going to cry. A moment later she put a finger to her lips and motioned Mahiette to come and see.

Mahiette came over silently and on tiptoe, as if she were approaching a deathbed.

It was indeed a sad sight which presented itself to the two ladies as they looked without moving or breathing through the barred window of the Trou-aux-Rats. The cell was narrow and had a pointed ceiling. In one corner there was a woman sitting, or rather crouching, on the stone floor. Her chin rested on her knees, which her crossed arms pressed tightly against her breast. Doubled up in this way, dressed in brown sackcloth which covered her entirely in large folds, her long gray hair falling over her face and down to her feet, at first glance she seemed to be only a strange shape standing out against the dark background of the cell, one of those phantoms, half light and half shadow, which are seen in dreams and in the extraordinary works of Goya, pale, motionless and sinister, crouching over a tomb or leaning against the bars of a dungeon. It was neither man, woman nor living creature; it was a figure, a sort of vision in which the real and the fantastic were contrasted like light and shade. An attenuated and severe profile could be dimly distinguished through the hair drooping down to the floor; at the bottom of her robe could be seen the tip of a bare foot, contracted against the cold, hard floor. The faint likeness of a human form discernible beneath this mournful exterior made one shudder.

She appeared to have neither animation, thought nor breath. Wearing only a thin robe of sackcloth, in January, sitting on the stone floor, without fire, in the darkness of a dungeon whose oblique opening admitted only the wind and never the sunlight, she did not seem to be suffering or even feeling. She looked as though she might have changed into stone with the dungeon or into ice with the season. Her hands were clasped and her eyes were fixed; at first glance one would have taken her for a specter, at second glance for a statue.

At intervals, however, her blue lips opened slightly and trembled for a moment, but did so as lifelessly and mechanically as leaves blown apart by the wind. And there was an expression of unspeakable and inalterable melancholy in her dull eyes as she incessantly stared into a corner of the cell which could not be seen from outside, seeming to focus all the somber thoughts of her anguished soul on some mysterious object there.

The three women, for Gervaise had joined the other two, looked in through the window. Their heads cut off the feeble ray of light entering the cell but the wretched woman still did not seem to notice them. "Let's not disturb her," whispered Oudarde, "she's praying."

Meanwhile Mahiette was staring with growing emotion at the gaunt, withered face and her eyes were filled with tears. "How strange!" she murmured. Then she put her head in between the bars of the window and managed to look into the corner toward which the poor recluse's eyes were turned.

When she drew back her head her cheeks were streaming with tears. "What do you call this woman?" she asked Oudarde.

"We call her Sister Gudule."

"I call her Paquette la Chantefleurie," said Mahiette. Then, placing a finger before her lips, she motioned the dumfounded Oudarde to put her head in through the window and look. Oudarde did so and saw, in the corner into which the recluse was staring in such somber ecstasy, a little pink satin shoe, embroidered with gold and silver. Gervaise also looked in and all three women, contemplating the unfortunate mother, burst into tears.

Neither their looks nor their tears, however, distracted the recluse. Her hands remained joined, her lips mute, her eyes fixed; and, for anyone who knew her story, the way she looked at that little shoe was heartbreaking.

The three women looked on without speaking, not daring even to whisper. That deep silence, that intense grief and that utter forgetfulness in which all had disappeared except one thing had the same effect on them as a high altar at Easter or Christmas. They stood in silent meditation, ready to kneel.

Finally Gervaise, the most curious of the three and therefore the least sensitive, tried to make the recluse speak:

"Sister! Sister Gudule!"

She repeated this appeal three times, raising her voice each time, but the recluse did not stir. Not one word, not one look, not one sigh, not one sign of life.

Then Oudarde said, in a kinder and gentler tone:

"Sister! Sister Saint Gudule!"

The same silence, the same motionlessness.

"What a strange woman!" cried Gervaise. "I don't think a cannon shot would awaken her."

"Maybe she's deaf," said Oudarde, sighing.

"Maybe she's blind," added Gervaise.

"Maybe she's dead," said Mahiette.

It is certain that if the soul had not yet left that inert, lethargic body, it had at least withdrawn and hidden itself at a depth to which the perceptions of the external organs could not penetrate.

"We'll just have to leave the cake on the window sill," said Oudarde. "But I'm afraid some child will steal it. What can we do to arouse her?"

Eustache, who so far had been absorbed in watching a small cart drawn by a large dog which had just passed in the street, suddenly noticed that the three ladies were looking at something through the window. Seized with curiosity, he climbed up on a post, stood on tiptoe and put his fat, ruddy face against the window, crying, "Mother, let me see!"

The recluse started at the sound of this loud, clear childish voice. She turned her head with the sharp movement of a steel spring, her long bony hands pushed the hair from in front of her eyes and she stared at the child in her bitter astonishment. "Oh, my God!" she cried all at once, hiding her head between her knees. "At least keep other mothers' children out of my sight!"

"Hello, madame," said the child gravely.

The shock had awakened the recluse from her trance. She shivered from head to toe, her teeth chattered, she raised her head a little and said, pressing her elbows against her hips and taking her feet in her hands in order to warm them, "It's so cold!"

"Poor woman," said Oudarde with deep compassion, "would you like a little fire?"

She shook her head.

"Well, then," said Oudarde, holding out a flask to her, "here's some spiced wine. It will warm you up. Drink it."

She shook her head again, looked steadfastly at Oudarde and said, "Water."

Oudarde insisted: "No, Sister Gudule, water isn't a drink for January. You must drink a little of this spiced wine and eat this cake we've baked for you."

She pushed back the cake which Mahiette held out to her and said, "Black bread."

"Here," said Gervaise, also moved to charity, taking off her woolen cloak, "this is a little warmer than what you have on. Put it around your shoulders."

She refused the cloak also and answered, "Sackcloth."

"But surely," said the kind-hearted Oudarde, "you must have noticed that yesterday was a holiday."

"I noticed it," said the recluse. "For the last two days I haven't had any water in my pitcher." Then she added, after a silence, "They forget about me when there's a holiday. And they're right. Why should the world think of me when I don't think of it? When the fire is out the ashes grow cold."

She let her head fall down between her knees again, as if tired from the effort of saying so much. The simple and charitable Oudarde, who took her last words as a complaint against the cold, said to her naïvely, "Would you like a little fire, then?"

"Fire!" exclaimed the recluse in a strange tone. "And would you make one for the poor little girl who's been in the cold ground for fifteen years?" She trembled in all her limbs, her voice quavered and she raised herself up to her knees. Suddenly she stretched out her thin white hand toward the child who was looking at her in astonishment. "Take that child away!" she cried. "The gypsy girl will be here soon!"

She then fell forward and her forehead struck sharply against the stone floor. The three ladies believed her to be dead. A moment later, however, she began to stir and they saw her drag herself on her knees and elbows over to the corner where the little shoe was. They could no longer see her and they dared not look at her but they heard the sound of countless kisses and sighs mingled with heart-rending cries and dull noises as if from a head striking against a wall. Then, after one of these blows, so violent that it startled all three of them, they heard nothing more.

"Has she killed herself?" said Gervaise, venturing to put her head in through the window. "Sister! Sister Gudule!"

"Sister Gudule!" repeated Oudarde.

"Good heavens!" exclaimed Gervaise. "She's not moving! Is she dead? Gudule! Gudule!"

"Wait," said Mahiette, who until then had been so choked with emotion that she could hardly speak. Leaning toward the window she called out, "Paquette! Paquette la Chantefleurie!"

A child blowing on the smoldering fuse of a firecracker and making it explode in his face could not have been more frightened than was Mahiette at the effect produced by this name abruptly pronounced in Sister Gudule's cell. The recluse trembled all over, stood up on her bare feet and rushed over to the window with such flaming eyes that the three women and the child all shrank back in terror. "Oh! Oh!" she shrieked with an appalling laugh. "It's the gypsy girl calling me!"

Just then a scene taking place at the pillory arrested her haggard gaze. Her brow wrinkled in horror and she stretched her skeleton arms outside her cell and screamed in an inhuman voice, "So it's you again, daughter of Egypt! It's you who's calling me, child-stealer! Curse you! Curse you! Curse you!"

CHAPTER FOUR

A Tear for a Drop of Water

THESE WORDS WERE, SO TO SPEAK, THE CONNECTING LINK BE-
tween two scenes which until then had been taking place
simultaneously, each on its own stage: one, which we have
just described, in the Trou-aux-Rats; the other, which we are
about to describe, at the pillory. The first was witnessed
only by the three ladies with whom the reader has just become acquainted; the spectators of the second consisted of
the crowd we have already seen gathering in the Place de
Grève around the pillory and the gallows.

The four sergeants who had been stationed at the four
corners of the pillory since nine o'clock had given the crowd
good reason to expect some kind of entertainment; not a
hanging, no doubt, but at least a flogging or a cutting off of
ears. They had gathered so thickly and closely around the
pillory that the sergeants had more than once been obliged
to force them back with their whips and the rumps of their
horses.

The people, accustomed to waiting for public punishments
and executions, did not manifest too much impatience. They
passed the time by looking at the pillory, which was a very
simple structure consisting of a cube of masonry about ten feet
high, hollow inside. A steep flight of rough-hewn stone steps
led to the top of it, on which there was a horizontal wheel
made of oak. The prisoner was tied to this wheel, kneeling
with his hands behind his back. A wooden shaft, moved by
a capstan concealed inside the structure, made the wheel revolve horizontally, thus successively exhibiting the prisoner's
face to every spectator. This was called "turning a criminal."

It is easy to see why this pillory was by no means as entertaining as the one at Les Halles. There was nothing archi-
tectural about it, nothing ornamental. There was no roof with
an iron cross above it, no octagonal lanterns, no slender pillars
spreading into flowered capitals at the top, no fantastic and
monstrous waterspouts, no carved woodwork and no fine sculpture deeply cut into the stone. Here the spectator was forced

to content himself with four plain stone walls and a bare, unimpressive gibbet alongside. It would have been a sorry feast for a lover of Gothic architecture but no one was ever less interested in monuments than the hardy onlookers of the Middle Ages, so they gave little thought to the beauty of a pillory.

The prisoner finally arrived, tied to the back of a cart. When he was hoisted to the top of the pillory and bound to the wheel with ropes and leather thongs a prodigious roar, mingled with laughter and cheers, went up from all parts of the square. The crowd had recognized Quasimodo.

It was an ironic twist of fate for him: pilloried in the same square in which he had been hailed and cheered as the Pope of Fools the day before. We may be sure, however, that no one present, including Quasimodo himself, clearly drew this parallel in his mind. Gringoire and his philosophy were lacking in the spectacle.

Presently Michel Noiret, Sworn Trumpeter of Our Lord the King, silenced the crowd and proclaimed the sentence according to the provost's orders. He then withdrew behind the cart with his uniformed assistants.

Quasimodo remained impassive. All resistance was made impossible for him by what was then called, in the language of criminal jurisprudence, "firm and rigorous bonds," which probably meant that they cut into his flesh. He let himself be led, shoved, carried, lifted and bound to the wheel without showing any emotion except savage and stupid surprise. He was known to be deaf; he now seemed to be blind also. He made no protest when he was stripped to the waist, made to kneel on the wheel and tightly bound to it, except that from time to time he breathed heavily, like a calf with its head dangling over the side of a butcher's cart.

"The stupid oaf!" exclaimed Jehan Frollo to his friend Robin Poussepain (for the two students had naturally followed the prisoner). "He has no more idea of what's happening to him than a bird shut up in a box!"

The crowd burst into loud laughter when they saw Quasimodo's bare hump, protruding chest and hairy shoulders. During this merriment a short, robust man wearing the livery of the City of Paris climbed to the top of the pillory and walked over to the prisoner. His name quickly spread through the crowd: Master Pierrat Torterue, Sworn Torturer of the Châtelet.

He began by placing an hourglass on one corner of the pillory, then he took off his coat. In his right hand he held a whip made of long braided white leather thongs, armed with sharp splinters of metal. With his left hand he carelessly rolled up his right sleeve.

Meanwhile Jehan Frollo had raised his blond, curly head above the crowd by climbing upon Robin Poussepain's shoulders. "Step up and watch, ladies and gentlemen," he shouted, "they're now going to flog Master Quasimodo, a marvelous piece of architecture, with a dome for a back and twisted columns for legs!" And the crowd laughed, especially the children and young girls.

The torturer finally stamped his foot and the wheel began to turn. Quasimodo rocked under his bonds. The stupefaction which abruptly appeared in his deformed face drew fresh shouts of laughter from the spectators. Suddenly, just as the rotation of the wheel presented Quasimodo's monstrous back to Master Pierrat, he raised his arm and the thin lashes of his whip whistled sharply through the air and landed furiously on the wretched prisoner's shoulders.

Quasimodo jumped as if he had been awakened from a deep sleep. He was beginning to understand. He twisted in his bonds and a violent contraction of surprise and pain strained the muscles of his face, but not a sound came from his lips. He merely swung his head back and forth like a bull which has been stung by a gadfly.

A second blow followed the first, then a third, then another and another. The wheel continued to revolve and the blows continued to rain down. Blood began to trickle down Quasimodo's swarthy shoulders and when the thin lashes of the whip tore through the air they sprinkled it over the crowd. He resumed, in appearance at least, his original impassivity after trying for a while, quietly and without great external effort, to break his bonds. His eye had flashed, his muscles had swelled and the ropes, thongs and chains holding him had been pulled taut. It was a powerful, desperate effort, but the bonds held firm. He then sank down exhausted and his stupefied expression gave way to one of deep and bitter hopelessness. He closed his single eye and let his head fall to his breast as if he were dead.

From then on he did not stir. Nothing could make him flinch, neither the constant flow of his blood, nor the blows, which redoubled in violence, nor the rage of the torturer, who had worked himself into a kind of intoxicated fury, nor the shrill whistling of the horrible lashes.

At length an official of the Châtelet, dressed in black and

sitting astride a black horse, pointed his ebony wand toward the hourglass. The torturer stopped. The wheel stopped. Quasimodo's eye opened slowly.

The flogging was over. Two of the torturer's assistants washed the prisoner's bleeding shoulders and rubbed them with some kind of ointment which almost instantly closed up his wounds. Then they threw a yellow cloth over him. Meanwhile Pierrat Torterue was shaking the blood off his whip.

But Quasimodo's punishment was not yet finished. He still had to undergo that hour on the pillory which Master Florian Barbedienne had so judiciously added to the sentence pronounced by Messire Robert d'Estouteville. The hourglass was therefore turned over and the hunchback was left bound to the wheel in order that justice might be fully satisfied.

We have already noted that Quasimodo was widely hated, and not entirely without reason. There was hardly a spectator in the crowd who did not have, or did not think he had, some complaint against the malicious hunchback of Notre Dame. Their joy had been unanimous on seeing him appear on the pillory; and the harsh punishment he had just suffered and the pitiful state in which it had left him, far from softening their hearts, only made their hatred fiercer by arming it with the sting of laughter.

Once the "public vengeance," as it is still called in our legal jargon, was satisfied, therefore, private vengeance took its turn. The women in the crowd were especially vehement. They all had some grudge or other against Quasimodo, some for his maliciousness and others for his ugliness; the latter were the most furious.

"Antichrist!" shouted one of them.

"Look at that beautiful tragic face!" shrieked another. "It would get him elected Pope of Fools all over again if today were yesterday!"

"Now we know what he looks like on the pillory. I hope we'll get to see him on the gallows next!"

"His face would make a woman miscarry better than any drug!"

Countless other insults assailed him, along with threats, laughter and, now and then, stones.

Quasimodo was deaf but he saw clearly and the fury of the crowd was expressed no less energetically in their faces than in their words. Besides, the stones explained the laughter quite effectively.

At first he bore it all with resignation. But gradually his

patience, which had braced itself under the torturer's whip, gave way under all those petty stings. He looked over the crowd threateningly but, bound as he was, his look was powerless to drive away those flies biting at his wounds. He then strained against his bonds and made the old wheel creak on its axle with his frenzied struggles, but this only increased the derision and jeering of his persecutors.

Finding that he was unable to break loose, he became calm again, except for an occasional sign of rage which made his chest heave. No shame was visible in his face; he was too far from society and too close to nature even to know the meaning of that emotion. But anger, hatred and despair slowly covered his face with a dark cloud.

This cloud lifted for a moment when a priest riding a mule appeared in the square. When he first caught sight of him in the distance, Quasimodo's face softened. The rage which had contracted it was succeeded by a strange smile, full of gentleness and ineffable tenderness. It grew more distinct and radiant as the priest approached. The prisoner seemed to be watching the arrival of a deliverer. When he drew close enough to recognize Quasimodo, however, the priest lowered his eyes, turned his mule around and spurred it vigorously, as if he were in a hurry to escape a humiliating appeal and not at all anxious to be greeted by a poor devil in such a predicament. The priest was Dom Claude Frollo.

The cloud fell darker than ever over Quasimodo's face. The smile was still mingled with it for a time, but it was now bitter, hopeless and deeply sad.

Time passed. He had now been there for as least an hour and a half, lacerated, abused, constantly jeered at and almost stoned to death. Suddenly he began to struggle against his bonds again with redoubled desperation, shaking the wheel which supported him. Then, breaking the silence which he had so stubbornly kept till then, he cried out in a hoarse and furious voice which was like the roar of a wild animal: "Water!"

This cry of distress, far from arousing any compassion in the crowd, only added to their amusement. Not one voice was raised around the wretched prisoner except to jeer at his thirst. It is true that at that moment he was even more grotesque and repulsive than he was pitiful, with his crimson face streaming with perspiration, his wildly glaring eye, his mouth foaming with rage and pain and his tongue lolling out of it. It must also be said that, even if some charitable soul had been tempted to bring him a glass of water, there was such a stigma of shame and disgrace attached to the infamous steps of the pillory that it would have turned back the Good Samaritan himself.

A few moments later Quasimodo cast a despairing look at the crowd and repeated in a still more heart-rending voice, "Water!"

And everyone burst out laughing.

"Drink this!" cried a student, throwing in his face a sponge which had been dragged in the gutter.

A woman threw a stone at his head: "That will teach you to wake us up at night with your devilish ringing!"

"Now will you go on casting spells on us from the towers of Notre Dame?" shouted a cripple, endeavoring to strike him with one of his crutches.

"Here's something to drink out of!" said a man, hurling a broken pitcher at his chest. "You made my wife give birth to a two-headed baby just by passing in front of her!"

"Water!" said Quasimodo for the third time, panting.

Just then he saw a strangely dressed young girl step out of the crowd. She was accompanied by a little white goat with gilded horns and carried a tambourine in one hand.

His eye sparkled. It was the gypsy girl he had attempted to carry off the night before, an escapade which he was dimly aware of being punished for at that very moment. (This, by the way, was by no means true, for he was actually being punished only because he had the misfortune to be deaf and to be tried by a deaf judge.) He was sure she was coming to take her revenge also and deliver her blow like the others.

Choking with rage, he saw her climb quickly up the steps of the pillory. If the lightning in his eye had had the power to strike, she would have been blasted into a thousand pieces before she reached him. But without saying a word she came up to him as he writhed vainly to escape from her and, detaching a gourd from her belt, gently raised it to his parched lips.

A big tear welled up in his eye, which until then had been so dry and fiery, and slowly trickled down his deformed face. It was perhaps the first tear the unfortunate man had ever shed. His emotion was so great that he forgot to drink. The gypsy girl made a little pout of impatience, then, smiling, pressed the neck of the gourd against his mouth. He drank in long drafts, for his thirst was violent.

When he had finished, the poor wretch put out his blackened lips, no doubt in order to kiss the hand which had just come to his assistance. But the girl, who was perhaps not without misgivings as she remembered the violent attempt of the night before, pulled back her hand like a child who is afraid of being bitten by an animal. He looked up at her, his eye filled with reproach and unspeakable sadness.

The sight of that beautiful girl, fresh, pure, charming and at the same time so weak, coming thus to bring relief to so much misery, deformity and maliciousness would have been touching anywhere; on the pillory it was sublime. The people themselves were moved by it and began to cheer and applaud.

It was just then that the recluse, looking through the window of her cell, had seen the gypsy girl on the pillory and flung her sinister imprecation at her: "Curse you, daughter of Egypt! Curse you! Curse you!"

CHAPTER FIVE

End of the Story of the Cake

LA ESMERALDA TURNED PALE AND STAGGERED AS SHE CLIMBED down from the pillory. The voice of the recluse still pursued her: "Come down now, gypsy devil! But you'll be up there again some day!"

"The recluse is raving again," murmured the people but they did nothing else, for such women were feared and therefore sacred. In those days people were extremely reluctant to attack a person who prayed night and day.

The time had come to release Quasimodo. He was untied and the crowd dispersed.

Mahiette, walking away with her two companions, suddenly stopped short. "By the way, Eustache," she said, "what have you done with the cake?"

"Mother," said the child, "while you were talking to that lady through the window a big dog came up and took a bite out of my cake, so I ate some of it too."

"What! Did you eat all of it?"

"It was the dog, Mother. I told him not to but he wouldn't listen to me. So I ate some too."

"What a terrible child!" said his mother, smiling and scolding at the same time. "I tell you, Oudarde, he eats every cherry
in our orchard all by himself. His grandfather says he's sure to
be a great captain when he grows up. . . . Don't you ever let me
catch you doing anything like that again, young man! Greedy
little pig!"

Book V

CHAPTER ONE

On the Danger of Confiding in a Goat

SEVERAL WEEKS HAD ELAPSED. IT WAS NOW THE BEGINNING OF
March. The sun, which Dubartas, that classic ancestor of pe-
riphrasis, had not yet named the "grand duke of candles," was
no less bright and cheerful for that. It was one of those spring
days which are so mild and beautiful that all Paris, pouring
into the public squares and promenades, celebrates them like
Sundays. On these days of light, warmth and serenity there
is one time in particular when one should go and admire the
façade of Notre Dame: the moment when the sun, already
sinking in the west, looks the cathedral almost full in the face.
Its rays, increasingly horizontal, slowly withdraw from the
pavement of the square and climb up the façade, making the
countless sculptured figures stand out against their shadows
while the great central rose-window flames like a Cyclops'
eye reflecting the glare of the forge.

It was just at that hour that, opposite the lofty cathedral
reddened by the setting sun, on a stone balcony over the porch
of a rich Gothic house on the corner of the square and the
Rue du Parvis, a group of beautiful young girls were playfully
laughing and talking together. From the length of their veils,
hanging from their pointed caps down to their heels; from the
fineness of the embroidered bodices which covered their
shoulders while revealing, following the charming fashion of

103

the day, the beginning of their virginal bosoms; from the opulence of their petticoats, which were even finer than their outer skirts (a wonderful refinement!); from the gauze, silk and velvet of which all these garments were made; and especially from the whiteness of their hands, which attested their idleness and laziness, it was easy to see that they were rich and noble heiresses. They were, in fact, Demoiselle Fleur-de-Lys de Gondelaurier and her companions, Diane de Christeuil, Amelotte de Montmichel, Colombe de Gaillefontaine, and the little Bérangère Champchevrier. All these girls of good family were gathered at the house of the widowed Madame de Gondelaurier for the expected visit of Monseigneur de Beaujeu and his wife, who were to come to Paris in April for the purpose of selecting maids of honor for Madame la Dauphine Marguerite on the occasion of her reception in Picardy. Now all the gentry for a hundred miles around were eager to obtain this honor for their daughters, many of whom had already been sent or brought to Paris. Those we have just mentioned had been entrusted by their parents to the care of the discreet and venerable Madame Aloïse de Gondelaurier, widow of a former Master of the King's Crossbowmen, living with her only daughter in her house on the Place du Parvis Notre Dame in Paris.

The balcony on which the girls were talking opened onto a room richly hung with fawn-colored Flemish leather stamped with gold foliage. The parallel beams which crossed the ceiling distracted the eye with a thousand strange carvings, painted and gilded. Splendid enamels glittered here and there on the carved lids of coffers and a porcelain boar's head crowned a magnificent sideboard. Madame de Gondelaurier, whose fifty-five years were as distinctly indicated by her clothing as by her face, was seated beside a high fireplace at one end of the room in a luxurious red velvet armchair. Beside her stood a young man with a proud but somewhat vain and swaggering look, one of those handsome fellows who arouse the admiration of all women but only make serious and perceptive men shrug their shoulders. He was wearing the brilliant uniform of the King's Archers, which resembled so closely the costume of Jupiter, which we have already admired at the beginning of this story, that there is no need to inflict a second description on the reader.

Some of the young ladies were sitting in the room, others on the balcony; some on velvet cushions, others on carved oaken stools. Each held on her lap a portion of a large tapestry on which they were all working together, while one end of it lay on the matting that covered the floor.

Like any group of young ladies when there is a young man among them, they were talking to one another in low tones mingled with stifled giggles. As for the young man, whose presence was enough to bring out all that feminine vanity, he showed very little interest in them; while they were all vying with one another to attract his attention, he seemed to be primarily occupied in polishing the buckle of his sword belt with one of his doeskin gloves.

From time to time the old lady would speak to him in a low tone and he would answer as best he could with a sort of awkward and forced politeness. From the smiles, winks and other significant little gestures which she exchanged with her daughter Fleur-de-Lys, during her conversation with the captain, it was easy to see that it concerned some engagement and forthcoming marriage between the two young people. And from his coolness and embarrassment it was easy to see that, as far as he was concerned at least, love no longer had any part in the matter. Discomfort and boredom were written clearly on all his features.

The worthy lady, convinced, like any other mother, of the overwhelming superiority of her daughter's merits, did not notice the young officer's lack of enthusiasm and made strenuous efforts to call his attention to the incomparable grace with which Fleur-de-Lys plied her needle or unwound her thread.

"Look," she said, pulling him by the sleeve in order to bring his ear close to her lips, "look at the way she bends down!"

"Yes, I see," replied the young man; then he fell back into his cold, absent-minded silence.

A moment later he had to lean down again and Madame de Gondelaurier said to him, "Have you ever seen a prettier or more charming face than your fiancée's? Did anyone ever have fairer skin or hair? Aren't her hands lovely? Isn't her neck as graceful as a swan's? How I envy you sometimes! You're so lucky to be a man, wicked libertine that you are!"

"Of course," he answered, thinking of something else.

"Then why don't you talk to her?" said Madame de Gondelaurier, suddenly pushing him toward her daughter. "Say something to her. You've become shy all of a sudden!"

We can assure the reader that shyness was not one of the captain's virtues or failings. He nevertheless tried to do as he was told.

"Tell me," he said, approaching Fleur-de-Lys, "what's the subject of this tapestry you're working on?"

"I've already told you three times," answered Fleur-de-Lys peevishly. "It's the grotto of Neptune."

It was obvious that she was much more clearly aware of the captain's coldness and absent-mindedness than her mother. He felt called upon to make some attempt at conversation with her.

"And for whom are you making this work of art?" he asked.

"For the Abbey of Saint-Antoine-des-Champs," she answered without raising her eyes.

The captain picked up one corner of the tapestry and said, "Who's this husky fellow blowing into a trumpet with his cheeks all puffed out?"

"That's Triton."

There was still a somewhat sulky intonation in Fleur-de-Lys' curt answers. The young man realized that it was necessary to whisper something in her ear, some gallant compliment or other. He leaned down but he could find nothing tenderer or more intimate in his imagination than this: "Why does your mother always wear a skirt with her coat of arms embroidered on it like our grandmothers used to do under Charles the Seventh? You ought to tell her it's not fashionable nowadays and that it makes her look like a walking mantelpiece. I can assure you no one else sits down on his coat of arms these days."

Fleur-de-Lys looked up at him with her lovely eyes full of reproach. "Is that all you can assure me of?" she whispered.

Meanwhile the worthy Madame de Gondelaurier, delighted to see them leaning near each other and whispering, said, as she fondled the clasp of her prayer book, "What a touching picture of young love!"

The captain, more and more embarrassed, came back to the tapestry. "It's really a fine piece of work!" he said loudly.

At this point Colombe de Gaillefontaine, another lovely blonde, timidly ventured a word to Fleur-de-Lys in the hope that the captain would answer: "Have you seen the tapestries in the Hôtel de la Roche-Guyon, Mademoiselle de Gondelaurier?"

"Isn't that the building that encloses the Lingère-du-Louvre gardens?" laughingly asked Diane de Christeuil, who had beautiful teeth and therefore laughed on all occasions.

"Isn't it near that big old tower from the ancient wall of Paris?" asked Amelotte de Montmichel, a pretty brunette with curly hair.

"You must be talking about the mansion that used to belong to Monsieur de Bacqueville in the time of Charles the Sixth," said Madame de Gondelaurier. "There are some really magnificent tapestries in it."

"Charles the Sixth! Charles the Sixth!" muttered the young captain to himself, curling his mustache. "My God, what a memory the old lady has for anything ancient!"

Madame de Gondelaurier went on: "Very beautiful tapestries; such wonderful work that it's considered to be unequaled."

Just then Bérangère de Champchevrier, a slender little seven-year-old girl who had been looking at the square through the railing of the balcony, suddenly cried out, "Oh, look at the pretty dancer down there in the square and all those people watching her dance with a tambourine!"

"It's probably some gypsy girl," said Fleur-de-Lys, nonchalantly turning her eyes toward the square.

"Let's see! Let's see!" cried her lively companions, running to the edge of the balcony while Fleur-de-Lys, made pensive by her fiancé's coldness, followed them slowly. The captain, relieved that the incident had cut short an embarrassing conversation, went back inside the room with the satisfied air of a soldier relieved from duty. Being in the presence of Fleur-de-Lys should have been an easy and pleasant duty, however, and it had formerly seemed so to him, but he had grown gradually disinterested until now the prospect of his forthcoming marriage was more disagreeable to him every day. Besides, he was fickle by nature and, if the truth must be known, he had rather vulgar tastes. Although of very noble family, his military life had caused him to take on many of the habits of a common soldier. He liked the tavern and everything that went with it. His family had given him some education and taught him fairly polished manners but he had entered the army too young and every day the veneer of the gentleman was worn away a little more by the harsh chafing of his sword belt. While he continued to visit Fleur-de-Lys periodically out of simple human decency, he felt doubly embarrassed with her: first because, having dispersed his love in so many other quarters, he had little of it left for her; second, because in the midst of so many stiff-necked, respectable ladies he was afraid that his tongue, accustomed to blasphemous and obscene oaths, might inadvertently lapse into the language of the tavern. It is not difficult to imagine the effect this would have produced.

With all this, however, he still had great pretensions to elegance and fine manners. The reader may reconcile these things as best he can; I am only noting the facts.

The captain had been standing for some time leaning against the carved mantelpiece when Fleur-de-Lys suddenly turned around and spoke to him. After all, the poor girl had been sulking only in self-defense. "Didn't you once tell me about a gypsy girl you rescued from some bandits one night about two months ago?" she asked.

"Yes, I think I did," answered the captain.

"Well, perhaps it was the same gypsy girl who's dancing down there in the square. Come see if you recognize her, Phoebus."

A secret desire for reconciliation was perceptible in this gentle invitation to come over beside her. Captain Phoebus de Châteaupers walked slowly out onto the balcony.

"Look at that girl dancing down there," said Fleur-de-Lys, tenderly placing her hand on his arm. "Is that your gypsy?"

Phoebus looked down and said, "Yes—I recognize her by the goat."

"Oh! What a pretty little goat!" exclaimed Amelotte, clasping her hands in admiration.

"Are its horns made of real gold?" asked Bérangère.

Without moving from her armchair, Madame de Gondelaurier joined in: "She must be one of those gypsies who came in through the Gibard Gate last year."

"Mother," said Fleur-de-Lys gently, "that gate is called the Gate of Hell nowadays." She knew how irritated the captain was by her mother's antiquated way of speaking. He was, in fact, sneering and muttering to himself, "Gibard Gate! Gibard Gate! That's for Charles the Sixth to pass through!"

"Look!" cried Bérangère, who had suddenly raised her eyes, which were constantly in motion, to the top of the towers of Notre Dame. "Who's that man in black up there?"

All the young ladies looked up. There was a man leaning with his elbows on the topmost balustrade of the northern tower, the one nearest the Place de Grève. It was a priest. They could clearly see his ecclesiastical robe and his face, which was resting on his hands. He was as motionless as a statue, his eye staring into space.

"It's the Archdeacon of Josas," said Fleur-de-Lys.

"You must have good eyes to be able to recognize him from here," remarked Colombe.

"Look at the way he's watching the dancer!" said Diane.

"She'd better be careful!" said Fleur-de-Lys. "He doesn't like gypsies."

"It's a shame he's looking at her that way," added Amelotte; "she's a wonderful dancer."

"Phoebus," said Fleur-de-Lys, "since you know her, why don't you call her up here? That would be amusing."

"Oh, yes!" cried all the young ladies, clapping their hands.

"But that's ridiculous!" replied Phoebus. "She's probably forgotten me and I don't even know her name. However, since you want me to, ladies, I'll try." He leaned over the balustrade and called out, "Mademoiselle!"

She was not beating her tambourine at that moment. She turned her head in the direction from which the call had come, saw Phoebus and stopped short. He beckoned to her. She continued to look at him, then blushed as if a flame had come up into her cheeks. Placing her tambourine under her arm, she walked past the gaping spectators toward the door of the Gondelaurier mansion, slowly, unsteadily and with the troubled look of a bird which has yielded to the fascination of a snake.

A moment later she appeared on the threshold, blushing, speechless, breathless, her large eyes cast down, not daring to take another step into the room.

Her appearance had a strange effect on the group of young ladies. They were all animated by a vague desire to please the handsome officer; his splendid uniform was the point at which all their coquettishness was aimed and ever since his arrival there had been among them a secret rivalry which they would hardly have admitted to themselves but which nevertheless betrayed itself in everything they said and did. And since they all possessed nearly the same degree of beauty, they were fighting with equal weapons and each one could hope to win the victory. But the arrival of the gypsy girl suddenly destroyed this equilibrium. Her beauty was so exquisite that from the moment she appeared in the doorway of the room she seemed to illuminate it with a kind of light peculiar to herself. In the confined space of that room, against the dark background of tapestries and carvings, she seemed incomparably more beautiful and radiant than she had in the public square. The noble young ladies were dazzled in spite of themselves. Each felt herself wounded in her beauty, so to speak. They therefore shifted their battle front by a tacit agreement. Women's instincts understand and respond to each other much more quickly than men's intelligences. A common enemy had just appeared on the scene; they were all aware of it and they all rallied for the attack. One drop of wine is enough to redden a whole glass of water; to tinge a whole company of pretty women with malice it is enough to introduce an even prettier woman among them—especially when there is only one man present.

The reception they gave to the gypsy girl was therefore marvelously icy. They looked her over from head to toe, then looked at one another in perfect understanding. Meanwhile she was waiting to be spoken to, so overcome by emotion that she dared not raise her eyes.

The captain was the first to break the silence. "What a charming creature!" he said in a tone of intrepid smugness. "Don't you think so, Fleur-de-Lys?"

This remark, which a more discreet admirer would have kept to himself, was not designed to dissipate the feminine jealousy arrayed against the girl. Fleur-de-Lys answered with a saccharine affectation of disdain: "Not bad."

The others whispered among themselves. Finally Madame de Gondelaurier, who was just as jealous for her daughter's sake as the others were for themselves, spoke to the dancer: "Come in, my girl."

"Come in, my girl!" repeated little Bérangère with mock dignity.

The gypsy girl approached the noble lady.

"My dear girl," said Phoebus pompously, "I don't know if I have the extreme good fortune to be recognized by you . . ."

She interrupted him with a smile and a look of infinite sweetness. "Oh, yes!" she said.

"She has a good memory," observed Fleur-de-Lys.

"You were certainly in a hurry to get away from me the other evening," said Phoebus. "Are you afraid of me?"

"Oh, no!" replied the gypsy girl.

There was something in the way she said this "Oh, no!" immediately after the "Oh, yes!" which cut Fleur-de-Lys to the quick.

"You left behind you," went on the captain, whose tongue was becoming loosened in talking to a girl of the street, "a rather wicked-looking, one-eyed hunchback—the bishop's bell-ringer, I believe. I hear he's an archdeacon's bastard and a devil by birth. He has some odd name which I can't remember right now; it's the name of some holiday or other. Anyway, he tried to carry you off, as if you were made for churchmen! That's going too far! Tell me, what the devil did he want with you?"

"I don't know."

"I've never heard of such insolence! A bellringer carrying off a girl as if he were a viscount! A low-born oaf poaching on the game of gentlemen! But he paid dearly for it. Pierrat Torterue is the roughest groom who ever curried a scoundrel. If it's any satisfaction to you, I can assure you he gave your bellringer's hide a thorough tanning."

"Poor man!" said the gypsy girl, to whom his words had brought back the memory of the scene on the pillory.

The captain burst out laughing. "By God!" he exclaimed "Your pity's about as well placed as a feather in a pig's rump! I'll be as pot-bellied as a pope if . . ." He stopped short. "Excuse me, ladies; I'm afraid I was about to forget myself."

"He's only speaking to the creature in her own language," said Fleur-de-Lys in a low voice. Her resentment was growing more intense at every moment and it was by no means diminished when she heard the captain, enchanted with the gypsy girl and even more enchanted with himself, repeating with naïve and soldierlike gallantry, "A very pretty girl, by God!"

"She's rather barbarously dressed," said Diane, laughing to show her fine teeth.

This remark was like a flash of light to the others. It showed them the gypsy's vulnerable point. Unable to find fault with her beauty, they attacked her clothes.

"That's true, my girl," said Amelotte. "Where did you learn to run around the street like that without a neckerchief?"

"What a terribly short skirt!" added Colombe.

"My dear," said Fleur-de-Lys acidly, "that gilded belt will get you picked up by the sergeants of the Châtelet some day."

"If you'd cover your arms decently, my girl," said Diane with an implacable smile, "they wouldn't be so sunburned."

The spectacle of these beautiful young ladies, with their venomous tongues, twisting, gliding and writhing around the street-dancer was worthy of a more intelligent spectator than Phoebus. They were cruel and gracious at the same time; they maliciously searched and pried into every part of her poor costume of tinsel and rags. There was no end to the laughter, sarcasm, haughty condescension and spiteful humiliation which they inflicted on her. They were like those young ladies of ancient Rome who amused themselves by thrusting gold pins into the breast of a beautiful slave girl; or like a pack of graceful greyhounds circling, with distended nostrils and eager eyes, around a poor doe of the forest which their master's look forbids them to devour.

After all, what was a wretched street dancer to these young high-born ladies? They seemed to take no account of her presence; they spoke of her, before her and to her as if she were some unclean yet rather pretty object.

She was not insensitive to these pinpricks. She flushed from time to time with shame and anger and an exclamation of contempt seemed to be hesitating on her lips; she made that disdainful pout which we have already described but she kept silent. She stood motionless, looking at Phoebus with sadness and resignation. But there was also happiness and tenderness in her look. She seemed to be restraining herself for fear of being sent away.

As for Phoebus, he laughed and took up her defense with a mixture of insolence and pity. "Don't listen to them," he said, clinking his gold spurs. "Your clothes may be a little outlandish, but that shouldn't matter to a pretty girl like you."

"It's obvious that beautiful gypsy eyes make a deep impression on the King's Archers!" exclaimed Colombe with a sarcastic smile.

"Why not?" retorted Phoebus.

At this reply carelessly tossed off by the captain, the young ladies all began to laugh but a tear also appeared in Fleur-de-Lys' eye. The gypsy girl, who had looked down at the floor, looked up at Phoebus again with an expression of joy and pride. Her beauty was especially radiant at that moment.

Madame de Gondelaurier, who had been observing the scene, felt offended and bewildered. "Good heavens!" she cried out suddenly. "What's this crawling between my legs?"

It was the goat, which had just arrived in search of its mistress and which had began by entangling its horns in the mass of cloth which the noble lady's clothes piled up at her feet when she was seated. This was a diversion. The gypsy girl, without a word, disengaged her goat.

"Oh! There's the little goat with golden hooves!" cried Bérangère, jumping with joy.

The gypsy girl crouched and pressed the head of the affectionate goat against her cheek. She seemed to be asking it to forgive her for having left it.

Meanwhile Diane leaned over and whispered in Colombe's ear: "Good heavens! I don't know why I didn't think of it sooner: that's the gypsy girl with the goat. They say she's a witch and that her goat does very miraculous imitations."

"Well, then," said Colombe, "let's have the goat entertain us too and perform a miracle for us."

Diane and Colombe eagerly addressed the gypsy girl: "Let's see you make your goat perform a miracle."

"I don't know what you mean."

"A miracle, something magic . . . witchcraft, in other words."

"I still don't know what you mean."

Just then Fleur-de-Lys noticed a small embroidered leather bag hanging from the goat's neck. "What's that?" she asked.

The girl looked up at her and answered gravely, "It's my secret."

"I'd give a lot to know what your secret is," thought Fleur-de-Lys.

Madame de Gondelaurier stood up and said irritably, "Well, now, if you're not going to entertain us, what are you doing in here?"

Without answering, the gypsy girl began to walk toward the door. But the closer she came to it the more slowly she walked. All at once she turned, looked at Phoebus with tearful eyes and stopped.

"Wait a minute!" cried the captain. "That's no way to leave. Come back and dance for us awhile. By the way, what's your name?"

"La Esmeralda," she said without taking her eyes off him.

At this strange name the young ladies burst into loud laughter.

"That's a fine name for a girl!" said Diane.

"It's easy to see she's a witch," remarked Amelotte.

"My dear girl," said Madame de Gondelaurier, "that's not a Christian name at all!"

Meanwhile, unnoticed by the others, Bérangère had drawn the goat into a corner with a biscuit. The two of them had instantly become fast friends. The curious child had unfastened the little bag hanging from the goat's neck, opened it and emptied its contents onto the floor; they consisted of an alphabet, each letter of which was inscribed on a little block of wood. As soon as they were spread out on the floor, the goat began to perform what was no doubt one of its "miracles": it selected certain letters and gently pushed them into a certain order. They soon formed a word which the goat had evidently been well trained to write. Bérangère clasped her hands in admiration and called out joyously, "Look what the goat just did!"

Fleur-de-Lys ran over and shuddered. The letters arranged on the floor spelled out this word: PHOEBUS.

"Did the goat write that?" she asked in a faltering voice.

"Yes," answered Bérangère.

It was impossible to doubt it, for the child did not know how to spell.

"So that's her secret!" thought Fleur-de-Lys.

In the meantime her mother, the other young ladies, the gypsy girl and the captain had all come over to look. When she saw the blunder the goat had made, La Esmeralda blushed, guilty prisoner before a judge. He looked at her with a smile of turned pale and began to tremble before the captain like a surprise and self-satisfaction.

"Phoebus !" whispered the young ladies, thunderstruck. "That's the captain's name!"

"You have a wonderful memory!" said Fleur-de-Lys to the petrified gypsy girl. Then she burst into tears. "Oh!" she sobbed sorrowfully, hiding her face in her hands. "She's a witch!" And she heard a still bitterer voice cry out from the depths of her heart, "She's a rival!" Then she fainted.

"My daughter! My daughter!" cried her panic-stricken mother. "Get out of here, gypsy from hell!"

La Esmeralda gathered up the unlucky letters in the twinkling of an eye, made a sign to Djali and went out one door while Fleur-de-Lys was carried out another.

CHAPTER TWO

On the Fact that a Priest and a Philosopher Are Two Different Persons

THE PRIEST WHOM THE YOUNG LADIES HAD NOTICED AT THE top of the northern tower, looking down so attentively at the street dancer, was Archdeacon Claude Frollo.

The reader will no doubt remember the mysterious cell which the archdeacon had reserved for himself in this tower. Every day, one hour before sunset, he shut himself up in it and sometimes spent the whole night in it. On this particular day, just as he arrived before its low door and was about to unlock it with the complicated key which he always carried with him, the sound of a tambourine and castanets struck his ear. It was coming from the square below. The cell, as we have already seen, had only one window, which faced toward the rear of the church. Claude Frollo hurriedly drew back his key and in an instant he was standing outside at the top of the tower in that somber, thoughtful attitude in which the young ladies noticed him.

All Paris was spread out beneath him, with the countless spires of its houses and buildings, its circular horizon of rolling hills, its river winding under the bridges, its people swarming in the streets, the clouds of its smoke and its mountain range of roofs pressing in closely upon the cathedral. But in all the city, the archdeacon saw only one spot: the square in front of Notre Dame; and in all that crowd he saw only one figure: the gypsy girl.

It would have been difficult to determine the nature of his look and of the gleam which appeared in his eyes. It was a fixed look, yet full of agitation and tumult. And from the immobility of his whole body and the fixed smile on his face, one might have thought that his eyes were the only living part of him.

The gypsy girl was dancing. She twirled her tambourine on the tip of her finger and tossed it up in the air as she danced a Provençal saraband. Light, agile and joyous, she did not feel the weight of the formidable gaze which fell on her head.

The crowd thronged around her. From time to time a man dressed in a loose-fitting yellow and red coat would make them widen the circle, then sit down again on a chair several feet away from the dancer and take the head of the goat between his knees. He seemed to be her companion, but Claude Frollo, from his lofty point of observation, could not distinguish his features.

As soon as the archdeacon noticed this stranger his attention seemed to be divided between him and the dancer and his face grew more and more somber. All at once he stood upright and a tremor ran through his body. "Who can that man be?" he muttered. "She's always been alone till now."

He then plunged back into the winding staircase and went down. The door to the belfry was ajar as he passed and he saw something which surprised him: Quasimodo was also looking down into the square so intently that he was not aware of his foster-father's presence as he passed by. "That's strange!" murmured Claude. "I wonder if it's the gypsy girl he's looking at." He continued to descend the staircase. A few minutes later he stepped through the door at the bottom of the tower and into the square.

"What happened to the gypsy girl?" he asked, mingling with a group of the spectators who had been attracted by the sound of the tambourine.

"I don't know," said the man beside him. "She disappeared just a minute ago. Somebody called to her from that house over there and I think she went into it to do a dance for them."

Instead of the gypsy girl, on the same carpet on which she had been performing her capricious dance a moment before, the archdeacon now saw only a man dressed in yellow and red who, in order to earn a few small coins in his turn, was walking around the circle of spectators with his elbows pressed tightly against his sides, his head thrown back, his neck outstretched and a chair between his teeth. On the chair he had tied a cat which one of the neighbors had lent him and which was now yowling lustily with fright.

"Good heavens!" cried the archdeacon when the acrobat, streaming with perspiration, passed in front of him with his pyramid of chair and cat. "What is Master Pierre Gringoire doing here?"

The archdeacon's stern voice threw such commotion into the poor devil's soul that he lost the balance of his edifice and sent the chair and the cat tumbling down upon the heads of the spectators amid a storm of jeers. It is probable that the philosopher (for it was indeed Pierre Gringoire) would have had a serious account to settle with the owner of the cat and with the people who had been bruised by his falling chair if he had not taken advantage of the tumult to slip into the church, where Claude Frollo motioned him to follow.

The cathedral was already gloomy and deserted. The lamps in the chapels had begun to twinkle like stars in the darkness. Only the great central rose window, whose myriad colors were illuminated by a horizontal ray of sunshine, glowed in the shadows like a cluster of diamonds and cast its dazzling reflection on the far end of the nave.

After they had taken several steps, Dom Claude stopped beside a pillar and looked steadfastly at Gringoire. This look was not the one which the poet had been fearing, ashamed as he was at having been surprised by such a grave and learned man while wearing such an outlandish costume, for there was no trace of mockery or sarcasm in the priest's eyes; they were serious, calm and piercing. The archdeacon was the first to break the silence:

"Come here, Master Pierre. I want you to explain a few things to me. First of all, why is it that, after not seeing you at all for two months, I suddenly find you in a public square all decked out in ridiculous clothes, half red and half yellow, like a Caudebec apple?"

"I agree with you, sir," said Gringoire sheepishly. "It's certainly a ridiculous outfit and I feel as uncomfortable in it as a cat with a gourd clapped over its head. And I realize how shameful it is for a philosopher to run the risk of being beaten by the sergeants of the watch in such a sorry disguise. But what else can I do, my reverend master? It's all the fault of my old coat, which ignobly deserted me at the beginning of winter on the pretext that it was falling to shreds. What was I to do? Civilization is not yet far enough advanced to allow us to go naked, as Diogenes advocated, and January is not a likely time to try to make mankind take such a great step forward. When this red and yellow garment presented itself, I took it. So here I am, dressed in the costume of a buffoon, like Saint Genest."

"You've taken up a fine trade!" said the archdeacon.

"I agree, master, that it's nobler to philosophize and write poetry than to balance cats in the street, but what am I to do? The most sublime poetry is worth less to the stomach than a piece of cheese. As you know, I wrote that famous morality play for Marguerite of Flanders; but the city won't pay me for it because they claim it wasn't good enough—as if they could order the tragedies of Sophocles for four crows apiece! I was about to starve to death when I fortunately noticed that I have rather strong jaws, so I said to them, 'Do tricks of strength and equilibrium and earn yourselves something to chew on!' A gang of vagabonds, who have become my closest friends, taught me twenty different kinds of Herculean feats and now every evening I give my teeth the bread they've earned during the day. I admit it's a shameful way to use my intellectual faculties and that man wasn't made to spend his life beating a tambourine and biting into chairs. But, reverend master, a man also has to earn a living."

Dom Claude listened in silence. Suddenly his deep-set eyes took on such a wise and penetrating expression that Gringoire felt them boring into the depths of his soul.

"That's all very well, Master Pierre, but why is it that you've become the companion of that gypsy dancer?"

"Why, that's because she's my wife and I'm her husband."

The archdeacon's eyes blazed. "How could you do such a

thing, wretched scoundrel!" he cried, furiously gripping Gringoire's arm. "How could you have so utterly forsaken God as to lay hands on that girl?"

"I swear by my hope of heaven," replied Gringoire, trembling in every limb, "that I've never touched her, if that's what's troubling you."

"What were you saying about husband and wife, then?"

Gringoire hastened to relate as succinctly as possible the events with which the reader is already acquainted: his adventure in the Court of Miracles and his wedding performed by the breaking of a jug. He stated, furthermore, that his marriage was still unconsummated, that every night La Esmeralda denied him his conjugal rights as she had done on their wedding night. "It's a bitter disappointment to me," he said in conclusion, "but it's all because I had the misfortune to marry a virgin."

"What do you mean?" asked the archdeacon, whose agitation had gradually subsided during Gringoire's story.

"It's rather difficult to explain," answered the poet. "It's a superstition, According to an old scoundrel that we call the Duke of Egypt, my wife was a foundling. She wears a charm around her neck which is supposed to make her meet her parents some day, but it will lose its power if she loses her virtue. As a result, we both remain extremely virtuous."

"So," said Claude Frollo, whose face was brightening more and more, "you believe the girl has never been touched by any man?"

"What can a man do against a superstition? She has that idea in her head and nothing can get it out. I'm sure it's extremely rare to see such nunlike chastity preserved so rigidly in the midst of all those other loose-living gypsy girls, but she has three things which protect her: first, there's the Duke of Egypt, who has taken her into his care, perhaps in the hope of selling her to some merry abbot later; next, there's the whole tribe, who hold her in extraordinary veneration, as if she were a second Virgin Mary; finally, there's a little dagger which she always carries on her somewhere in defiance of the provost's decree and which leaps into her hand as soon as anyone presses her waist. She's a proud little wench, I can assure you of that!"

The archdeacon continued to ply Gringoire with questions. La Esmeralda was, in Gringoire's opinion, a pretty, charming and harmless creature; a naïve, exuberant girl, ignorant of everything and enthusiastic about everything, still unaware of the difference between a man and a woman, even in her

dreams; fond, above all, of dancing, noise and open air. Her
character was no doubt due to the wandering life she has always led. Gringoire had managed to learn that, while she was
a little child, she had roamed all over Spain and Catalonia
and believed that she had even gone as far as Sicily and the
Kingdom of Algiers. The gypsies, said Gringoire, were vassals
of the King of Algiers. In any case, he was sure that she had
come to France from Hungary at an early age. From all these
countries she had retained scraps of old jargons and foreign
ideas and songs, which made her speech as motley as her costume, which was half Parisian and half African. The people
of the sections of the city which she frequented liked her for
her gaiety, her kindness, her lively manner, her dancing and
her singing. In all of Paris she believed herself to be hated by
only two persons, of whom she often spoke with fright. One
was the recluse of Roland Tower, who had some mysterious
grudge against gypsies and who cursed her every time she
passed by the window of her cell; the other was a priest who
never saw her without looking at her and speaking to her in
a way which frightened her. This latter fact troubled the archdeacon considerably but Gringoire did not notice his agitation; two months had been long enough to make the absent-
minded poet forget the singular details of the evening when
he first met La Esmeralda and the archdeacon's presence in
the affair. Except for these two persons, she was afraid of
nothing and no one; she was not a fortune teller, so she was
safe from the acusations of witchcraft which were so often
made against gypsy women. And then Gringoire was a brother
to her, if not a husband. Actually, the philosopher bore his
platonic marriage quite patiently; at least he was always sure
of a bed and something to eat. Every morning he left the
Court of Miracles with his wife and helped her make a har-
vest of small coins, spent every evening under the same roof
with her, allowed her to bolt herself in her room, then slept
the sleep of the just. It was a pleasant life, he said, and quite
conducive to meditation. Also, in his heart and soul, the
philosopher was not at all sure he was madly in love with her;
he loved her goat almost as much. It was a charming, gentle
and intelligent animal, a learned goat. Nothing was commoner
in the Middle Ages than those trained animals which aroused
great wonder and often led their masters and mistresses to the
stake. The magic feats of this particular goat, however, were
quite innocent. Gringoire explained them in detail to the
archdeacon, who appeared to be greatly interested. In most

cases it was only necessary to hold out the tambourine in a certain way to make the goat perform the trick desired. It had been trained that way by La Esmeralda, who had such an exceptional talent for those things that it had taken her only two months to teach the goat to spell out the word "Phoebus."

"Phoebus!" exclaimed the archdeacon. "Why Phoebus?"

"I don't know," replied Gringoire. "It may be a word which she thinks has some magic power or other. She often repeats it to herself when she thinks she's alone."

"Are you sure," said Claude with a penetrating look, "that it's only a word and not a name?"

"Whose name?"

"How should I know?"

"My theory is that gypsies are inclined to be sun worshipers, hence Phoebus."

"That doesn't seem as clear to me as it does to you, Master Pierre."

"Well, it doesn't matter to me. As far as I'm concerned, she can mutter her Phoebus all she likes. One thing is sure at least: Djali likes me almost as much as she does."

"Who's Djali?"

"That's her goat."

The archdeacon rested his chin on his hand and remained thoughtful for a moment. Suddenly he turned to Gringoire again and said, "Will you swear to me that you've never touched her?"

"Who, Djali?"

"No, that woman."

"My wife? I swear I've never touched her."

"Are you often alone with her?"

"Every evening, for an hour or so."

Dom Claude frowned. "Swear to me by your mother's womb," he said, "that you have never so much as laid a finger on that creature."

"I'll also swear it by my father's head if you like, for the two things aren't entirely unrelated. But, reverend master, will you allow me to ask you a question also?"

"You may."

"Why are you so interested in this?"

The archedeacon's pale face became as red as a young girl's cheek. He stood for a moment without answering, then said with visible embarrassment, "Listen to me, Master Pierre: you're not damned yet, as far as I know. I'm interested in your welfare. The slightest contact with that demon of a gypsy girl will make you the vassal of Satan. As you know, it's always the body that brings about the damnation of the soul. Woe unto you if you ever come near that woman. That's all."

"I tried once," said Gringoire, scratching his ear. "That was on our wedding night. But I got nowhere."

"How could you do such a thing, Master Pierre?" said the priest, his face darkening.

"Another time," continued the poet, smiling, "I looked in through the keyhole before I went to sleep and I saw the most delightful lady who ever went to bed wearing only a slip."

"Go to the devil!" cried the archdeacon with a terrible look. Then, violently shoving the startled Gringoire aside, he stalked rapidly away into the shadows of the cathedral.

CHAPTER THREE

The Bells

SINCE HIS MORNING ON THE PILLORY, THE PEOPLE LIVING around the Cathedral of Notre Dame noticed that Quasimodo's bell-ringing ardor had cooled. He had formerly rung the bells on all occasions: peals of the great bells for high mass, rich octaves running up and down the smaller bells for a wedding or a christening, all mingled in the air like an embroidery of all sorts of delightful sounds, making the old church vibrant and sonorous with perpetual rejoicing. The people felt the constant presence of a spirit of sound and caprice singing by means of those brazen throats. That spirit now seemed to have vanished; the cathedral seemed gloomy and readily given to silence. Holidays and funerals had their simple peals, dry and bare, exactly what the ritual called for and nothing more. Of the double sound which makes a church—the organ within and the bells without—only the organ remained.

Yet Quasimodo was still there. What was troubling him? Was it that the shame and desperation of the pillory still lingered in his heart, that the torturer's lashes were still resounding in his mind, that his sadness at having been given such treatment had extinguished everything in his soul, including his passion for the bells? Or was it that Marie had a rival in his heart, that he was neglecting the great bell and her fourteen sisters for something more lovable and beautiful?

It happened that in the Year of Our Lord 1482 the Annunciation fell on Tuesday, March 25. On that day the air was so pure and light that Quasimodo's love for his bells returned to a certain extent. He climbed up the stairs of the northern tower as the beadle was pushing open the doors of the church, which at that time were enormous panels of heavy wood covered with leather, bordered by gilded iron nails and framed by delicate carvings.

When he reached the high loft of the belfry, Quasimodo gazed at the bells for some time, shaking his head sorrowfully as if something foreign had interposed itself between him and them. But when he had set them in motion, when he felt that cluster of bells stirring under his hand, when he saw (for he could not hear) the palpitating octave running up and down that sonorous scale like a bird hopping from branch to branch, when the demon of music had taken possession of the poor deaf creature, he became happy once again, his heart expanded and his face brightened. He paced to and fro, animating his six singers by voice and gesture, like the conductor of an orchestra spurring on his intelligent virtuosos.

"Go on, Gabrielle, go on!" he cried, "Pour out all your sound into the square! Today is a holiday . . . Don't be lazy, Thibault; you're slowing down. Go on! Go on! Are you getting rusty, you shirker? That's good! Faster! Faster! Make them all deaf like me! Guillaume! Pasquier's doing much better than you are and you're much bigger! Harder! Harder! It's the Annunciation today. The sun is shining. We need a fine peal. Poor Guillaume! You're all out of breath!"

He was completely absorbed in urging on his bells, which were all leaping and shaking their gleaming rumps like a noisy team of Spanish mules goaded by the vehement cries of their driver, when, looking down into the square, he saw an oddly dressed girl unrolling a carpet on the pavement. A little goat was already standing on it and a group of spectators had begun to cluster around the two of them. This sight abruptly altered his train of thought and froze his musical enthusiasm. He stopped, turned his back on the bells and fixed on the dancing girl that tender, dreamy look which had astonished the archdeacon on another occasion. Meanwhile the forgotten bells all died down simultaneously, to the great disappointment of the lovers of bell-ringing who had been contentedly listening to the peal from the Pont-au-Change and who now walked away as baffled as a dog who has been shown a bone and then given a stone instead.

CHAPTER FOUR

The Archdeacon's Cell

ONE FINE MORNING IN THE SAME MONTH OF MARCH, OUR young student, Jehan Frollo, noticed as he was dressing himself that no metallic jingle came from his purse. "Poor purse!" he said, pulling it from his pocket. "Not one single coin! How cruelly you've been disemboweled by dice, steins of beer and the pleasures of Venus! There you are, all empty, wrinkled and limp!"

He dressed himself sadly. An idea occurred to him as he was lacing his boots. He rejected it at first, but he could not get it out of his head entirely. He put on his vest inside out, an obvious sign of some violent inner struggle. Finally he threw his cap on the floor and cried out, "All right! Come what may, I'll go to see my brother! I'm sure to get a sermon, but maybe I'll also get a little money." Then, throwing on his fur-trimmed coat and picking up his hat, he rushed out of the room.

As he passed by the Rue de la Huchette, walking down the Rue de la Harpe, his olfactory nerves were tickled by the odor coming from the spits which were incessantly turning there. He cast a loving glance at them but, having nothing with which to buy his breakfast, he heaved a deep sigh and went on his way. He did not even take time to throw a stone in passing, as was then the custom, at the statue of Périnet Leclerc, who surrendered Paris to the English in the time of Charles VI, a crime for which his effigy, battered by stones and covered with mud, did penance for three centuries on the corner of the Rue de la Harpe and the Rue de Buci, as if on a perpetual pillory.

A short time after crossing the Petit-Pont, Jehan found himself before Notre Dame. He then became undecided again and walked around the statue of Monsieur Legris for a few moments, repeating to himself in anguish, "The sermon is sure, but the money is doubtful." He stopped a beadle coming out of the cloister and asked him, "Where is the Archdeacon of Josas?"

"I believe he's in his cell in the tower," was the answer, "but I advise you not to disturb him unless you've been sent by either the pope or the king."

"Ah!" thought Jehan, clapping his hands, "this is a fine chance to see that famous sorcerer's den of his!"

His mind made up by this reflection, he walked resolutely through the small black door and began to climb the winding staircase leading to the top of the tower. "We'll see!" he said to himself on the way. "By the Holy Virgin, it must be a sight worth seeing, that cell which my reverend brother keeps as carefully hidden as his pudendum! They say he lights up the flames of hell there and cooks the philosopher's stone. Well, I care about as much for the philosopher's stone as I do for a pebble in the street, and I'd much rather find an omelet on his stove than the biggest philosopher's stone in the world!"

He stopped for a moment to catch his breath and swore at the endless steps by countless cartloads of devils, then continued his ascension. A short time after he had passed the belfry he came to a recess in which there was a low pointed door with a heavy lock on it. "This must be it," he said to himself.

The door was not locked. He pushed it gently and put his head in through the crack.

The reader is no doubt familiar with the works of Rembrandt, that Shakespeare of painting. Among his many wonderful etchings there is one which depicts, supposedly, Doctor Faustus and which it is impossible to contemplate without astonishment. In the middle of a dark room is a table laden with hideous objects: skulls, spheres, alembics, compasses and parchments covered with hieroglyphics. The doctor is before this table, dressed in a loose greatcoat with a fur cap pulled down to his eyebrows. Only the upper half of his body is visible. Half risen from his immense armchair, pressing his clenched fists against the table, he is looking with curiosity and terror at a great luminous circle of magic letters which is gleaming on the wall in front of him. The cabalistic sun seems to flicker before one's eyes and fill the dimly lit room with its mysterious radiance. It is both horrible and beautiful.

Something rather similar presented itself to Jehan's view

when he ventured to put his head through the crack of the door. He saw the same kind of dimly lit room. There were also a large armchair and table, compasses, alembics, animal skeletons hanging from the ceiling, a sphere lying on the floor, glass jars containing gold leaves, skulls lying on sheets of vellum covered with letters and figures, thick piles of manuscripts—in short, all the rubbish of medieval science and all covered with dust and cobwebs. But there was no circle of luminous letters and no doctor contemplating the flaming vision like an eagle gazing at the sun.

The cell was not deserted, however. There was a man sitting in the armchair and leaning over the table with his back to the door. Jehan could see only his shoulders and the back of his head but he had no difficulty recognizing that bald head on which nature had made a permanent tonsure, as if she had wished to mark the archdeacon's irresistible ecclesiastical calling by an outward symbol.

Jehan had opened the door so gently that his brother Claude was unaware of his presence. The curious student took advantage of the opportunity to examine the cell. To the left of the armchair, beneath the high window, was a large stove which he had not noticed at first. On it was a disorderly array of vials, bottles and retorts. Jehan observed with disappointment that there was no saucepan. Furthermore, there was no fire in the stove and it did not seem to have been lit for quite some time. A glass mask, which the archdeacon no doubt used to protect his face when he was working with some dreadful substance or other, was lying in a corner, covered with dust and apparently forgotten. Beside it was an equally dusty pair of bellows, the upper surface of which bore this inscription spelled out in copper letters: Spira, spera.

Numerous other inscriptions were, according to the custom of alchemists, written all over the walls, some in ink, others scratched with a piece of metal. Gothic, Hebrew, Greek and Roman letters were all jumbled together and the inscriptions all ran into one another, the more recent ones effacing the older ones. They formed a confused mixture of all human philosophies, dreams and wisdom. And they were all crossed at random by stars, figures of men and animals and intersecting triangles, which made each wall bear no small resemblance to a sheet of paper on which a monkey has been scratching with an ink-filled pen.

All in all, the cell gave a general impression of neglect and dilapidation and the bad condition of the utensils seemed to indicate that their owner had been distracted from his work for some time by other preoccupations.

As he pored over a manuscript ornamented with strange paintings, Claude Frollo seemed to be incessantly tormented by some idea which intruded itself into his meditations. Such, at least, was Jehan's impression as he heard him say, with the thoughtful pauses of a daydreamer thinking aloud: "Yes, according to both Manou and Zoroaster, the sun in born of fire and the moon is born of the sun. Fire is the soul of the universe. Its elementary atoms are constantly spreading and flowing over the world in infinite currents. At the points where these currents intersect in the sky, they produce light; at their points of intersection on earth, they produce gold. . . . Gold and light are the same thing. The difference between them is only the difference between the visible and the palpable, the liquid and the solid states of the same substance; the difference between water vapor and ice, nothing more. . . .This is no dream, it is the universal law of nature. . . . But how is science to go about fathoming this universal law? This light shining on my hand is gold! Its atoms are dispersed according to a certain law and they have only to be condensed according to a certain law! But how to do it? . . . Some have tried to bury a ray of sunlight. . . . Averroës—yes, it was Averroës—buried one under the first pillar to the left of the sanctuary of the Koran in the great mosque of Cordova; but the vault was not to be opened to see if the operation was successful until eight thousand years later."

"My God!" thought Jehan. "That's a long time to wait for a crown!"

"Others have thought," continued the archdeacon to himself, "that it would be better to work with a ray from Sirius. But it's very difficult to obtain a pure ray from Sirius because of the light from other stars mixed in with it. . . . Flamel believed it was better to work with earthly fire. . . . The diamond is in coal and gold is in fire. . . . But how to get it out? . . . Magistri states that there are certain women's names which have such a sweet and mysterious charm that it is necessary only to pronounce them during the operation. . . . Let's read what Manou has to say on the subject: 'Where women are honored, the divinities rejoice; where they are despised, it is useless to pray to God. . . . A woman's mouth is constantly pure; it is running water, a ray of sunshine. . . . A woman's name must be pleasant, sweet and imaginative; it must end in long vowels and sound like a word of blessing.'

. . . Yes, the sage is right; Maria, La Sophia, La Esmeral—
Damnation! Always the same thought!"

He slammed the book shut and passed his hand over his
forehead, as if to drive out the idea that was obsessing him.
Then he took from the table a nail and a small hammer
whose handle was curiously painted with cabalistic letters.
"For some time now," he said with a bitter smile, "all my
experiments have failed. I'm possessed by a fixed idea which
pierces my brain like a red-hot iron. I haven't even been able
to discover the secret of Cassidorus, who made his lamp burn
without either wick or oil, a feat which ought to be quite easy
to perform. . . . One miserable thought is all it takes to make
a man weak and mad. How Claude Pernelle would laugh at
me! She was unable to distract Nicolas Flamel from his great
works for even a moment. Why, here I am with the magic
of Zechiele in my hand! Each time that formidable rabbi
struck this nail with this hammer, one of his enemies, even if
he were two thousand leagues away, would sink one cubit into
the earth until he was eventually swallowed up. The King of
France himself sank into the pavement of Paris up to his
knees for having inconsiderately knocked on the rabbi's door.
. . . Well, I have the hammer and the nail but they're no
more formidable in my hands than any other hammer in the
hands of a carpenter. . . . Yet all I have to do is to find the
magic word which Zechiele pronounced when he struck the
nail."

"That ought to be a mere bagatelle!" thought Jehan.

"Let's try!" continued the archdeacon eagerly. "If I succeed
I'll see a blue spark fly from the head of the nail . . . *Emen-
hétan; Emen-hétan!* . . . No, that's not it . . . *Sigéani!
Sigéani!* . . . May this nail open a grave for any man who
bears the name of Phoebus. . . . Damnation! Always, still,
forever the same idea!"

He threw down the hammer angrily. Then he slumped so
deeply into the armchair and onto the table that Jehan lost
him from sight behind the enormous back of the chair. For
several minutes he saw nothing except the archdeacon's
clenched fist pressing down on a book.

The student watched his brother with surprise. He, who
wore his heart on his sleeve, who observed no other law in
the world except the good law of nature, who let his passions
flow according to their inclinations and in whom the lake of
powerful emotions was always dry because he was constantly
making new channels to drain it, he did not know how furi-

ously the sea of human passions ferments and boils when it is refused any outlet, how it swells, how it overflows, how it wears away the heart, how it breaks out in inward sobs and stifled convulsions until it finally breaks down all the dikes restraining it. Claude Frollo's austere and icy exterior, that cold surface of rigid and inaccessible virtue, had always deceived Jehan. The lighthearted student had never reflected on the lava which boils furiously deep under the snowy crest of Mount Etna.

We do not know whether these ideas suddenly crossed his mind at that moment but, feather-brained as he was, he at least realized that he had seen something he should not have seen, that he had just surprised his elder brother's soul in one of its most secret struggles and that he must not let him know it. Seeing that the archdeacon was still motionless, he quietly drew back his head and made a noise of footsteps outside the door, as of someone arriving and giving notice of his approach.

"Come in," called out the archdeacon, "I've been expecting you; I left the door unlocked for you."

Jehan stepped in boldly. The archdeacon, extremely embarrassed by such a visit in such a place, started in his chair. "What!" he exclaimed. "It's you, Jehan! What are you doing here?"

"Brother," replied the student, making an effort to achieve the proper piteous and humble expression and toying with his cap in an innocent way, "I've come to ask you for . . ."

"What?"

"Some advice which I need very much." He dared not add, "And for some money, which I need even more." This second half of his sentence remained unspoken.

"Jehan," said the archdeacon coldly, "I am extremely dissatisfied with you."

"Alas!" sighed the student.

Dom Claude turned his chair around and said, "I'm glad you came just now."

This was a formidable introduction. Jehan braced himself.

"Jehan, complaints about you are brought to me every day. What do you have to say about the beating you gave the young Viscount Albert de Ramonchamp?"

"Oh, that was nothing. He was just a mischievous page who amused himself by running his horse through the mud to splash students."

"And what about this Mahiet Fargel, whose robe you tore? 'Tunicam dechiraverunt' says the complaint."

"Why, it was only an old hood!"

"The complaint says 'tunicam,' not 'capettam.' Don't you understand Latin?"

Jehan did not answer.

"Yes," continued the archdeacon, shaking his head, "that's what learning has come to nowadays. The Latin language is hardly understood, Hebrew is unknown and Greek is so little esteemed that it is not considered ignorant for even the most learned men to pass over a Greek word without reading it."

These reflections made him silent and he stopped speaking. Jehan, who had all the cunning of a spoiled child, decided that the moment was favorable to venture his request. He began in an extremely gentle tone:

"Brother, do you really hate me so much as to glare at me so ferociously because of a few little blows given in fair fighting with some worthless urchin. quibusdam marmosetis? You see, brother Claude, I do know my Latin!"

But this fawning hypocrisy did not have its usual effect on his stern elder brother. He did not lose one wrinkle of his frown. "Come to the point," he said dryly.

"All right, I will!" replied Jehan bravely. "Here it is: I need money."

At this audacious declaration the archdeacon's countenance assumed a pedagogic and paternal expression. "You know, Jehan," he said, "that our fief of Tirechappe brings in only thirty-nine livres a year. That isn't much."

"I need money," repeated Jehan stoically.

"You also know that the ecclesiastical judge ruled that our twenty-one houses were held in full fee of the bishopric and that we could redeem this homage only by paying the bishop two marks of silver gilt at six livres each. I haven't been able to save those two marks yet, as you well know."

"I know I need money," said Jehan for the third time.

"What do you want to do with it?"

This question brought a gleam of hope to Jehan's eyes. He resumed his fawning attitude: "Look, brother Claude, I don't want it for any bad purpose. It's not so I can show off in taverns with your money or parade through the streets of Paris in gold brocade. It's for an act of charity."

"What do you mean?" asked Claude, slightly taken aback.

"Two of my friends want to buy a layette for the child of

a poor widow. It will cost three florins and I'd like to contribute my share."

"Do you really expect me to believe such a story? And who ever heard of a layette costing three florins?"

Jehan decided to take the bull by the horns once again. "All right," he said, "I might as well tell you: I want the money to pay for a little visit to Isabeau la Thierrye at the Val d'Amour tonight."

"Wretched libertine!" cried the archdeacon. "Get out of here, I'm expecting someone."

Jehan made one last effort: "Brother Claude, at least give me enough to buy something to eat."

"How are you doing in your study of the decretals of Gratian?"

"I lost my notebooks."

"How are you doing with the Latin humanities?"

"Someone stole my copy of Horace."

"How are you doing with Aristotle?"

"Why, don't you know one of the Fathers of the Church said that heretics have always sought refuge in the tangled underbrush of Aristotle's metaphysics? I don't need to know anything about Aristotle. I don't want his metaphysics to destroy my religion."

"Young man," retorted the archdeacon, "in the last ceremonial entry of the king there was a gentleman named Philippe de Comines who had this motto embroidered on the trappings of his horse: *Qui non laborat non manducet* [He who will not work shall not eat]. I advise you to meditate on these words."

Jehan remained silent for a moment, staring angrily at the floor. He then turned abruptly toward Claude and said, "So, dear brother, you refuse to give me enough to buy a crust of bread!"

"*Qui non laborat non manducet.*"

At this reply from the inflexible archdeacon, Jehan hid his head in his hands, like a woman sobbing, and cried out with an expression of despair, "*Ototototototoï!*"

"What does that mean?" asked Claude, astonished by the unexpected outburst.

"Why, it's Greek," said the student, looking up at him with his impertinent eyes, into which he had just rubbed his fists in order to make them look as though they were red from weeping. "It's an anapest by Aeschylus which admirably expresses sorrow." He then burst into such hearty, contagious laughter that even the archdeacon smiled. After all, it was Claude's own fault for having so thoroughly spoiled his younger brother.

"Oh, brother Claude," said Jehan, emboldened by the archdeacon's smile, "just look at my worn-out boots! Have you ever seen a sadder sight in your life?"

The archdeacon promptly resumed his original sternness. "I'll send you some new boots," he said. "But no money."

"Not even a little, brother Claude?" begged Jehan. "I'll learn Gratian by heart, I'll believe firmly in God, I'll be a real Pythagoras of learning and virtue. But please, just give me a little money now! Starvation is staring me in the face! Don't let it devour me!"

Dom Claude shook his head. *"Qui non laborat . . ."*

"All right, then, go to the devil!" interrupted Jehan. "From now on I'll gamble and fight and spend all my time in taverns and brothels!" As he said this he threw his cap in the air and snapped his fingers like castanets.

The archdeacon looked at him darkly and said, "Jehan, you have no soul."

"In that case, according to Epicurus, I'm lacking only something which no one can describe, made out of something which has no name."

"Jehan, you must think seriously of redeeming yourself. You're on a slippery downward path; do you know where you're going?"

"Yes, to the tavern."

"The tavern leads to the pillory."

"It's as good a guide as any."

"The pillory leads to the scaffold."

"The scaffold is a balance which has a man at one end and the whole world at the other; it's a fine thing to be the man."

"The scaffold leads to hell."

"At least it's warm down there."

"Jehan, Jehan! You'll come to a bad end!"

"At least I've had a good beginning."

In the silence which followed, footsteps were heard on the stairs.

"Quiet!" said the archdeacon, putting his finger to his lips. "Here comes Master Jacques. Listen, Jehan, never breathe a word about anything you may hear or see in this room. Quick, hide under the stove and don't make a sound!"

Jehan crawled under the stove. Then a brilliant idea occurred to him. "By the way, brother Claude," he said, "I'd like a florin for keeping quiet."

"Silence! I promise to give you one."

"Give it to me now."

"Here, take it!" said the archdeacon, angrily tossing him his purse. Jehan drew back under the stove and the door opened.

CHAPTER FIVE

The Two Men in Black

THE MAN WHO ENTERED WORE A BLACK ROBE AND A GLOOMY expression. The first thing about him which struck our friend Jehan (who had naturally placed himself so as to be able to see and hear everything) was the deep sadness of both his clothes and his face. There was a certain gentleness spread over that face, but it was the hypocritical gentleness of a cat or a judge. He was a man of about sixty, with gray hair, wrinkles, white eyebrows, a pendulous lower lip and large hands. When Jehan saw that he was probably only some magistrate or doctor and that his nose was very far from his mouth, a sure sign of stupidity, he drew back into his hole, annoyed at the prospect of spending an indefinite length of time in such an uncomfortable position and in such bad company.

Meanwhile the archdeacon had not even stood up to receive his visitor. After several moments of silence in which he seemed to be finishing some interrupted meditation, he pointed to a stool near the door and said, "Sit down, Master Jacques."

"Thank you, master," answered the man in black.

The difference in the way each man pronounced the word "master" showed that their relationship was that of teacher and disciple.

"Well," said the archdeacon after another silence which Master Jacques was careful not to interrupt, "have you succeeded?"

"Alas, master," said the other man with a sad smile, "I keep puffing away and I have all the ashes anyone could want but still no gold."

Dom Claude made an impatient gesture. "I'm not talking about that, Master Jacques Charmolue. I'm asking you about the trial of that sorcerer, Marc Cenaine I think you called him, the butler of the Court of Accompts. Has he admitted his sorcery? Have you been able to get anything out of him by torture?"

"I'm afraid we haven't had that consolation yet, master," replied Master Jacques with the same sad smile. "That man is as hard as a stone. I don't think he'd tell us anything if we boiled him in oil. But we're doing the best we can. All his joints are already dislocated, but nothing has done any good so far. He's a terrible man. I don't know what to do with him."

"Have you found anything else in his house?"

"Yes," said Master Jacques, fumbling in his purse. "We found this parchment. There are two words on it which we don't understand." He unrolled the parchment as he spoke.

"Give it to me," said the archdeacon. "This is pure magic, Master Jacques!" he cried as soon as he took one glance at it. "*Emen-hétan!* That's the cry of the witches when they arrive at their sabbath. *Per ipsum, et cum ipso, et in ipso!* That's the command which chains down the devil in hell! *Hax, pax, max!* That's medicine, a protection against the bite of a mad dog. Master Jacques, you are the king's attorney in the Ecclesiastical Court and I tell you this parchment is abominable!"

"We'll put the man to the torture again," promised Master Jacques. "Here's something else we found in his house," he added, reaching into his purse again. He drew out a vessel of the same family as those which covered Dom Claude's stove.

"Ah!" said the archdeacon. "An alchemist's crucible!"

"I confess I tried it out on my stove," said Master Jacques with his timid, awkard smile, "but it didn't succeed any better than my own."

The archdeacon examined the vessel. "Look what's inscribed on his crucible: *Och! Och!* That's the word·which drives away fleas! This Marc Cenaine is ignorant. I'm sure you'll never make any gold with this!"

"Speaking of errors," said the king's attorney, "I looked at the doorway of the cathedral again before I came up here. Are you quite sure it's the beginning of the book of natural philosophy that's represented on the side nearest the Hôtel-

Dieu and that among those seven nude figures the one with the wings on his heels is Mercury?"

"Yes," replied the archdeacon. "Augustino Nypho wrote about it; he was that Italian doctor who had a bearded demon who taught him all things. Besides, I'll go down with you in a while and point it all out to you."

"Thank you, master," said Charmolue with a low bow. "By the way, when would you like me to have that little witch arrested?"

"What witch?"

"That gypsy girl: you know, the one who comes to dance in the square. She has a goat that's possessed by the devil; it reads, writes and understands mathematics like Picatrix. The trial is always prepared and you may be sure it won't take long. She's a pretty girl, though, that little dancer! Such lovely black eyes! When shall we begin?"

The archdeacon was extremely pale. "I'll let you know," he mumured in a scarcely audible voice. "Go on with Marc Cenaine for the moment."

"Don't worry," said Charmolue, smiling. "I'll have him strapped down to the leather bed again as soon as I get back. But he's a devil of a man. He's wearing out Pierrat Torterue himself!"

Dom Claude appeared to be plunged in gloomy meditation. "Master Pierrat . . . I mean Master Jacques, go on with Marc Cenaine."

"Very well, Dom Claude. Poor man! What a martyrdom he'll have suffered before we're through with him! But he ought to know better than to go to witches' sabbaths. A butler of the Court of Accompts, too! As for the gypsy girl— Esmeralda, her name is—I'll await your orders. . . . Oh, yes —as we go out the door downstairs I'd like you to explain that painting of a gardener you can see when you come into the church. It's the Sower, isn't it? . . . Master, what are you thinking about?"

Dom Claude, lost in his own thoughts, was not listening. Charmolue followed the direction of his gaze and saw that it was fixed on a large cobweb which spanned the narrow window of the cell. Just then a careless fly, seeking the March sunshine, flew into the web and became entangled in it. As soon as it felt the web shake, an enormous spider rushed over to the fly and seized it. The archdeacon, as if suddenly awakened from a trance, pulled back Charmolue's arm with convulsive violence. "Master Jacques!" he cried out, "don't interfere with the workings of fate!"

The king's attorney looked at him with fright. His arm felt as though it were being gripped by a pair of iron pincers. The archdeacon's eyes gleamed fiercely as he stared at the spider and the fly.

"Yes, yes," he said in a voice which seemed to come from deep inside him, "there's the symbol of it all. The fly soars through the air, young and happy; it's seeking springtime, open air and freedom. But it flies into the fateful web and the spider comes out, the hideous spider! Poor little dancer! Poor predestined fly! Don't interfere, Master Jacques. It's fate! . . . Alas, Claude, you're that fly—and the spider, too! You were flying toward knowledge, light and sunshine; you thought only of reaching the open air, the dazzling light of eternal truth. But, blind fly, senseless doctor, in your flight toward that shining window which opens onto that other world, that world of clarity, intelligence and knowledge, you didn't see the subtle spider's web spread by fate between you and the light! You rushed into it, wretched madman, and now you're struggling against it with your head crushed and your wings broken! Don't interfere, Master Jacques, don't interfere!"

"I won't, I promise," said Charmolue, looking at him without understanding. "But please let go of my arm, master. You have a grip like a vise!"

The archdeacon did not hear him. "Fool!" he continued, still staring at the cobweb. "Even if you could break through that horrible web with your feeble wings, do you think you could reach the light? Alas, how would you get past that windowpane on the other side of the web, that transparent obstacle, that unbreakable wall of crystal which separates all philosophies from the truth? Oh, how vain science is! How many wise men have come flying from afar to dash their heads against that wall! How many clashing systems buzz vainly against that eternal windowpane!"

He was silent. His last reflections, which gradually turned his thoughts away from himself and toward science, seemed to have calmed him. Jacques Charmolue brought him completely back to reality by asking him this question: "Tell me, master, when will you come to help me make gold? I'm very anxious to succeed."

The archdeacon nodded with a bitter smile. "Master Jacques," he said, "read the *Dialogus de Energia et Operatione*

Daemonum, by Michael Psellus. What we're doing is not entirely innocent."

"Not so loud, master! I suspected that myself. But surely it's all right for a king's attorney to try his hand at alchemy when he earns only thirty crowns a year. Just the same, let's talk a little lower."

Just then the sound of chewing coming from under the stove reached the anxious Charmolue's ears. "What's that?" he asked.

It was Jehan, who, extremely cramped and bored in his hiding-place, had managed to find an old crust of bread and a small triangle of moldy cheese and was eating it unceremoniously as both his consolation and his breakfast.

"It's my cat making a meal of a mouse," replied the archdeacon hastily.

This explanation satisfied Charmolue. "Of course, master," he said with a respectful smile, "all great philosophers have always had some sort of pet animal."

Dom Claude, fearing that Jehan might take it into his head to play some other prank, reminded his worthy disciple that they had a number of figures on the doorway of the cathedral to study together. They both left the cell, to the great relief of Jehan, who was beginning to have serious fears that his chin and his knee might grow together.

CHAPTER SIX

The Effect Which May Be Produced by Seven Oaths Uttered in the Open Air

"GOD BE PRAISED!" CRIED JEHAN AS HE CAME OUT OF HIS hiding-place. "They're gone at last! *Och! Och! Hax, pax, max!* Fleas! Mad dogs! The devil! I've had enough of their talk! My head's ringing like a bell! And moldy cheese on top of all that! Enough! Now let's take my kind brother's purse and go change his money into bottles!"

He looked into the precious purse with love and admiration, brushed off his clothes, whistled a tune, looked around to see if there was anything in the cell worth taking, picked up several glass amulets to give as jewels to Isabeau la Thierrye and finally pushed open the door, which his brother had left unlocked as a last bit of indulgence and which Jehan now left unlocked as a last bit of malice.

Halfway down the dark spiral staircase he brushed against something which moved out of the way with a growl. He assumed it was Quasimodo, which struck him as so funny that he descended the rest of the staircase holding his sides with laughter. He was still laughing when he stepped out into the square.

"Ah, the good solid pavement of Paris!" he cried, stamping his foot. "That damned staircase is enough to make the angels of Jacob's ladder out of breath! What a fool I was to squeeze myself into that stone gimlet sticking up into the sky, just so I could eat a piece of moldy cheese and see the rooftops of Paris through a narrow window!"

After he had taken several steps he perceived Dom Claude and Jacques Charmolue contemplating the sculpture of the doorway of the cathedral. He approached them on tiptoe and overheard the archdeacon saying to Charmolue: "It was William of Paris who had a figure of Job carved into this lapis lazuli. Job represents the philosopher's stone, which must also be tried and tormented in order to become perfect."

"What do I care about that?" thought Jehan. "I'm the one who has the purse!"

Just then he heard a loud voice behind him articulating a formidable series of oaths: "By the blood of God! By the belly of God! Blood and thunder! By the body of God! By the navel of the devil! By the beard of the pope! Hell and damnation!"

"That could be no one except my friend Captain Phoebus!" exclaimed Jehan.

The name "Phoebus" reached the ears of the archdeacon just as he was explaining to Charmolue the dragon hiding its tail in a bath from which arises a cloud of smoke and the head of a king. He shuddered, stopped speaking and turned around to see his brother Jehan walking up to a tall officer standing in front of the Gondelaurier mansion.

Captain Phoebus de Châteaupers was leaning against the corner of his fiancée's house, swearing like a pagan.

"By God, Captain Phoebus," said Jehan, shaking his hand, "you swear with admirable enthusiasm!"

"Hell and damnation!" replied the captain.

"Hell and damnation to you too!" said Jehan. "Tell me, noble captain, what's the cause of this torrent of eloquence?"

"Excuse me, Jehan. A horse going at top speed can't stop short; I was swearing at full gallop. I just came from seeing those pious prudes up there. Every time I leave them my throat is full of oaths and I have to spit them out or they'll choke me."

"Would you like to have a drink?" asked Jehan.

This suggestion calmed the captain. "I'd like to, but I don't have any money."

"I have some."

"Really? Let's see it."

Jehan majestically exhibited the purse to the captain. In the meantime the archdeacon had left the dumfounded Charmolue and walked over to within several feet of the two friends. But they were so absorbed in the contemplation of the purse that they did not notice him.

"A purse in your pocket is like the moon in a bucket of water, Jehan," said Phoebus. "You can see it, but it isn't really there. I'll bet it has nothing but stones in it."

"Take a look at the stones I pave my pocket with, then," said Jehan coldly, pouring out the contents of the purse on a nearby curbstone with the air of a Roman saving the fatherland.

"Good God!" exclaimed Phoebus. "Look at all that money! It's dazzling!"

Jehan remained dignified and impassive. A few coins rolled into the gutter and the captain bent down to pick them up. Jehan held him back and said, "Shame on you, Captain Phoebus de Châteaupers!"

Phoebus counted the money, then turned gravely to Jehan and said, "Do you realize how much there is here? Did you rob someone?"

Jehan threw back his blond, curly head and said haughtily, "I have a brother who's both an archdeacon and an imbecile."

"By the horns of God!" exclaimed Phoebus.

"Let's go have a drink," said Jehan.

"Where shall we go? To the *Pomme d'Eve?*"

"No, captain, we're going to the *Vielle Science.*"

"But the wine is better at the *Pomme d'Eve.* Also, it has a vine beside the door which cheers me up while I'm drinking."

"All right, then, we'll go to the *Pomme d'Eve.*"

The two friends headed for the tavern. It is useless to add that they had picked up the money and that the archdeacon followed them. Was this the Phoebus whose cursed name had been intruding itself into all his thoughts ever since his conversation with Gringoire? He did not know, but at least it was a Phoebus, and that magic name was enough to make the archdeacon follow stealthily behind the two carefree companions, listening to their words and observing their slightest gestures with attentive anxiety. He had no difficulty in hearing everything they said, for they spoke very loudly, not at all embarrassed at having their conversation overheard by the passers-by. They spoke of duels, women, drinking and escapades.

As they turned a corner, the sound of a tambourine came to them from a nearby crossing. Dom Claude heard the officer say to the student, "Come on, let's walk faster."

"Why, Phoebus?"

"I'm afraid that gypsy girl will see me."

"What gypsy girl?"

"The one with the goat."

"La Esmeralda?"

"That's right; I always forget her devilish name. Hurry up, she'd recognize me if she saw me. I don't want her to speak to me in the street."

"Do you know her?"

Here the archdeacon saw Phoebus grin, lean near Jehan's ear and whisper a few words to him. Then he burst out laughing and threw back his head with a triumphant air.

"Really?" said Jehan.

"I swear."

"Tonight?"

"Tonight. "

"Are you sure she'll come?"

"Don't be silly, Jehan, it's sure!"

"Captain Phoebus, you're a lucky man!"

The archdeacon heard this entire conversation. His teeth chattered and he trembled visibly from head to toe. He stood still for a moment, leaned against a post as if he were drunk, then resumed his pursuit of the two merry companions. When he caught up with them again they were singing an old drinking song at the top of their lungs.

CHAPTER SEVEN

The Phantom Monk

THE FAMOUS TAVERN KNOWN AS THE Pomme d'Eve WAS
located near the university on the corner of the Rue de la Ron-
delle and the Rue du Bâtonnier. It was a large room with a
low vaulted ceiling supported in the middle by a thick yellow
wooden pillar. There were tables everywhere, gleaming tin
mugs hanging on the wall, always a crowd of drinkers and ac-
commodating women, a window looking onto the street, a
vine beside the door and, over this door, a creaking sheet of
iron with a woman and an apple painted on it, rusted by the
rain and swinging in the wind on an iron rod.

Night was falling. The street was dark. The tavern, full
of candles, could be seen glowing from far away, like a forge
in the night. Through its broken windows could be heard
the sound of clinking glasses, drunken reveling, cursing and
quarreling. Through the mist which the heat of the room
spread over the front window a hundred confused figures
could be seen swarming inside. People walking by on serious
errands went past this tumultuous scene without looking
at it. Now and then some ragged little street urchin would
stand on tiptoe to look in and shout the old refrain with which
it was customary to taunt drunkards: "Aux Houls, saouls,
saouls, saouls!"

One man, however, walked imperturbably back and forth
in front of the noisy tavern, constantly looking into it and
never going any further from it than a sentry from his box. He
was muffled up to the nose in a cloak which he had just
bought in a nearby shop, probably to protect himself against
the cold of the March evening, and perhaps also in order
to conceal his clothes. He stopped before the window from
time to time, listened, looked and stamped his feet.

The door of the tavern finally opened. This was apparently
what he was waiting for. Two drinkers came out. A ray of
light from the doorway illuminated their jovial faces for a
moment. The man in the cloak went off to take up a point of
observation under a porch across the street.

"Hell and damnation!" said one of the drinkers. "It's almost seven o'clock—time for my rendezvous!"

"I must say you seem very greedy, Phoebus," said his companion thickly.

"Jehan, you're drunk."

The man watching from the other side of the street appeared to have recognized the two friends, for he slowly followed the zigzag path which the student imposed on the captain, who, a more seasoned drinker, was in much firmer control of himself. Listening to them attentively, the man in the cloak was able to overhear this interesting bit of conversation:

"Try to walk straight, will you? You know I have to leave you. It's almost seven o'clock and I have an appointment with a woman."

"Go ahead, then, leave me! I see stars and tongues of fire! You're like the Château de Dampmartin, bursting with laughter!"

"By my grandmother's warts, Jehan, you're raving like a lunatic! . . . By the way, do you have any money left?"

"I never make mistakes, professor."

"Jehan! Answer me! You know I'm supposed to meet that girl at the end of the Pont Saint-Michel, that I can take her only to Falourdel's and that I'll have to pay the old woman for the room. She'd never give me credit. Jehan! Please tell me if we drank up everything in the archdeacon's purse. Don't you have anything left at all?"

"The awareness of having well spent the other hours is an excellent sauce at table."

"Stop talking nonsense and tell me if you have any money! Give it to me or I'll search your pockets myself!"

"Sir, the Rue de la Verrerie is at one end of the Rue Galiache and the Rue de la Tixeranderie is at the other."

"That's right, Jehan, the Rue Galiache, that's very good—but for the love of God, come to your senses! I need some money and I need it now!"

"Silence, everyone, and pay special attention to the chorus."

Jehan began to sing. Phoebus interrupted him. "All right, you scholar from hell!" he roared. "May you be strangled with your mother's entrails!" He gave a violent shove to the drunken student, who reeled against a wall, then slowly slid down it to the pavement. With a remainder of that brotherly compassion which is never totally absent from the heart of a drinker, Phoebus rolled Jehan with his foot onto one of those poor man's pillows which Providence provides on all the street corners of Paris and which the rich disdainfully refer to as heaps of garbage. The captain arranged Jehan's head on an inclined plane of cabbage stalks; the student immediately began to snore in a magnificent bass. The rancor in the captain's heart was not yet entirely extinguished, however. "So much the worse for you if the devil's cart picks you up as it passes!" he said to the sleeping student, then walked away.

The man in the cloak, who had not stopped following him, paused hesitantly for a moment before the young man stretched out on the pavement, heaved a deep sigh, then continued to follow the captain.

As he turned into the Rue Saint-André-des-Arcs, Phoebus noticed that he was being followed. When he happened to look around he saw a sort of shadow creeping behind him along the walls. When he stopped, it stopped. When he moved on, it moved on also. This caused him very little anxiety, for his pockets were empty.

He stopped before the Collège d'Autun, where he had gone through what he liked to call his studies. From his days as a mischievous schoolboy he had retained the habit of never passing before the building without inflicting on the statue of Cardinal Pierre Bertrand, which stood to the right of the doorway, that kind of affront about which Priapus complains so bitterly in Horace's satire, *Olim Truncus Eram Ficulnus*. He and his fellow students had carried on the custom so assiduously through the years that the inscription, "*Eduensis episcopus*," had been almost worn away.

As he stood before the statue, the street was completely deserted. When he nonchalantly prepared to move on, however, he saw the shadow approaching him slowly, so slowly that he had time to observe that it wore a cloak and a hat. It came up to him, then stood as motionless as the statue of Cardinal Bertrand, staring at him with eyes full of that vague light which comes from the eyes of a cat at night.

The captain was brave and would scarcely have minded meeting a robber with a sword in his hand. But this walking statue, this petrified man, made a chill run through him. At that time there were rumors current about a phantom monk who prowled the streets of Paris at night. These rumors flashed confusedly across his mind. He remained speechless for several minutes, then finally said, with a forced laugh, "Sir, if you're a robber, as I hope you are, you're like a heron attacking a nutshell. I'm a ruined scion of an honorable family.

You'll do better to try your luck in the college here: in the chapel there's a piece of wood from the true cross, mounted in silver."

The hand of the shadow came out from beneath its cloak and seized Phoebus's arm with the force of an eagle's claw. At the same time the shadow spoke: "Captain Phoebus de Châteaupers!"

"How the devil do you know my name?" exclaimed Phoebus.

"Your name is not all I know," said the man in a sepulchral voice. "You have an appointment tonight."

"Yes, I have," said Phoebus, astounded.

"At seven o'clock."

"In a quarter of an hour."

"At Falourdel's."

"That's right."

"With a woman."

"I plead guilty."

"Whose name is . . ."

"La Esmeralda," said Phoebus lightly. His carefree manner had come back to him by degrees.

At this name the man shook Phoebus' arm furiously and said, "Captain Phoebus de Châteaupers, you're lying!"

The captain flushed, drew back violently and clapped his hand to his sword. "By Christ and Satan!" he cried. "That's something that isn't often said to a Châteaupers! You don't dare repeat it!"

"You're lying," said the man coldly.

The captain gnashed his teeth. The phantom monk had vanished; he now saw only a man and an insult. "All right, then," he said, choking with rage, "draw your sword! Right now! There's going to be blood on this pavement before we're through!"

The man did not stir. When he saw his adversary ready to attack, he said bitterly, "You're forgetting your appointment, captain."

The passions of men like Phoebus are like boiling milk, whose ebullition can be stopped by a few drops of cold water. These words made him lower his sword which was glittering in his hand.

"Captain," continued the man, "tomorrow, or the day after tomorrow, or a month from now, or ten years from now, you'll find me ready to cut your throat. But first go to your appointment."

"It's true," said Phoebus, as if to himself, "that a girl and a sword are two fine things to meet in the same evening but I see no reason why I should give up one for the other when I can have both." He put his sword back into its scabbard.

"Go to your appointment," said the stranger.

"Thank you for your courtesy," said Phoebus with some embarrassment. "We'll have time enough tomorrow to slash each other. I'm grateful to you for allowing me to spend a pleasant evening before then. I'd hoped to be able to lay you out in the gutter and still arrive in time for my appointment, especially since it's fashionable in such cases to keep the lady waiting for a while. But you seem to be a husky fellow and it will be safer to postpone our encounter till tomorrow, so I'll go to my appointment now." He paused and scratched his ear. "Horns of God! I was forgetting: I have no money for the room and the old hag will want to be paid in advance. She doesn't trust me."

"Take this, it will be enough."

Phoebus felt the stranger's cold hand slip a large coin into his. He could not help taking the money and clasping the hand which had given it to him. "By God!" he exclaimed. "You're a good fellow!"

"I give you the money on one condition," said the stranger. "Prove to me that I was wrong and that you were telling the truth. Let me hide somewhere in the room from where I can see whether the woman is really the one you say."

"I have no objection to that," replied Phoebus. "There's a small room next to the one I'll be using. You can watch to your heart's content from there."

"Let's go, then," said the man.

"At your service," said the captain. "For all I know, you may be the devil in person but for tonight we'll be friends. Tomorrow I'll pay you all my debts, with both my purse and my sword."

They began to walk rapidly. After several minutes the sound of the river announced that they were on the Pont Saint-Michel, which was then covered with houses. "First I'll take you to the room," said Phoebus to his companion, "then I'll go to meet the young lady."

His companion did not answer. He had not said a word from the time they began walking side by side. Phoebus stopped in front of a low door and pounded on it. It opened to reveal an old woman and an old lamp, both trembling. The old woman was bent almost double and was dressed in rags. Her head shook and her hands, face and neck were covered with wrinkles. Her lips turned inward beneath her gums and she had tufts of white whiskers all around her mouth, which gave her the sly look of a cat. The interior of her den was no less dilapidated than herself. The walls were of chalk and black beams ran across the ceiling. There were cobwebs in every corner and a cluster of rickety tables and chairs in the center of the room. Against one wall was a fireplace without a mantelpiece; a filthy child was playing in the ashes. At the back of the room was a wooden staircase, or rather a ladder, which led up to a trap door in the ceiling.

Phoebus's mysterious companion pulled his cloak up around his eyes when he stepped inside. The captain put his coin into the old woman's hand and said, "We want a room." She carefully placed the money in a drawer and turned to show them the way. While her back was turned, the ragged little boy who had been playing in the ashes stealthily opened the drawer and took out the coin. In its place he left a dried leaf which he had pulled off a piece of firewood.

The old woman motioned the two men to follow her and climbed up the ladder ahead of them. On reaching the floor above, she set down her lamp on a chest and Phoebus, who knew the house well, opened a door leading into a dark room. "Enter, my friend," he said to his companion. The man in the cloak obeyed without a word. The door closed behind him and he heard Phoebus bolt it, then go back down the ladder after the old woman, who took the lamp with her.

CHAPTER EIGHT

The Usefulness of Windows Overlooking the River

CLAUDE FROLLO (FOR WE ASSUME THAT THE READER, MORE intelligent than Phoebus, has seen in this whole adventure no other phantom monk than the archdeacon) groped around for several moments in the dark hole in which the captain had bolted him. It was a low attic room with a triangular cross-section. There was no window of any kind and the sloping roof was not high enough to allow a man to stand upright. Claude therefore crouched in the dust and loose plaster, which crunched under his feet. His head was burning hot. He felt around him on the floor, found a piece of broken glass and pressed it against his forehead. Its coolness relieved him a little.

What was taking place in the archdeacon's dark soul at that moment? In what fateful order did he arrange in his thoughts La Esmeralda, Phoebus, Jacques Charmolue, Jehan, whom he had loved so much and whom he had abandoned in the gutter, his reputation, which would perhaps be dragged through the mud because of his presence in this infamous house, and the adventures he had just been through?

He had been waiting for a quarter of an hour, during which it seemed to him that he had aged a hundred years, when he suddenly heard the ladder creak; someone was coming up. The trap door opened and a light appeared. There was a rather wide crack in the worm-eaten door of his hiding place. He put his face against it and looked into the next room. The old woman with the catlike face was the first to enter. She was followed by Phoebus, twirling his mustache, and the graceful figure of La Esmeralda. The archdeacon saw her appear like a dazzling vision rising from the earth. He trembled; a cloud passed before his eyes, his heart began to pound violently and everything seemed to whirl around him. Then he lost consciousness.

When he returned to his senses, Phoebus and La Esmeralda were alone, sitting on the wooden chest beside the lamp. At one end of the room the archdeacon saw a dilapidated bed. Beside it was a window whose cracked panes revealed a patch of sky and the moon resting in the distance on a bed of fluffy clouds.

The girl was blushing, palpitating and speechless. The officer, to whom she dared not raise her eyes, was beaming. Mechanically, and with charming awkwardness, she traced incoherent designs on the lid of the chest with her finger. Her little goat was lying at her feet.

The pounding of the blood in his temples made it difficult for Dom Claude to hear what they were saying. An amorous conversation is a rather commonplace thing. It is essentially a perpetual "I love you," an extremely bare and insipid phrase for a disinterested listener. But Dom Claude was not a disinterested listener.

"Please don't despise me, Captain Phoebus," said the girl without raising her eyes. "I feel I'm doing something wrong."

"Despise you!" exclaimed the officer in a tone of self-assured gallantry. "Why should I despise you, my dear?"

"For coming here with you."

"I see we don't understand each other. I ought to hate you, not despise you."

The girl looked at him in alarm. "Hate me! For what?"

"For being so difficult to persuade."

"It was because I'm breaking a vow. I'll never find my parents now, the amulet will lose its power . . . but it doesn't matter! I have no need of parents now!"

"The devil take me if I understand what you're saying!"

La Esmeralda was silent for a moment, then a tear welled up in her eye, a sigh escaped from her lips and she said, "Oh, Captain Phoebus, I love you so!"

There was such an aura of chastity and charming virtue around her that Phoebus did not feel entirely at ease. Her last words emboldened him, however. "You love me!" he cried ecstatically and put his arm around her waist. This was what he had been waiting for.

The archdeacon watched him and tested with his finger the point of a dagger which he kept concealed under his cloak.

"Phoebus," said the girl, gently removing the captain's tenacious hands from her waist, "you're kind, noble and handsome. You saved my life, even though I'm only a poor gypsy girl. For years I dreamed of an officer who would save my life. I was dreaming of you before I ever saw you, my Phoebus. My dream had a fine uniform like yours and noble features and a sword. You have a beautiful name. I love your name and I love your sword. Draw your sword, Phoebus, and let me see it."

"What a child you are!" said the captain, smiling, as he unsheathed his sword. La Esmeralda examined it carefully, especially the figure engraved on the hilt, kissed it and said to it, "You're the sword of a brave man. I love my captain."

As she bent over it, Phoebus took advantage of the opportunity to kiss her on the neck. She looked up and blushed to the roots of her hair. The archdeacon gnashed his teeth in the darkness.

"Phoebus," she said, "let me talk to you. Walk a little, so I can see how tall you are and hear your spurs jingle. You're so handsome!"

The captain stood up to comply with her request, scolding her with a self-satisfied smile: "You're such a child! By the way, have you ever seen me in my full-dress uniform?"

"No, alas!" she replied.

"That's something really fine to look at!"

He sat down beside her again but much closer this time. "Listen to me, darling . . ." he began but she put her lovely hand over his lips in a gesture of playful grace.

"No," she said, "I won't listen to you. Do you love me? I want you to tell me if you love me."

"Do I love you, angel of my life!" cried the captain, half-kneeling before her. "My body, my blood, my soul, everything is yours, everything is for you! Yes, I love you and I've never loved anyone but you!"

He had repeated this little speech on so many other similar occasions that he delivered it all in one breath, without making a single mistake. At this passionate declaration, La Esmeralda looked up at the dingy ceiling, which took the place of the sky, with an expression of angelic bliss. "Oh," she murmured, "this is the moment when one ought to die!" As for Phoebus, the moment was a good opportunity to steal another kiss, which tortured the wretched archdeacon in his corner.

"Die!" cried the amorous captain. "What are you saying, my beautiful angel? This is the time to live! Die at a wonderful moment like this? My God, what a ridiculous idea! Listen, my dear Similar—Esmenarda—Excuse me, but you have such a prodigiously outlandish name that I can never get it straight in my mind."

"Oh," said the poor girl, "I thought it was pretty because it was so unusual. But since you don't like it, I'll change it to something else."

"Let's not worry about such a trifle, my darling. It's a name that takes a while to get used to, that's all. Once I know it by heart it won't give me any more trouble. Listen, my dear Similar, I love you passionately. I love you so much it's a miracle. And I know a young lady who's bursting with rage because of it."

"Who's that?" interrupted the jealous girl.

"What does it matter to us? Do you love me?"

"Oh, yes!"

"Well, then, it's all settled! You'll see how I love you, too. May the devil impale me on his pitchfork if I don't make you the happiest woman in the world! We'll have a little nest somewhere and I'll parade my soldiers under your window. I'll take you to the grand ceremonies at the Grange de Rully. It's a magnificent sight: eighty thousand armed men, thirty thousand suits of armor, all sorts of banners flying—an array fit for the devil himself, in other words! I'll take you to see the lions at the Hôtel-du-Roi; they're real wild animals. All women like that."

For some time the girl, absorbed in her own charming thoughts, had been listening dreamily to the sound of his voice without heeding the meaning of his words.

"Oh, you'll be happy, all right," went on the captain, at the same time gently unfastening her belt.

"What are you doing?" she asked sharply. His movement had aroused her from her reverie.

"Nothing," he answered. "I was just thinking that you ought to take off this streetdancer's costume when you're with me."

"When I'm with you, my Phoebus!" said the girl tenderly. Then she became pensive and silent once again.

The captain, emboldened by her gentleness, took her waist without any resistance on her part, then began to unlace her blouse. The panting archdeacon saw her lovely bare shoulder appear. She made no protest; she did not even seem to notice what Phoebus was doing. His eyes gleamed.

Suddenly she turned to him. "Phoebus," she said with an expression of infinite love, "instruct me in your religion."

"My religion!" cried the captain with a burst of laughter. "Good God! What do you want to do with my religion?"

"It's so we can get married," she replied.

The captain's face took on an expression of mingled surprise, scorn and lust. "Oh," he said, "are we getting married?"

The girl turned pale and her head drooped sadly.

"Listen, darling," said Phoebus tenderly, "what good does marriage do? Do people love each other any more after some priest has spouted Latin at them?"

As he said this in his softest voice, he moved extremely near to her, his caressing hands once again took up their position around her slender waist, his eyes shone more and more brightly, and it was obvious that he was approaching one of those moments when even Jupiter abandoned himself so utterly that Homer was obliged to call in a cloud to his aid.

Meanwhile Dom Claude was observing everything. The darkskinned, broad-shouldered priest, who had been condemned until then to the austere virginity of the cloister, quivered at the sight of that scene of love and voluptuous passion. The beautiful young girl's surrender to the ardent young man seemed to pour molten lead into his veins. He felt extraordinary movements within himself. His eye followed the removal of each pin with lascivious jealousy.

Suddenly Phoebus pulled off her blouse completely. The

poor girl, who had until then remained pale and pensive, awakened from her reverie with a start. She abruptly pushed the enterprising officer away, blushing and speechless with shame, and hid her bosom with her arms.

The captain's abrupt action had revealed the amulet which she wore around her neck. "What's that?" he asked, seizing this pretext to approach the frightened girl again.

"Don't touch it!" she cried. "It's my guardian charm. It will bring me back to my family if I remain worthy of it. Please leave me alone, Captain Phoebus! Have mercy on me! Please give me back my blouse!"

Phoebus stepped back and said coldly, "I see now that you don't love me."

"I don't love you!" cried the wretched girl, throwing her arms around his neck and pulling him down beside her. "I don't love you, my Phoebus! How can you tear my heart out by saying such a cruel thing? Take me, Phoebus, take everything, do whatever you like with me, I'm yours! What do I care about the amulet? What do I care about my mother? I love you! Look at me, Phoebus, my beloved Phoebus; I came to you of my own free will. My soul, my life, my body, it's all one thing and it's all yours. No, we won't be married; you don't want to. What am I, after all? I'm only a wretched girl from the gutter, but you, my Phoebus, you're a gentleman! What a silly idea, a street dancer marrying an officer. I must have been mad even to think of it! No, Phoebus, I'll be your mistress, your amusement, your pleasure, whenever you want me, but I'll belong to you. That's all I was made for; what do I care if I'm disgraced and despised, as long as I'm loved! I'll be the proudest and happiest woman in the world! And when I'm old and ugly, Phoebus, when I'm no longer fit for you to love, you'll let me serve you. Other women will embroider your scarves. I'll be the servant who takes care of them. You'll let me polish your spurs, brush your clothes and dust your boots. You will have the mercy to let me do that, won't you, Phoebus? But for now, take me! All this belongs to you, my Phoebus, but love me! All we gypsies need is open air and love!"

As she spoke thus, with her arms around his neck, she looked at him supplicatingly with a smile on her lips and tears in her eyes, her delicate bosom rubbing against the rough embroidery of his doublet as she twisted her lovely half-nude body. The captain, intoxicated with desire, pressed his burning lips against her beautiful bare shoulders. Her head thrown back, her eyes staring blindly up at the ceiling, she quivered under his kiss.

Suddenly, above his head, she saw a livid, convulsive face with eyes like those of a soul in hell. Near it was a hand clutching a dagger. It was the face and the hand of the archdeacon, who had broken down the door. Phoebus did not see him. The girl was speechless before the terrifying apparition. She saw the dagger plunge down toward Phoebus. He uttered an oath and fell to the floor. She fainted. Just before she lost consciousness altogether, she thought she felt a touch of fire on her lips, a kiss more burning than the torturer's red-hot iron.

When she came back to her senses, she was surrounded by soldiers of the watch, the captain was being carried out bathed in his own blood, the priest had disappeared, the window overlooking the river was wide open and she heard someone saying, "She's a witch who just stabbed a captain."

Book VI

The Coin Changed into a Dried Leaf

GRINGOIRE AND THE WHOLE COURT OF MIRACLES WERE IN A state of extreme anxiety. La Esmeralda had been missing for a month. No one had seen her goat, either, which doubled Gringoire's sorrow. She had disappeared one evening and not been heard from since. All search had proved fruitless. Several of Gringoire's malicious colleagues told him they had seen her that evening near the Pont Saint-Michel walking off with an officer; but Gringoire was a skeptical philosopher and, besides, he knew better than anyone else how virtuous his wife was. He had no doubts on that score.

Nevertheless he could not account for her disappearance. It caused him such great pain that he would have grown much thinner if such a thing had been possible. He forgot everything else, even his literary pursuits, including his great work entitled *De Figuris Regularibus et Irregularibus*, which he intended to have printed as soon as he could lay his hands on enough money.

One day as he was walking sadly past the Tournelle Criminelle he noticed a considerable crowd around one of the doors of the Palace of Justice. "What's happening?" he asked a young man who was coming out.

"I don't know," answered the young man. "They say there's a woman being tried for the murder of an officer. Since there seems to be some witchcraft involved in it, the bishop and the ecclesiastical judge have intervened in the case and my brother, the Archdeacon of Josas, spends all his time at the trial. I wanted to talk to him but I couldn't get through the crowd to him, which annoys me greatly because I need money."

"Alas, I wish I were able to lend you some," said Gringoire. "There are holes in my pockets but they weren't made by coins." He dared not tell the young man that he knew his brother the archdeacon, whom he had not seen since the scene in the church, a neglect of which he felt ashamed.

The student went on his way and Gringoire began to follow the crowd going up the great staircase. In his opinion there was nothing so good for dispelling a melancholy mood as the spectacle of a criminal trial, for the judges were usually amusingly stupid. The people with whom he had mingled walked along and elbowed each other in silence. After a period of slow and monotonous shuffling down a long, dark corridor which wound through the palace like an intestinal canal, he arrived at a low door opening into a room which his tall stature enabled him to examine above the undulating heads of the crowd.

The room was large and dark, which made it look still larger. Night was falling; the high pointed windows admitted only a dim light which died away before it reached the vaulted room. Here and there several candles on tables lighted up the heads of clerks bent over stacks of paper. One end of the room was occupied by the crowd; on both sides there were lawyers sitting at tables and at the back, on a raised platform, there were a great number of judges with frozen, sinister faces, the last rows of whom were almost invisible in the shadows. A large statue of Christ could be dimly discerned above their heads. The whole room bristled with pikes and halberds, which the light from the candles seemed to tip with fire.

"Who are those people over there, lined up like prelates at a council?" said Gringoire to a man standing next to him.

"Those are the Counselors of the Great Chamber on the right and the Counselors of the Inquest on the left," answered the man.

"And who's that red-faced, sweaty man above them?"

"That's the presiding magistrate."

"And what about those sheep behind him?" asked Gringoire, who, as we have already noted, did not like the magistrature, which may have been partly due to the grudge he bore against the Palace of Justice after his dramatic misadventure there.

"Those are the Royal Masters of Requests."

"And who's the boar in front of them?"

"That's the Clerk of the Court of Parliament."

"And the crocodile to his right?"

"Master Philippe Lheulier, King's Advocate Extraordinary."

"And the big black cat to his left?"

"Master Jacques Charmolue, King's Attorney in the Ecclesiastical Court."

"And what are all those worthy men doing there?"

"They're conducting a trial."

"Whose trial? I don't see a prisoner."

"It's a woman and you can't see her from here. She has her back to us and she's hidden by the crowd. She's over there where you can see that cluster of halberds."

"Who is she?" asked Gringoire. "Do you know her name?"

"No, I just arrived. But I suppose it's a question of witchcraft because the ecclesiastical judge is attending the trial."

"Well, then," said our philosopher, "we're going to see the gentlemen of the magistrature eating human flesh. It's as entertaining a spectacle as any other."

At this point the people standing around Gringoire and his informant imposed silence on them. An important witness was testifying.

The witness was an old woman who was so muffled up that she looked like a walking bundle of rags. She stood in the middle of the room and addressed the court:

"Gentlemen, it's as true as it is that my name is Falourdel and that I've been established for forty years on the Pont Saint-Michel and always paid my rent and taxes. I'm a poor old woman now, gentlemen, but I was once a pretty girl . . . Several days before it happened, people had been telling me, 'Don't spin too much at night, Falourdel, because the devil likes to comb old women's distaffs with his horns. Last year the phantom monk was seen near the Temple but now he's prowling around near your house. Be careful he doesn't come knocking at your door some night.'

"Well, one night I was spinning when someone knocked on my door. I opened it and two men came in. One of them was dressed in black and the other was a handsome officer. I couldn't see anything except the eyes of the one in black and they were like burning coals. Everything else was covered up by his cloak and his hat.

"They asked me for a room. I let them have one upstairs, my cleanest one, and they gave me a crown. I put it into a drawer and said to myself, 'That will buy me some tripe tomorrow at the slaughterhouse.' We went upstairs. As soon as I turned my back, the man in black disappeared. That surprised me a little. The officer came back downstairs with me and went out. I'd spun about a quarter of a skein when he came back with a pretty young girl—a real little beauty, gentlemen; she'd have been dazzling if she'd been dressed up right. She had a black goat with her—or maybe it was white, I can't remember. That made me a little uneasy. If the officer wanted to bring a girl with him, it was no concern of mine, but a goat was something different. I don't like those animals. They have beards and horns. They're almost like men. And they make you think of witchcraft, too. But I didn't say anything. I had the crown. That was right, wasn't it, gentlemen?

"I took the captain and the girl to the room upstairs and left them alone—alone with the goat, at least. I came back downstairs and started spinning again. My house has two stories and the back of it faces the river, like all the other houses on the bridge. The windows of both stories overlook the river. Well, I kept spinning and I couldn't stop thinking about the phantom monk. I suppose it was the goat that made me think about it. Also, the girl was rather strangely dressed. All at once I heard someone cry out upstairs, then I heard something fall on the floor and the sound of the window being opened. I ran to my window, which is underneath, and I saw something black go flying past and fall into the river. It was a ghost dressed up like a priest. The moon was shining and I saw it very clearly. It swam over toward the right bank. I was trembling like a leaf. I called for help. The gentlemen of the watch came in and started beating me before they even took the trouble to find out what had happened. Finally I managed to explain things to them and we went upstairs. My poor room was all covered with blood, the captain was stretched out on the floor with a dagger in his neck, the girl was pretending to be dead and the goat was frightened out of its wits. 'I'll be washing this floor for two weeks,' I said to myself. They carried out the officer—poor young man!—and the girl, who had her clothes half off. But the worst of it was that when I went to get the coin the next day to buy some tripe with, I found only a dried leaf in the drawer where it had been."

A murmur of horror arose from the audience. "A ghost and a goat—there's witchcraft in it, all right,'" said a man standing near Gringoire. "And that dried leaf!" added another. "No doubt about it," said a third, "she's a witch in league with the phantom monk to rob officers." Gringoire himself was not far from finding the story likely and frightening.

"Witness," said the presiding magistrate solemnly, "have you anything else to tell the court?"

"No, sir," answered the old woman, "except that in the report they call my house a filthy hovel, which is an outrageous lie. The houses on the bridge may not be palaces but several butchers live there and they're rich men with clean and beautiful wives."

The magistrate who looked like a crocodile to Gringoire stood up. "Silence!" he said. "I must ask you, gentlemen, not to lose sight of the fact that a dagger was found on the accused. Witness, have you brought the leaf into which the coin the demon gave you was transformed?"

"Yes, sir. Here it is."

A clerk handed the dead leaf to the crocodile, who shook his head in a sinister manner and passed it on to the presiding magistrate, who passed it on to the king's attorney and so on until it had gone all around the room. "It's a birch leaf," said Master Jacques Charmolue. A new proof of witchcraft.

A counselor took the floor: "Witness, you say that two men went upstairs with you, the officer and the man in black, who disappeared at first but whom you later saw swimming in the Seine dressed as a priest. Which of those two men gave you the coin?"

The old woman thought for a moment and said, "It was the officer." A murmur arose from the audience once again. "Aha!" thought Gringoire. "That changes things."

Meanwhile Master Philippe Lheulier, King's Advocate Extraordinary, intervened in the questioning: "Let me remind you, gentlemen, that in a deposition written down while he was on his deathbed, the murdered officer stated that as soon as the man in black spoke to him, it occurred to him that he might be the phantom monk. He also stated that the phantom strongly urged him to go to his appointment with the accused and that when he, the captain, told him that he had no money, he gave him a crown. This was the same coin with which he later paid for the room. It was therefore a coin of hell!"

This conclusive remark appeared to dispel all the doubts of Gringoire and the other skeptics in the audience.

"You have already seen the documents, gentlemen," added

the king's advocate. "You may refer to the deposition of Captain Phoebus de Châteaupers."

At this name the accused stood up. Her head was visible above the crowd. To his horror, Gringoire recognized La Esmeralda.

She was pale; her hair, formerly so gracefully plaited and sprinkled with sequins, was disheveled; her lips were blue; her hollow eyes were frightening. "Phoebus!" she said bewilderedly. "Where is he? Please, gentlemen, before you kill me, tell me if he's still alive!"

"Silence, prisoner!" said the presiding magistrate. "That does not concern you."

"Have pity on me! Tell me if he's alive!" she replied, clasping her hands, which made her chains rattle.

"Very well, then," said the king's advocate dryly, "he's on the point of death. Now are you satisfied?"

The wretched girl sank down into her seat again without a word. There were no tears in her eyes and her face was as white as that of a waxen statue.

The presiding magistrate bent down toward a man standing below him. "Usher," he said, "bring in the other prisoner."

All eyes turned toward a small door, which opened and, to Gringoire's extreme agitation, admitted a pretty goat with gilded horns and hooves. The graceful animal stopped for a moment on the threshold, craning its neck as if it were standing on a high rock with a vast horizon around it. Then it saw the gypsy girl and, leaping over the table and the head of a clerk, it was at her knees in two bounds. It rolled joyfullly at her feet, soliciting a word or a caress, but she did not stir.

"Why, that's the same wicked goat!" cried the old woman. "I recognize both of them."

"If the court so desires," said Jacques Charmolue, "we shall now proceed to the examination of the goat."

Nothing was more common in those days than the trial of an animal for witchcraft. In the accounts of the provostry for 1466, for example, we find a detailed list of the expenses of the trial Gillet-Soulart and his sow, "executed for their crimes at Corbeil." Every item is set down: the cost of the sow's grave, the five hundred bundles of wood, the bread and three pints of wine for the prisoner's last meal, fraternally shared by the executioner, and the cost of keeping and feeding the sow for eleven days during the trial. Sometimes justice did not even stop at animals: the capitularies of Charlemagne and of Louis le Débonnaire decree punishment for luminous phantoms who have the audacity to appear in the air.

"We hereby warn the demon with which this goat is possessed and which has thus far resisted all attempts to exorcise it," continued Jaques Charmolue, "that if it persists in its wickedness or tries to frighten the court, we shall be forced to demand that it be sentenced to the gallows or the stake."

Gringoire broke out into a cold sweat. Charmolue picked up the gypsy girl's tambourine, held it out to the goat in a certain way and asked, "What time is it?" The goat looked at him intelligently, raised one of its gilded hooves and stamped seven times. It was actually seven o'clock. A movement of terror ran through the crowd.

Gringoire could no longer contain himself. "The goat is sealing its own doom!" he cried out. "Can't you see it doesn't know what it's doing?"

"Silence in the audience!" said the usher sharply.

By holding the tambourine in various ways, Jacques Charmolue made the goat perform other tricks which we have already described. And, by an optical illusion peculiar to judicial proceedings, the same spectators who had once applauded Djali's innocent pranks in the street were now terrified by them under the roof of the Palace of Justice. The goat was undoubtedly the devil.

It was still worse when Charmolue emptied out on the floor a leather bag containing movable letters which had been hanging from Djali's neck and the crowd saw the goat spell out the fateful name "Phoebus." The witchcraft of which the captain had been a victim seemed proved beyond the shadow of a doubt and in everyone's eyes La Esmeralda, that lovely dancer who had dazzled them so often with her grace, was now a horrifying witch.

She gave no sign of life while this was taking place. Nothing seemed to penetrate into her thoughts—neither Djali's fond advances, the threats of the judges, nor the muttered imprecations of the audience. In order to attract her attention it was necessary for a sergeant to shake her unmercifully.

"Prisoner," said the presiding magistrate solemnly, "you are of the gypsy race, which is given to evil ways. On the night of March 29, in complicity with the powers of darkness and the bewitched goat which is now on trial with you, you stabbed and killed Captain Phoebus de Châteaupers with the aid of charms and magic practices. Do you persist in denying it?"

"Horrible!" cried the girl, hiding her face in her hands. "My Phoebus! This is hell on earth!"

"Do you persist in denying it?" repeated the magistrate coldly.

"Yes, I deny it!" she said loudly, standing up.

"Then how do you explain the evidence against you?"

"I've already told you," she said in a broken voice. "I can't explain it. A priest I don't know . . . a horrible priest who was always pursuing me . . ."

"Exactly. The phantom monk."

"In view of the prisoner's obstinacy," said Master Jacques Charmolue gently, "I recommend the application of torture."

"Granted," said the presiding magistrate.

The poor girl shuddered. She stood up at the order of the soldiers, however, and walked with rather firm steps, preceded by Charmolue and the priests of the Ecclesiastical Court, between two rows of halberdiers toward a low door which suddenly opened and then closed behind her and which seemed to Gringoire like a monstrous mouth which had just devoured her. A plaintive bleating was heard as soon as she had disappeared; it was the little goat crying.

The proceedings were suspended. When a counselor remarked that the gentlemen of the court were tired and that there would be a long wait until the end of the torture, the presiding magistrate replied that a judge must sacrifice himself for the sake of his duty.

"What a malicious wench," said one old judge, "to make herself be put to the torture when we haven't had our supper."

CHAPTER TWO

Sequel to the Coin Changed into a Dried Leaf

AFTER GOING UP AND DOWN SEVERAL STEPS IN THE CORRIDORS, which were so dark that they were lighted by lamps in broad daylight, La Esmeralda was shoved into a sinister round room situated at the bottom of one of those large towers which still rise up through the layer of modern buildings with which the new Paris has covered the old. There were no windows in this dungeon; the only opening was the entrance, which was barred by a heavy iron door. There was no lack of light, however. A furnace was built into the thickness of the wall. A large fire was burning in it, filling the entire room with a flickering red glare. By this light the prisoner could see all around the room a number of frightful-looking instruments whose uses were unknown to her. In the middle of them was a leather mattress, lying almost flat on the floor. Above it hung a strap with a buckle, one end of which was fastened to a copper ring held between the teeth of a grotesque monster carved into the stone of the ceiling. Tongs and pincers were heating inside the furnace. This inferno was called simply the "questioning room."

Pierrat Torterue, Sworn Torturer of the Châtelet, was seated nonchalantly on the leather bed. His assistants, two square-faced gnomes wearing leather aprons, were turning over the irons on the coals.

The poor girl tried to summon up her courage but she was horror-stricken when she entered that room.

The sergeants of the bailiff of the palace ranged themselves on one side and the priests of the Ecclesiastical Court on the other. In one corner there was a clerk sitting at a table with an inkstand on it. Jacques Charmolue approached the gypsy girl with a gentle smile. "My dear girl," he said, "do you still persist in your denial?"

"Yes," she answered in a voice which was scarcely audible.

"In that case," said Charmolue, "we shall have the painful duty of questioning you more insistently than we would like to. Please be so kind as to sit down on this bed. Master Pierrat, make room for this young lady and close the door."

Pierrat stood up and grumbled, "If I close the door my fire will go out."

"Well, leave it open, then," said Charmolue.

Meanwhile La Esmeralda remained standing, terrified at the sight of that leather bed on which so many wretched prisoners had writhed in agony. At a sign from Charmolue, the two assistants took hold of her and forced her to sit down on it. They did not hurt her but at their touch and the contact of the leather, she felt the blood rush to her heart. She cast a bewildered glance around the room. It seemed to her that the ugly instruments of torture were moving toward her, ready to climb up her body to bite and pinch her.

"Where's the doctor?" asked Charmolue.

"Here I am," answered a man in black whom she had not noticed before. She shuddered.

"For the third time," said Charmolue in his caressing voice, "do you persist in denying the actions of which you are accused?"

This time her voice failed her and she could only nod her head.

"You persist?" said Charmolue. "Then I'm very sorry but I must do my duty."

"How shall we begin, sir?" asked Pierrat.

Charmolue hesitated a moment with the ambiguous grimace of a poet searching for a rhyme. Finally he said, "We'll begin with the boot."

The unfortunate girl felt herself so forsaken by God and mankind that her head drooped down to her breast like an inert object. The torturer and the doctor approached her at the same time, while the two assistants began to rummage in their hideous arsenal. She started convulsively at the clanking of the frightful irons. "Oh, my Phoebus!" she murmured so softly that no one heard her. Then she resumed her statue-like immobility and silence. The sight of her would have rent the heart of anyone except a judge. She was like a poor sinful soul questioned by Satan at the crimson wicket of hell.

The callous hands of Pierrat Torterue's assistants brutally stripped the shapely leg and the little foot which had so often charmed the onlookers with their grace and beauty in the streets of Paris. "What a pity!" murmured the torturer as he considered their delicate forms.

Soon, through a cloud which spread itself before her eyes, she saw the "boot" approaching; soon she saw her foot disappear into the frightful apparatus, pressed in between two iron-clad boards. Then terror lent her strength. "Take it off!" she shrieked wildly. She stood up all disheveled and cried out, "Mercy!" She tried to throw herself at Charmolue's feet but her leg was caught in the heavy block of wood and iron and she sank down helplessly.

At a sign from Charmolue she was put back on the bed and two brutal hands fastened around her slender waist the strap which hung down from the ceiling.

"For the last time, will you admit the actions of which you are accused?" asked Charmolue with imperturbable benignity.

"I'm innocent!"

"Then how do you explain the evidence against you?"

"Alas, sir, I can't explain it."

"Yet you still deny your crimes?"

"Yes, I deny everything!"

"Begin," said Charmolue to Pierrat.

Pierrat turned the screw, the "boot" tightened and the

wretched girl uttered one of those horrible shrieks which have no spelling in any human language.

"Stop," said Charmolue to Pierrat. "Now will you confess?" he asked La Esmeralda.

"I confess everything!" she cried. "I confess! I confess! Mercy!"

She had not reckoned her strength when she confronted the torture. The poor girl, whose life until then had been so light-hearted and gentle, was vanquished by the first pain.

"It is my duty to tell you," said Charmolue, "that you must expect death as the result of your confession."

"I hope so," she said. She fell back onto the leather bed half-unconscious, letting herself hang by the strap buckled around her waist.

"Come, come, my girl, hold yourself up a little," said Master Pierrat, raising her.

"Clerk, write this down," said Charmolue. "Gypsy girl, do you confess having participated in orgies, sabbaths and other rites of hell in company with phantoms, demons and witches? Answer."

"Yes," she said so softly that her voice was lost in her breathing.

"Do you confess having seen the ram which Beelzebub causes to appear in the clouds to summon witches to their sabbaths and which can be seen by them alone?"

"Yes."

"Do you confess having worshiped the heads of Baphomet, the abominable idols of the Templars?"

"Yes."

"Do you confess having had commerce with the devil in the shape of the goat which is on trial with you?"

"Yes."

"Finally, do you confess having murdered a captain named Phoebus de Châteaupers on the night of March 29 with the aid of the devil and of the phantom commonly known as the phantom monk?"

She fixed her dazed eyes on Charmolue and replied mechanically, without shock or convulsion, "Yes." It was obvious that her spirit was completely broken.

"Finish writing all that down, clerk," said Charmolue. Then, addressing the torturers: "Unfasten the prisoner and have her taken back to court." When the "boot" had been taken off he examined her foot, which was still numb from the pain it had undergone. "Well, I see there's no great harm done," he said. "You cried out in time. You'll still be able to dance, my girl."

Then he addressed his colleagues of the Ecclesiastical Court: "Justice is finally enlightened now! That's a great relief, gentlemen. This young lady will bear witness that we've acted with all possible gentleness."

CHAPTER THREE

Conclusion of the Coin Changed into a Dried Leaf

WHEN SHE CAME BACK INTO THE COURTROOM, PALE AND LIMP-ing, she was received with a general murmur of pleasure. On the part of the spectators it came from the feeling of satisfied impatience which one experiences in the theater at the end of the final intermission when the curtain goes up and the last act is about to begin. On the part of the judges it came from the hope of having supper soon. The little goat also bleated for joy. It tried to run toward its mistress but it had been tied to a bench.

Night had now fallen. The candles, whose number had not been increased, gave off so little light that the walls of the room could not be seen. All objects were enveloped in a sort of shadowy mist, through which the apathetic faces of several judges were scarcely visible. Opposite them, at the far end of the long room, they could see a vague spot of whiteness standing out against the dark background. It was the accused.

She dragged herself to her place. When Charmolue had majestically installed himself in his place, he sat down, then stood up and said, without too strongly betraying the vanity of his success, "The accused has confessed to everything."

"Gypsy girl," said the presiding magistrate, "have you admitted all the charges of witchcraft, prostitution and murder?"

She was heard sobbing in the darkness. "Anything you like," she answered feebly, "but kill me quickly!"

"Master Charmolue," said the presiding magistrate, "the court is now ready to hear your report."

Charmolue exhibited an enormous notebook and began to read, with abundant gestures and exaggerated emphasis, a

Latin oration in which all the evidence of the trial was drawn out in Ciceronian periphrases and quotations from Plautus, his favorite comic author. We regret that we cannot treat our readers to this remarkable oration. The manner in which the speaker delivered it was truly extraordinary. But he had not finished the introduction when he suddenly stopped short in the middle of a resounding sentence and his eyes, which were usually so gentle and even rather stupid, became fiery with rage. "Gentlemen," he cried (this time in French, for it was not in his notebook), "Satan is so closely connected with this affair that there he is, attending our proceedings and mocking their dignity!" So saying, he pointed to the little goat, which, seeing Charmolue's gesticulations, had thought it appropriate to do likewise and had sat down on its rump, reproducing to the best of its ability, with its front paws and bearded head, the animated gestures of the King's Attorney in the Ecclesiastical Court. It will be remembered that this was one of Djali's most amusing tricks. The incident was a final proof of guilt and it had a powerful effect. The goat's feet were tied together and Jacques Charmolue resumed his eloquence. At the end of a long and admirable harangue he concluded by demanding that the prisoner be required to pay a fine and do public penance before the Cathedral of Notre Dame, then be taken to the Place de Grève with her goat and executed. When his oration was finished he put on his cap and sat down.

Another man in a black robe stood up beside the accused. It was her lawyer. The judges, still without their supper, began to mutter.

"Be brief," said the presiding magistrate.

"Gentlemen of the court," began the lawyer, "since the defendant has confessed to her crimes, I have only one thing to say. Here is a passage from the Salic law: 'If a witch has eaten a man and is convicted of so doing, she shall pay a fine of eight hundred deniers.' May it please the court to sentence the defendant to pay a fine."

"That clause is obsolete," said the King's Advocate Extraordinary.

"Nego," replied the lawyer.

"Put it to a vote!" said a counselor. "The crime has been proved and it's late."

The judges "voted by cap" without leaving the room, for they were in a hurry. They were seen taking off their caps one after the other as the presiding magistrate addressed the question to them in a low voice. The poor prisoner seemed to be looking at them but her eyes no longer saw what was before them. Finally the clerk began to write and handed a long parchment to the presiding magistrate. Then the wretched girl heard the spectators stirring, the pikes clanging together and a cold voice pronouncing these words:

"Gypsy girl, on the day which shall please Our Lord the King, at the hour of noon, you shall be taken in a cart, barefooted and stripped to your slip, before the central doorway of the Cathedral of Notre Dame and there do public penance with a wax candle weighing two pounds in your hand. From there you shall be taken to the Place de Grève, where you shall be hanged on the gallows of the city; and this your goat likewise. And you shall pay to the Ecclesiastical Court three gold lions in reparation of the crimes, committed by you and confessed by you, of witchcraft, magic, fornication and the murder of Phoebus de Châteaupers. May God have mercy on your soul."

"Oh, it's a dream!" murmured La Esmeralda. She felt rough hands dragging her away.

CHAPTER FOUR

"Abandon Hope, All Ye Who Enter Here"

IN THE MIDDLE AGES, WHEN A BUILDING WAS COMPLETED there was almost as much of it below the ground as above it. Unless it was built on piles, like the Cathedral of Notre Dame, a palace, fortress or church always had a double bottom. Sometimes it was a sepulcher, although in palaces and fortresses it was oftener a prison, or perhaps both at once. These mighty edifices did not merely have foundations; they also had roots, so to speak, which branched out into rooms, galleries and stairways like those of the upper structure. The vaults of a building were another building into which one walked down rather than up, and which piled up underground stories below the upper ones, like those inverted forests and mountains which are reflected on the surface of a lake beneath those which rise from its banks.

In the Bastille Saint-Antoine, the Palace of Justice and the Louvre, these underground edifices were prisons. The further the stories of these prisons plunged into the ground, the narrower and darker they became; they were so many zones pervaded by different shades of horror. Dante was unable to find anything better for his hell. These funnel-like dungeons usually ended in a deep hole, in which Dante put Satan and in which society put those who were condemned to death. Once a prisoner was buried there he bade farewell to light, air, hope and life itself. He would come out only to go to the gallows or the stake. Sometimes he would simply remain there to rot; human justice called this "forgetting." He felt himself cut off from the rest of mankind by a mountain of stones; the entire prison was an enormous, complicated lock which shut him off from the living world.

It was into a dungeon of this kind that La Esmeralda was put, with the colossal Palace of Justice over her head, lost in darkness, buried, entombed, walled up. Anyone who could have seen her in that state, after having seen her laughing and dancing before, would have shuddered. Cold as night, cold as death, not one breath of air in her hair, not one human sound in her ears, not one glimmer of light in her eyes, crushed by chains, crouching beside a jug and a piece of bread on a little heap of straw in the puddle of water formed by the oozing of the walls, motionless, almost breathless, she was almost too numb to suffer. Phoebus, the sunlight, the open air, the streets of Paris, her dancing and the applause which it brought forth, the sweet words of love with the officer, then the priest, the dagger, the blood, the torture, the gallows—all this was still running through her mind, sometimes like a bright, golden vision, sometimes like a hideous nightmare; but it was no longer anything but a horrible and confused struggle which took place in the shadows, or a faraway music which was being played up on earth and which could not be heard at the depth to which she had fallen.

She was neither awake nor asleep. She could no longer distinguish waking from sleeping, dreams from reality or day from night. Everything was mingled, broken, floating and confused. She no longer felt, knew or thought anything. No living creature was ever plunged more deeply into annihilation.

She was so numb, frozen and petrified that she hardly noticed the sound of a trap door which was opened from time to time above her without admitting the slightest ray of light and through which a hand tossed her a crust of black bread.

This periodic visit from the jailer was the only communication which remained between her and mankind.

The moisture filtering through the moldy stones of the ceiling condensed into drops of water which fell at regular intervals. She listened stupidly to the sound of those drops as they fell into the puddle beside her. They were the only movement around her, the only clock which marked the time, the only sound which reached her from all the sounds made on the face of the earth, except that she occasionally felt something cold passing over her foot or her arm, which made her shudder.

She did not know how long she had been there. She remembered that a death sentence had been pronounced somewhere against someone, that she had been led away and that she had awakened in darkness, silence and cold. When she tried to crawl on her hands and knees, iron rings had cut into her ankles and chains had rattled. She noticed that she was completely walled in and that beneath her there was a heap of straw and a stone floor covered with water. But there was no light or opening of any kind. She sat on the straw or, sometimes, in order to change her posture, on the bottom step of a stone staircase that was in her dungeon. For a while she tried to count the black minutes measured by the dripping of the water; but her mind soon discontinued this melancholy task of a sick brain and plunged her into a deep stupor.

Finally one day or one night (for noon and midnight were the same color in her sepulcher) she heard above her a sound which was louder than the one usually made by the jailer when he brought her bread and water. She looked up and saw a reddish gleam through the cracks in the trap door in the ceiling. Then the door grated on its rusty hinges and she saw a lantern, a hand and the lower parts of the bodies of two men. The light dazzled her so painfully that she closed her eyes.

When she opened them the lantern had been placed on a step of the staircase and a man was standing before her. A black cloak hung down to his feet and a hood of the same color hid his face. He was like a black shroud standing erect. She stared at him for several minutes; they were like two statues facing each other. Only two things seemed to be alive in that cavern: the wick of the lamp, which was crackling because of the humidity of the atmosphere, and the water dripping from the ceiling.

The prisoner finally broke the silence: "Who are you?"
"A priest."

The word and the tone in which it was pronounced made her start. He continued in a muffled voice: "Are you prepared?"

"For what?"

"To die."

"Oh! Will it be soon?"

"Tomorrow."

Her head, which had been raised in joy, fell back to her bosom. "That's a long time!" she murmured. "Why couldn't they do it today?"

"You must be very unhappy," said the priest after a silence.

"I'm very cold." She took her feet in her hands and her teeth chattered. The priest appeared to be glancing around the cell from under his hood. "No light! No fire! Water on the floor!" he said. "It's horrible."

"Yes," she answered, with the astonished air which misery had given her, "daylight belongs to everyone. Why have they given me only night?"

"Do you know why you are here?" asked the priest after another silence.

"I think I knew once," she said, passing her fingers over her brow, as if to aid her memory, "but I can't remember now." Suddenly she burst into tears like a child. "I want to get out of here, sir," she said. "I'm cold, I'm afraid and there are animals that crawl along my body."

"Very well, then, follow me," said the priest, taking her arm. The poor girl was frozen to the marrow of her bones, yet his hand gave her a sensation of intense cold. "Oh!" she murmured, "that's the icy hand of death! Who are you?"

The priest pushed back his hood. She looked at his face. It was the same sinister face which had pursued her for so long, the diabolical head which had appeared above the beloved head of her Phoebus, the eyes which she had seen glowing next to a dagger.

This apparition, which had always been so fateful for her, which had pushed her from disaster to disaster, awakened her from her stupor. It seemed to her that the veil which had been formed over her memory was suddenly torn aside. All the details of her horrible adventure, from the scene in the house on the Pont Saint-Michel to her trial and death sentence, rushed back into her mind at once, not vague and confused, as they had been till then, but distinct, vivid and terrible. Half-obliterated by her suffering, her memories were revived by the sight of the somber face before her as fire brings out the letters written on a piece of paper in invisible ink. It seemed to her that all the wounds in her heart had opened and were all bleeding at once.

"Ah!" she cried, trembling convulsively and putting her hands over her eyes: "It's the priest!" Then she dropped her arms listlessly and sat down, staring at the floor, mute and still trembling. The priest looked at her like a hawk which has circled for a long time high in the sky over a poor lark cowering in the grass, silently narrowed the circles of its flight, then suddenly pounced on its prey like a bolt of lightning and gripped it panting in its claws.

She began to murmur softly, "Finish! Finish! Strike the last blow!" She thrust her head down between her shoulders in terror, like a lamb waiting for the butcher's cudgel to descend.

"Do I horrify you?" he asked finally. She did not answer. He repeated the question. Her lips contracted as if she were smiling. "The executioner is mocking the condemned," she said. "The months he's pursued me, threatened me, terrified me! If it weren't for him, oh, God, how happy I'd be! He's the one who cast me into this abyss! He's the one who killed . . . who killed him! My Phoebus!" She burst out sobbing, raised her eyes to the priest and said, "Who are you? What have I done to you? Why do you hate me so?"

"I love you!" cried the priest.

Her tears stopped abruptly. She stared at him, stupefied. He fell to his knees and looked at her with fiery eyes.

"Do you understand? I love you!" he cried once again.

"What love!" she exclaimed, shuddering.

"It's the love of the damned."

They both remained silent for several moments, crushed by the weight of their emotions, he frantic, she dazed. "Listen," he said at length, with a strange calmness which had come back to him, "I'll tell you everything. I'll tell you what until now I have hardly dared tell myself when I furtively questioned my conscience in those deep hours of the night when there are so many shadows that it seems as if God Himself no longer sees us. Listen: before I saw you I was happy."

"So was I!" she sighed weakly.

"Don't interrupt me. Yes, I was happy, or at least I thought I was. I was pure and my soul was full of limpid clarity. No one held his head more proudly than I. Priests consulted me on chastity and theologians on doctrine. Yes, knowledge was everything for me. More than once my flesh was aroused by the passing of a female form. The force of a man's sex and blood which, as a foolish adolescent, I thought I had smothered for life, had more than once convulsively shaken the chain of iron vows which attach me to the cold stones of the altar. But then fasting, prayer, study and the austerity of the cloister would make my soul once again master of my body. I shunned women. Also, I had only to open a book and all the impure vapors of my brain vanished before the splendor of science. After a few minutes I would feel the heavy things of the earth flying far away and I was calm again, dazzled and serene in the presence of the tranquil radiance of eternal truth. As long as the devil sent to attack me only vague shadows of women who passed before my eyes in the church or in the streets and who hardly ever entered my thoughts, I was able to overcome him easily. Alas, if I haven't maintained the victory it's God's fault for not making men and the devil of equal strength. Listen: one day . . ." He stopped and she heard him heave a deep, painful sigh. He continued:

"One day I was looking out of the window of my cell. . . . What book was I reading then? Oh! All that's a whirl in my head. I was reading. The window overlooked the square. I heard the sound of a tambourine and music. Annoyed at being disturbed in my meditation, I looked down into the square. There were others looking at what I saw, yet it wasn't a sight made for human eyes. There, in the middle of the square—it was noon, bright sunlight—a creature was dancing. Such a beautiful creature that God would have preferred her to the Virgin Mary, would have chosen her for His mother and wanted to be born of her if she had existed when He made Himself a man! Her eyes were black and splendid; some of her black hair shone in the sunlight like threads of gold. Her feet vanished in their movement like the spokes of a rapidly turning wheel. Around her head, in her black tresses, there were pieces of metal which sparkled in the sunlight and formed a crown of stars on her forehead. Her arms, lithe and brown, clasped and unclasped themselves around her waist like two scarves. The form of her body was amazingly beautiful. Oh, that resplendent form, which stood out like something luminous in the light of the sun itself! Alas, dear girl, it was you. . . . Surprised, intoxicated, fascinated, I stood there looking at you. I watched you so intently that suddenly I shivered with fright, for I felt that fate had seized me."

Overcome, the priest stopped again for a moment. Then he went on: "Half spellbound already, I clutched for something

to break my fall, I reminded myself of the traps which Satan
had set for me before. The creature before my eyes had that
superhuman beauty which can come only from either heaven
or hell. She was not simply a girl made from our common
clay and poorly illuminated inside by the flickering light of a
woman's soul. She was an angel! But an angel of flame, not of
light. Just as I was thinking this, I saw a goat beside you, an
animal of the witches' sabbath, looking at me and laughing.
The noonday sun tipped its horns with fire. Then I saw the
devil's trap and I no longer had any doubt that you had come
from hell to bring about my perdition. I believed it."

He looked her coldly in the eye and added, "I still believe
it. . . . Meanwhile the charm was beginning to operate; your
dancing whirled in my brain; I felt the mysterious spell at
work inside me. Everything in my soul that should have been
awake was asleep and, like those who die in the snow, I found
pleasure in letting this sleep steal over me. Suddenly you began to sing. What could I do, wretch that I was? Your singing
was even more charming than your dancing. I tried to flee but
it was impossible. I was nailed, rooted in place. It seemed to
me that I had sunk up to my knees in the stone floor. I had to
stay there till the end. My feet were like ice and my head was
boiling. Finally—perhaps you took pity on me—you stopped
singing and went away. The reflection of the dazzling vision
and the echo of the enchanting music gradually died away
in my eyes and ears. Then I leaned against the window, stiffer
and more helpless than a statue. The vesper bells awakened
me. I stood up and fled but, alas, something in me had fallen
which could not be raised up again, something had arrived
from which I could not escape.

"Yes, from that day onward there was in me a man whom
I did not know. I had recourse to all my remedies: the cloister,
the altar, work and books—but all in vain. Oh, how hollow
science rings when you desperately dash a head filled with
passions against it! Do you know what I always saw between
me and my books from then on? It was you, your shadow,
the image of the luminous apparition which had one day
passed before me. But that image was no longer the same
color: it was dark, sinister and shadowy, like the black circle
that remains before the eyes of a man who has been rash
enough to look directly at the sun.

"Constantly hearing your voice in my head, constantly
seeing your feet dancing on my breviary, constantly feeling
your form brushing against my flesh at night, I wanted to

see you again, touch you, know who you were, see if I would
find you identical with the ideal image of you which had
remained with me and perhaps shatter my dream with the
aid of reality. In any case, I hoped that a new impression
would obliterate the first one, which had become intolerable
for me. I sought you out. I saw you again. But alas, when I
had seen you twice I wanted to see you a thousand times!
I wanted to see you forever. I no longer belonged to myself—
how can a man stop on that downward path to hell? The devil
had attached one end of his thread to my wings and the other
to your foot. I became a wanderer like you. I waited for you
in doorways and on street corners, I watched you from the
top of my tower. Every night I found myself more charmed,
more desperate, more bewitched and more lost!

"I found out who you were—a gypsy. How could I doubt
your magic then? I hoped that a trial would break the spell.
A witch once cast a spell on Bruno d'Ast; he had her burned
at the stake and he was cured. I knew that. I wanted to try
that remedy. At first I tried to have you prohibited from entering the square before the cathedral, hoping I might forget
you if I never saw you again, but you ignored the prohibition. You came back. Then I conceived the idea of carrying
you off. One night I tried it. There were two of us. We had
you in our hands when that cursed officer appeared on the
scene. He saved you, which was the beginning of your misfortune, along with mine and his. Finally, no longer knowing
what else to do, I denounced you to the Ecclesiastical Court.
I thought I'd be cured, like Bruno d'Ast. I also thought that a
trial would somehow bring us together, that in a prison I
could hold you, have you, that you'd be unable to escape from
me, that you'd possessed me so long that it was now my
turn to possess you. When one does evil, one must do it
thoroughly; it's madness to stop halfway! The extremity of
crime has a certain delirium of joy. A priest and a witch can
mingle in its ecstasy on the straw of a dungeon floor!

"I therefore denounced you. It was then that I frightened
you so whenever you saw me. The plot I was weaving against
you and the storm I was gathering over your head escaped
from me in threats and flashes of lightning. But I still hesitated. My plan had certain frightful aspects which made me
shrink back in terror.

"Perhaps I might have renounced it, perhaps my hideous
thoughts might have withered in my brain without bearing
fruit. I still believed that I had the choice of continuing or

stopping the process which I had begun. But an evil thought is inexorable and strives to become an action; where I thought myself all-powerful, fate proved to be more powerful than I. Alas! Alas! It was fate that took you and thrust you into the terrible workings of the mechanism I had constructed. . . . Listen; I'm about to finish.

"One day—also a sunny day—there passed before me a man who pronounced your name and laughed and had lust in his eyes. I followed him. You know the rest."

He was silent. The girl found only one word to say: "Phoebus!"

"Not that name!" cried the priest, seizing her arm violently. "Don't pronounce that name! It was that name that ruined both of us, wretched creatures that we are! Or rather we all ruined one another through the inexplicable workings of fate! . . . You're suffering, aren't you? You're cold, the darkness blinds you, the dungeon presses in on you; but perhaps you still have a glimmer of light within you, be it only your childish love for that hollow man who was playing with your heart. But as for me, I bear the dungeon inside myself; inside me there is winter, ice and despair; my soul is plunged in darkness. Do you know everything I have suffered? I attended your trial. I was seated on the bench of the Ecclesiastical Court. Yes, beneath one of those hoods were the writhings of the damned. When they took you away, I was there; when they questioned you, I was there. It was my crime, it was my gallows which I saw slowly rising above your head. At each testimony, each proof, each plea, I was there. I was there when that ferocious beast—oh! I didn't forsee the torture! Listen: I followed you into the torture chamber. I saw you undressed and handled half-naked by the infamous hands of the torturer. I saw your foot, which I would have given an empire to kiss only once and then die, I saw that foot crushed by the horrible boot which transforms the members of a living being into bloody jelly. While I was watching that, I slashed my chest with a dagger which I held beneath my cloak. When you shrieked, I plunged it into my flesh; if you had shrieked a second time I would have plunged it into my heart! Look. I think it's still bleeding."

He threw open his cassock. His chest was torn as if by the claws of a tiger and there was a rather wide and badly healed wound in his side. La Esmeralda recoiled in horror.

"Have pity on me!" said the priest. "You think yourself miserable but, alas, you don't know what misery is! Oh! To love a woman! To be a priest! To be hated! To love her with all the fury of your soul, to feel that for the least of her smiles you'd gladly give your blood, your entrails, your fame, your salvation, your life in this world and in the next! To regret not being a king, an emperor, an archangel, a god, in order to place a greater slave at her feet! To press her to you night and day in your dreams and thoughts, then see her in love with a soldier's uniform! And to have nothing to offer her except a wretched cassock which would only frighten and disgust her! To be present, with your jealousy and rage, while she lavishes treasures of love and beauty on a stupid braggart! To see that body, whose form burns into you, those sweet, delicate breasts and that flesh palpitating under the kisses of another! To love her feet, her arms, her shoulders, to think of her blue veins, of her brown skin until you writhe on the floor of your cell for nights on end, then see all caresses you've dreamed of giving her end in torture! To have succeeded only in making her lie down on a leather bed! Oh! Those are the real pincers heated in the fire of hell! Oh, happy is the man who is sawn in two or pulled apart by horses! Do you know what torture it is when for long nights your blood boils, your heart breaks, your head bursts and your teeth bite into your hands? Have mercy on me! Throw a few ashes on these burning coals! I beg you, wipe away the sweat that streams down my forehead! Torture me with one hand but caress me with the other!"

He rolled in the water on the floor and hammered his head against the stone steps. She listened to him and watched him. When he stopped speaking, exhausted and panting, she repeated softly, "Oh, my Phoebus!"

The priest crawled toward her on his knees. "I beg you," he cried, "if you have any pity at all, don't repulse me! I love you! I'm a wretched man! When you pronounce that name it's as though you were grinding all the fibers of my heart between your teeth! Mercy! If you've been sent from hell, I'll go there with you! I've done everything for that. Hell with you in it would be heaven for me; the sight of you is more charming than that of God! Will you take me? I would have thought the day a woman rejected a love like mine the mountains would move. Oh, if you wanted to . . . We could be so happy! We'd run away—I'd get you out of here—we'd go to the place that has the most sunlight, the most trees, the most blue sky. We'd love each other, we'd mingle our souls together and we'd have an undying thirst for each other which we'd constantly quench together from the inexhaustible well of love!"

She interrupted him with a terrible burst of laughter. "Just look at you, Father," she said, "you have blood under your fingernails!"

The priest remained for several instants as if petrified, staring at his hand. "Yes, that's right," he said finally, with strange gentleness, "abuse me, mock me, cover me with ignominy, but come with me! Hurry! You have only till tomorrow! The scaffold of the Place de Grève is always ready. It's horrible! To see you going there in that cart! Have mercy on me! I never really felt how much I love you till now. Come with me! You'll have time to learn to love me after I've saved you. You can hate me as long as you like. But come with me. Tomorrow! Tomorrow! The scaffold! Oh, save yourself! Save me!"

He seized her arm frantically and tried to pull her toward him. She stared at him steadfastly and said, "What has become of my Phoebus?"

"Oh!" cried the priest, releasing her arm. "Have you no pity?"

"What has become of Phoebus?" she repeated coldly.

"He's dead!"

"Dead!" she said, still cold and motionless. "Then why are you speaking to me of living?"

He was not listening to her. "Yes, yes," he said, as if talking to himself, "he must be quite dead. The blade went in very far. I think I touched his heart with the point."

She sprang at him like an enraged tigress and shoved him against the steps with supernatural strength. "Go away, monster!" she cried. "Go away, murderer! Let me die! May my blood and Phoebus' make an everlasting stain on your forehead! Be yours, priest? Never! Never! Nothing will bring us together, not even hell!"

The priest stumbled on the staircase. He silently disengaged his feet from the skirt of his cassock, picked up his lantern and began to climb slowly up the steps leading to the trap door. He opened it and went out. Suddenly La Esmeralda saw his head reappear. His face wore a hideous expression as he cried out to her in a voice full of rage and despair. "I tell you he's dead!"

She fell face downward. Nothing more was heard in the dungeon except the dripping of the water which rippled the pool in the darkness.

CHAPTER FIVE

The Mother

ONE MORNING, AS THE SUN OF MAY WAS RISING IN A DARK BLUE sky, the recluse of Roland Tower heard the sound of wheels, horses and clanking iron in the Place de Grève. She paid little attention to it, tied her hair down over her ears in order not to hear it and resumed her contemplation of the inanimate object that she had worshiped for fifteen years. Her daughter's little shoe, as we have already said, was the whole universe for her. All her thoughts were wrapped up in it and would be separated from it only by death.

That morning her grief seemed to be even more violent than usual. Those passing by the window of her cell heard her lamenting in a loud, monotonous and heart-rending voice: "Oh, my little girl! My poor, dear little child! I'll never see you again! It still seems like yesterday to me! Oh, God, if You were going to take her back so soon, You shouldn't have given her to me at all! Don't You know that our children are the fruit of our wombs and that a mother who has lost her child no longer believes in God? Oh, how could I have gone out that day? Oh, Lord! Lord! To snatch her away from me like that You must never have seen me with her, when I warmed her happily at my fire, when she smiled at me as she suckled, when I made her little feet walk up my bosom to my lips! If You'd seen that, dear God, You would have taken pity on my joy, You wouldn't have deprived me of the only love that remained in my heart! Was I such a wretched creature, Lord, that You couldn't even look at me before condemning me? Alas! Here's the shoe but where's the foot? Where's the child? My daughter! What have they done to you? Lord, give her back to me! I've prayed to You for fifteen years, isn't that enough? Give her back to me for one day, one hour, one minute—just one minute, Lord, then cast me into hell for all eternity! Oh, if only I could touch Your robe, I'd hang on to it with both hands till You gave me back my child! Have You no pity at the sight of her pretty little shoe, Lord? How can You condemn a poor mother to such torture for fifteen years? My daughter! I need my daughter! What does it matter to me that she's in heaven? I don't want Your angel, I want my child!"

The poor woman clutched the little shoe which had been her consolation and her despair for so many years and sobbed as wildly as she had done on the first day. For a mother who has lost her child it is always the first day. Her mourning clothes may wear out and fade; her heart remains black.

At that moment she heard the sound of fresh and joyous children's voices outside her cell. Each time she saw or heard children, the poor mother would rush into the darkest corner of her sepulcher, where she seemed to try to plunge her head into the stone in order not to hear them. This time, however, she jumped to her feet and listened attentively. One little boy had just said, "They're going to hang the gypsy girl today."

She rushed over to her window, which, as we have noted, overlooked the Place de Grève. She saw that a ladder had been erected near the permanent scaffold and that the hangman was engaged in adjusting the chains, which had been rusted by the rain. A few people were standing around looking on.

The laughing children were already far away. The recluse looked for a passer-by whom she might question. She noticed a priest standing near her window. He was pretending to read the public breviary, but he was actually much more concerned with the scaffold, toward which he cast a somber glance from time to time. She recognized the Archdeacon of Josas, a saintly man.

"Father," she said, "who's going to be hanged today?"

The priest looked at her without answering. She repeated her question. Then he said, "I don't know."

"I heard some children saying it was a gypsy girl," said the recluse.

"I think so," said the priest.

Paquette la Chantefleurie burst into hyenalike laughter.

"You have great hatred for gypsies, haven't you, sister?" asked the archdeacon.

"Do I hate them! They're witches, child stealers! They devoured my little girl, my child, my only child. They ate her!" The priest looked at her coldly. "There's one of them I hate above all others," she continued, "and whom I have cursed. She's young, about the age my daughter would be if her mother hadn't eaten my child. Every time that young viper passes in front of my cell my blood boils!"

"Well, then, sister, you can rejoice," said the priest, as cold as the statue on a sepulcher, "for she's the very one you're about to see hanged." His head fell to his breast and he walked slowly away.

The recluse wrung her hands for joy. "I predicted she'd be up there again some day!" she cried. "Thank you, Father."

She began to walk rapidly up and down before the bars of her window, disheveled, fiery-eyed, striking the wall with her shoulders; she was like a caged she-wolf which has been hungry for a long time and begins to feel that mealtime is approaching.

CHAPTER SIX

Three Human Hearts Differently Made

———————

PHOEBUS, MEANWHILE, WAS NOT DEAD. MEN OF THAT KIND are hard to kill. When Master Philippe Lheulier, King's Advocate Extraordinary, said to poor La Esmeralda, "He's on the point of death," it was either a mistake or a jest. When the archdeacon told her, "He's dead," the fact is that he knew nothing about the matter but he believed it, counted on it and hoped it. It would have been intolerable for him to give the woman he loved good news about his rival. Any man in his place would have done the same thing.

Phoebus' wound was serious, to be sure, but not so serious as the archdeacon flattered himself that it was. The surgeon to whom the soldiers of the watch had immediately carried him had grave doubts about his recovery for a week or so and even said so in Latin. Youth, however, won out in the end and, as often happens, prognostics and diagnostics notwithstanding, Nature amused herself by saving the patient in spite of the physician. It was while he was still lying on his sickbed in the surgeon's house that he had been questioned by Philippe Lheulier and the inquisitors of the Ecclesiastical Court, which annoyed him greatly. Then, one fine morning, finding himself better, he left his gold spurs in payment of the surgeon's fees and quietly departed. This, however, had no effect on the trial. Justice in those days had little concern for clarity and accuracy in criminal proceedings. The main thing was to see that the accused went to the gallows. The judges had ample proof against La Esmeralda. They believed that Phoebus was dead and that was enough for them.

Phoebus, for his part, had not fled far. He had simply rejoined his company, in garrison at Queue-en-Brie, a few relays from Paris. After all, he had no desire to make a personal appearance at the trial. He was vaguely aware that he would cut a ridiculous figure if he did so. Besides, he did not know exactly what to make of the whole affair. Irreligious and superstitious, like any soldier who is nothing but a soldier, when he thought over the adventure he was far from reassured about the goat, the strange way in which he had met La Esmeralda, the equally strange way in which she had made him aware of her love for him, the fact that she was a gypsy and, finally, the phantom monk. In all this he saw much more magic than love, probably a witch and perhaps the devil himself. It was a drama in which he had played a very awkward part, the part of the comedian who was the object of blows and laughter. He felt that kind of shame which La Fontaine has described so admirably: "As ashamed as a fox caught by a hen."

He hoped that the affair would not be noised about, that if he remained absent his name would hardly be mentioned, at least not outside the courtroom. He was not mistaken in this, for there were no newspapers in those days and since hardly a week went by without some counterfeiter being boiled in oil, some witch being hanged or some heretic being burned at the stake, the people of Paris were so accustomed to such sights that they scarcely took notice of them. An execution was a common occurrence; an executioner was only a kind of butcher, a shade darker than the others.

Phoebus, therefore, soon set his mind at ease with regard to the enchantress La Esmeralda, or Similar, as he called her, the stabbing he had received from her or the phantom monk (it made little difference to him who had done it) and the outcome of the trial. But no sooner had he emptied his heart on that score than the image of Fleur-de-Lys returned to it. His heart, like the physics of that time, abhorred a vacuum. Besides, Queue-en-Brie was a very dull place, a village of blacksmiths and milkmaids with chapped hands, a long string of houses and huts lining the highway for a mile or so.

Fleur-de-Lys was his next-to-the-last passion, a pretty girl with a delightful dowry. One morning, therefore, completely recovered from his wound and assuming that after two months the affair of the gypsy girl would be finished and forgotten, the amorous cavalier rode up to the door of the Gondelaurier mansion.

He noticed a rather large crowd gathering in front of the Cathedral of Notre Dame. He assumed that it was because of some religious festival or procession and gave it no further thought. He tied his horse to the ring at the gate and joyfully went up to see his beautiful fiancée.

She was alone with her mother. She was still troubled by the scene with the witch and her goat with its cursed alphabet as well as by Phoebus' long absence; but when she saw him walk in he looked so well, his uniform was so new, his sword belt was so shiny and he had such an impassioned air that she blushed with pleasure. The noble young lady herself was more charming than ever. Her magnificent hair was admirably arranged, she was dressed in sky-blue, which is so becoming to blondes, and her eyes were filled with that amorous languor which is even more becoming to them.

Phoebus, who had seen nothing in the way of beauty for quite some time except the country wenches of Queue-en-Brie, was enchanted with Fleur-de-Lys, which gave him such an eager and gallant manner that he was instantly forgiven for everything. Even Madame de Gondelaurier, still sitting maternally in her big armchair, did not have the heart to rebuke him. As for Fleur-de-Lys' reproaches, they died away in tender murmurs.

The young lady was still sitting beside the window, embroidering her grotto of Neptune. The captain stood leaning on the back of her chair as she scolded him affectionately:

"Where have you been keeping yourself for the last two months, you wicked man?"

"You're beautiful enough to make an archbishop dream of you," said Phoebus, slightly embarrassed by her question.

She could not help smiling. "Never mind my beauty," she said, "just answer my question."

"Well, I was called to garrison duty."

"Where, if you don't mind telling me? And why didn't you come to tell me good-by?"

"At Queue-en-Brie." He was delighted that the first question helped him to avoid the second.

"But that's very close to Paris. Why didn't you come to see me even once?"

Phoebus was not seriously embarrassed. "Why, I was . . . garrison duty. . . . Besides, I was sick."

"Sick!"

"Yes . . . wounded."

"Wounded!" The poor girl was extremely upset.

"Oh, there's no cause for alarm," said Phoebus carelessly. "It was nothing. A quarrel, a bit of swordplay—what does it matter to you?"

"What does it matter to me?" cried Fluer-de-Lys, looking up at him with tears in her eyes. "You can't mean what you're saying! What about the swordplay? I want to know everything!"

"Well, my dear, I had a few hard words with Mahé Fédy—you know, the lieutenant from Saint-Germain-en-Laye—and we both ripped open a few inches of each other's skin. That's all."

The lying captain knew very well that a duel always raises a man in a woman's estimation. Fleur-de-Lys looked into his eyes, overcome with fear, pleasure and admiration. She was not, however, entirely reassured. "I certainly hope your wound has healed, my Phoebus," she said. "I don't know your Mahé Fédy, but I'm sure he's a scoundrel. What did you quarrel over?"

At this point Phoebus, whose imagination was not overly creative, began to find himself at a loss to explain his prowess. "Oh, you know how those things are," he said. "It was nothing serious . . . something about a horse." Then, in order to change the subject, he asked, "Tell me, what's all that noise in the square?" He walked over to the window and said, "Why, there's a big crowd down there!"

"I heard that a witch is supposed to do public penance in front of the church this morning," said Fleur-de-Lys, "and then be hanged at the Place de Creve."

"What's the witch's name?"

"I don't know."

"What's she accused of?"

Fleur-de-Lys shrugged her white shoulders and repeated, "I don't know."

"There are so many witches nowadays," remarked her mother, "that they burn them without even knowing their names. You might as well try to know the name of every cloud in the sky. But it's nothing we need worry about; God has it all written down in His book." The venerable lady stood up and walked over to the window. "Good heavens!" she exclaimed. "You're right, Phoebus, there's quite a mob of people down there. My goodness, they're even standing on the roofs! You know, Phoebus, that reminds me of my younger days.

When Charles the Sixth made his entry there was a crowd like that too; I can't remember what year it was. When I talk to you about it, it seems like something very old to you, doesn't it? But it seems very young to me. The queen was riding behind the king on his horse and after them came all the lords with their ladies riding behind them the same way. I remember laughing at the sight of Amanyon de Garlande, who was very short, riding beside Sire Matefelon, a real giant of a knight who had killed heaps of Englishmen. It was a fine thing to see. A procession of all the noblemen of France, with their banners flying. It's so sad to think that nothing is left of all that now!"

The two lovers were not listening to the venerable dowager. Phoebus had returned to lean on the back of his fiancée's chair, a delightful position from which his lascivious gaze could plunge into all the openings of her blouse, which gaped so obligingly, letting him see so many exquisite things and imagine so many others that, dazzled by that skin which shone like satin, he said to himself, "How could a man love anything except a blonde?" They both kept silent. From time to time she looked up at him fondly and their hair mingled in the spring sunshine.

"Phoebus," she said suddenly in a low voice, "we'll be married in three months. Swear to me that you've never loved any other woman."

"I swear it, my beautiful angel!" answered Phoebus and his impassioned gaze joined the sincere tone of his voice to convince her. He may even have believed it himself at that moment.

In the meantime her mother, delighted to see the young couple on such excellent terms, had left the room to attend to some household matter. Phoebus noticed her absence and it made all sorts of strange ideas come into his head. Fleur-de-Lys loved him, he was her fiancé, she was alone with him and his former taste for her had revived, if not in all its freshness, at least in all its ardor. After all, it is no great crime to eat one's wheat before it is ripe. I do not know if these thoughts passed through his mind but in any case Fleur-de-Lys was suddenly alarmed by the look in his eyes. Then she noticed that her mother was gone.

"Good heavens!" she exclaimed, flushed and agitated. "It's very hot in here!"

"Yes, I think it's almost noon," said Phoebus. "The sun is rather hot. I'll draw the curtains."

"No!" cried the poor girl. "I need fresh air." Then, like a doe which feels the breath of the approaching pack, she stood up, ran over to the window, opened it and rushed out onto the balcony. Phoebus, annoyed, followed her.

The square presented a sinister and singular spectacle which quickly changed the nature of Fleur-de-Lys' alarm. An enormous crowd was overflowing into all the adjacent streets. The low wall which marked off a space in front of the cathedral would not have been sufficient to hold back the mob if it had not been lined with soldiers armed with pikes and arquebuses. Thanks to them, the space remained clear. The great doors of the cathedral were closed, contrasting with the innumerable windows overlooking the square, which were all open and displayed thousands of heads heaped up one on top of the other like the piles of cannon balls on an artillery range.

The surface of the crowd was gray and dirty. The spectacle which they were awaiting was evidently one of those which have the privilege of attracting the lowest elements of the population. There were more women than men and there was more laughter than shouting. From time to time some shrill voice would rise above the general clamor:

"Hey, Mahiet, who are they going to hang there?"

"Idiot! She's going to do public penance there, in her slip! God's going to cough Latin in her face. They always do it there, at noon. If it's the gallows you want, go to the Place de Grève."

"I'll go there afterward."

"Say, Boucandry, is it true she refused to have a confessor?"

"I think so."

"You see! The pagan!"

"It's the custom, sir. The bailiff of the palace delivers the prisoner to the Provost of Paris for execution if it's a layman, or to the Ecclesiastical Court of the bishopric if it's a churchman."

"Thank you, sir."

"Oh, the poor creature!" said Fleur-de-Lys, surveying the crowd with a sorrowful look. The captain, much more occupied with her than with that tattered mob, was amorously fingering her waist from behind. She turned around supplicating and smiling. "Please don't, Phoebus," she said. "If my mother comes in she'll see your hand!"

Just then the clock of Notre Dame slowly struck noon. A murmur of satisfaction arose from the crowd. The last vibration of the twelfth stroke had scarcely died away when a loud outcry went up from the square, the windows and the rooftops: "Here she comes!"

Fleur-de-Lys put her hands over her eyes in order not to see. "Would you like to go back in, darling?" asked Phoebus.

"No," she replied, opening from curiosity the eyes she had closed a moment before from fright.

A cart, drawn by a strong Norman work horse and completely surrounded by cavalrymen in purple uniforms with white crosses on them, had just entered the square. The sergeants of the watch opened a passage for it through the crowd by vigorously wielding their whips. Beside the cart rode a few officers of justice, recognizable by their black uniforms and the awkward way they sat their horses. They were led by Master Jacques Charmolue.

In the fateful cart sat a young girl with her hands tied behind her back. She had been stripped to her slip and her long hair (the custom at that time was to cut it off only when the prisoner was at the foot of the scaffold) fell loosely over her half-uncovered breasts and shoulders. Through that black, glossy hair could be seen a heavy gray rope wound around her neck like an earthworm around a flower, chafing her tender skin as it twisted and jerked.

The spectators at the windows could see her bare legs at the bottom of the cart. Obeying a last instinct of feminine modesty, she tried to keep them hidden under her. At her feet was a little goat, also tied up. Her slip had come loose and she was holding it up with her teeth. Her suffering seemed to be made even greater by being thus exposed nearly naked before all eyes.

"Look!" said Fleur-de-Lys excitedly to the captain. "It's that filthy gypsy girl with her goat!" She turned back to him as she said this. He stared at the cart and turned pale.

"What gypsy girl?" he stammered.

"What! Don't you remember . . ."

He stepped back to go inside. But Fleur-de-Lys, whose jealousy, once so keenly aroused by this same gypsy girl, had just been awakened again, shot him a penetrating and mistrustful glance. She now vaguely remembered having heard something about a captain being involved in the witch's trial.

"What's the matter with you?" she asked him. "The

sight of that woman seems to trouble you."

"Trouble me? Not in the least," said Phoebus with a forced smile.

"In that case, stay here," she retorted imperiously, "and we'll watch till the end."

The unlucky captain had no choice but to remain. However, it reassured him a little to see that the condemned girl never looked up from the bottom of the cart. It was La Esmeralda all right, no doubt of it. Even in her ultimate shame and despair she was still beautiful. The hollowness of her cheeks made her big black eyes seem even bigger and her livid profile was pure and sublime. Her spirit had been so thoroughly broken that, except for her modesty, she had completely abandoned herself. With each jolt of the cart her body bounced like something lifeless or broken. A tear could still be seen in her eye but it was motionless, as if frozen there.

The cart entered the square and stopped before the central doorway of the cathedral. The escort lined up on both sides. A hush fell over the crowd. In this solemn and expectant silence, the great doors opened, as if by themselves, accompanied by the shrill creaking of their hinges. The entire length of the church was revealed, vast, gloomy, draped in mourning, lighted only by a few candles flickering in the distance on the high altar, opening like the mouth of a dark cavern onto the light-flooded square. At the furthest extremity, in the shadow of the chancel, was the dim outline of a gigantic silver cross against the background of a piece of black drapery hanging from the ceiling to the floor. The entire nave was deserted but the heads of a few priests could be seen moving confusedly in the distant stalls of the choir. Just as the great doors swung open a solemn and monotonous chant burst from the depths of the cathedral. Chanted by old men lost in the faraway shadows, it was the Mass for the Dead. Chanted for that lovely creature, full of youth and life, caressed by the warm air of spring and bathed in sunlight.

The people stood listening in silence. The terrified and bewildered girl stared blindly into the somber interior of the church, her bloodless lips stirring as if she were praying. When the executioner's assistant came to help her climb out of the cart he heard her softly repeating the word "Phoebus."

Her hands were untied and she climbed down, along with her goat, which was also untied and was bleating with joy at feeling itself free again. She was made to walk barefooted over the harsh pavement to the bottom step of the cathedral. The rope around her neck trailed like a snake following her.

The chanting stopped. A great golden cross and a row of candles began to move in the darkness of the church. The pikes of the yeomen rattled. A moment later a long procession of priests in chasubles and deacons in dalmatics emerged and solemnly advanced toward the prisoner, chanting as they came. But her eyes were fixed on the one who was walking in front, immediately behind the cross bearer. She shuddered and whispered to herself, "There he is again—the priest!"

The archdeacon advanced chanting loudly, staring straight ahead with his head thrown back. When he first stepped out into the light from under the high pointed doorway, wrapped in a great silver cope with a black cross on it, he was so pale that some of the spectators thought one of the marble bishops kneeling on the tombstones in the choir must have risen and come forward to receive the condemned girl on the brink of the grave.

She, equally pale and frozen, was scarcely aware that a heavy lighted candle of yellow wax had been placed in her hands and she did not hear the shrill voice of the registrar reading the fateful text of her penance. When she was told to answer "Amen," she did so mechanically. She did not recover any life or strength until she saw the priest coming toward her alone after having motioned her guards to withdraw. She felt the blood rush to her head and a last spark of indignation was kindled in her heart.

The archdeacon approached her slowly. Even in that extremity she saw him stare at her nakedness with sensuality, jealousy and lust. "Young woman," he said loudly, "have you asked God to forgive your sins and failings?" he then leaned close to her ear (the spectators thought he was receiving her last confession) and whispered: "Now will you be mine? I can still save you."

She looked him in the eye and said, "Get away from me, you demon, or I'll denounce you!"

A hideous smile came over his face. "No one would believe you," he said. "You'd only be adding slander to your other crimes. Answer me quickly: will you be mine?"

"What have you done to my Phoebus?"

"He's dead."

Just then the archdeacon happened to look up. On the balcony of the Gondelaurier mansion on the other side of the square he saw the captain standing beside Fleur-de-Lys. He reeled and passed his hand over his eyes. When he looked again and saw that he was not mistaken he muttered a curse and his features contracted violently.

"All right, then, die!" he said to La Esmeralda between his teeth. Then, raising his hand over her head, he spoke in a loud and solemn voice:

"Go now, lingering soul, and may the mercy of God be with thee."

These were the dreaded words with which it was customary to end such somber ceremonies, the signal of the priest to the executioner. The crowd knelt.

"God have mercy on us," said the priest standing in the doorway.

"God have mercy on us," repeated the people in a murmur which rose up like the rumble of an angry sea.

"Amen," said the archdeacon. He turned his back on the prisoner, crossed his hands, rejoined the procession of priests and disappeared, along with the cross, the candles and the copes, beneath the shadowy arches of the cathedral. His sonorous voice faded away in the choir, chanting a verse of despair. At the same time, the intermittent clanging of the yeomen's iron-shod pikes slowly receding among the columns of the nave was like a clock-hammer striking the doomed girl's last hour.

She stood still, waiting to be disposed of. At a signal from Jacques Charmolue, two of the executioner's assistants, dressed in yellow, stepped forward and tied her hands again.

As she was about to climb back into the cart and begin her last journey, she was seized with a powerful longing for life and with anguish at having to leave it. She looked up at the sky, the sun, the silvery clouds interspersed with patches of blue; then she looked down at the earth around her, at the crowd, the houses. . . . Just as the man in yellow was tying her elbows together, she uttered a piercing cry, a cry of joy. There, on a balcony at one corner of the square, she had seen him—Phoebus! The judge had lied! The priest had lied! It was really Phoebus; she could not possibly doubt it. He was there—alive, handsome, dressed in his scarlet uniform with a plume on his hat and his sword at his side.

"Phoebus!" she shouted. "My Phoebus!" She tried to reach out to him, trembling with love and happiness, but her arms were tied behind her. Then she saw him frown as a beautiful young girl who was leaning on his arm looked up at him with disdainful lips and angry eyes. He spoke a few words to her and they both left the balcony, closing the door behind them.

"Phoebus!" she cried out wildly. "Do you believe it too?" Then a monstrous thought flashed into her mind: she remembered that she had been sentenced to death for the murder of Phoebus de Châteaupers.

She had borne up under everything till then, but this final blow was too much for her. She fell to the pavement and lay still.

"Lift her into the cart," said Jacques Charmolue.

No one had yet noticed a strange spectator standing in the Gallery of the Kings of France, immediately above the lofty central doorway of the cathedral. He had been watching everything so impassively and with his deformed face thrust so far forward that if it had not been for his red and purple clothes he might have been taken for one of those stone monsters through whose mouths the long gutters of Notre Dame have emptied for six hundred years. No detail of the ceremony had escaped him. And right at the beginning, while no one thought of observing him, he had tied a long knotted rope to one of the columns of the gallery, then resumed his quiet watch.

Suddenly, just as the executioner's assistants were about to carry out their orders, he climbed over the balustrade of the gallery and clutched the rope with his hands, knees and feet. The crowd saw him slide down the façade like a raindrop on a windowpane, run over to the executioner's assistants with the swiftness of a cat, fell them both with his enormous fists, take the gypsy girl in one arm as easily as a child picking up a doll and rush into the church, holding her above his head and shouting in a formidable voice, "Sanctuary!"

"Sanctuary! Sanctuary!" repeated the crowd and the clapping of ten thousand hands made Quasimodo's eye sparkle with joy and pride.

The shock brought La Esmeralda back to consciousness. She opened her eyes, looked at Quasimodo, then instantly closed them again, as if terrified at the sight of her deliverer.

Charmolue stood dumfounded, along with the executioner, his assistants and the entire escort. Within the walls of Notre Dame the prisoner was inviolable. The cathedral was a recognized place of refuge. All human justice expired at its threshold.

Quasimodo stopped in the great doorway. His broad feet seemed to rest as solidly on the floor of the church as the massive Roman pillars. His huge hairy head was thrust down between his shoulders like that of a lion, which also has a mane and no neck. The quivering girl lay limp between his horny hands like a piece of white cloth, but he held her with such care that he appeared to be afraid she might break or wither like a flower. Sometimes he looked as though he dared not touch her, even with his breath. Then, all at once, he would hug her to his bony chest as if she were his, the only thing he had in the world, his treasure; and his gnomelike eye, looking down on her, would flood her with tenderness, sorrow and pity.

At this sight the women laughed and wept and the whole crowd stamped with enthusiasm, for at that moment Quasimodo actually had a beauty of his own. Quasimodo, the orphan, the foundling, the outcast, had an appearance of noble grandeur. He felt himself strong and majestic. He looked proudly into the face of that society from which he was banished and in which he had just intervened so powerfully; he defied that human justice whose victim he had snatched away, those tigers whose jaws remained empty, those soldiers, judges and executioners, all that might of the king which he, a cripple, had overcome with the might of God.

It was touching to see the protection given by a creature so deformed as he to one so unfortunate as the condemned girl—the two ultimate miseries of nature and of society had come together to help each other.

After several minutes of triumph, he abruptly turned and plunged into the church with his burden. The people, fond of any display of prowess, strained their eyes to see him in the shadowy nave, regretting that he had withdrawn so soon from their acclamations.

Suddenly he appeared at one end of the Gallery of the Kings of France and ran wildly across it, holding up his conquest and shouting, "Sanctuary!" The crowd burst into applause again. When he reached the other end of the gallery he vanished once more into the church. A moment later he reappeared on the platform above, still running with the gypsy girl in his arms and still shouting, "Sanctuary!" And the crowd applauded once again. He finally made a third appearance at the top of the tower which housed the great bell. From there he seemed to show the girl triumphantly to the whole city and his thunderous voice, which others heard so seldom and which he himself never heard at all, roared savagely up at the sky, "Sanctuary! Sanctuary! Sanctuary!"

Book VII

CHAPTER ONE

Fever

CLAUDE FROLLO WAS NO LONGER IN NOTRE DAME WHEN HIS adopted son so abruptly cut through the fateful web in which the wretched archdeacon had caught the gypsy girl and also himself. When he came back into the sacristy he took off his alb, cope and stole, threw them into the hands of the dumfounded beadle, hurried out the private door of the cloister, ordered a boatman to take him to the left bank of the Seine, then plunged into the hilly streets of the university section, not knowing where he was going. At every step he met groups of men and women joyously hurrying toward the Pont Saint-Michel in the hope of arriving in time to see the witch hanged. Pale, bewildered, frantic, more blinded and frightened than an owl let loose in broad daylight and pursued by a band of children, he no longer knew what he thought or even what he imagined. He walked and ran, taking any street at random, but always pushed forward by the Place de Grève, the horrible Place de Grève which he was dimly aware of behind him.

He continued until he had gone all the way around the Montagne Sainte-Geneviève and left the city by the Saint-Victor Gate. He went on fleeing as long as he could see the line of towers enclosing the university and the scattered houses of the suburbs; but when a ridge finally cut him off entirely from that hateful Paris, when he could believe himself to be a hundred leagues away from it, in the open fields, he stopped and it seemed to him that he began to breathe again.

Then a throng of hideous ideas rushed into his mind. He saw clearly into his soul and shuddered. He thought of the unfortunate girl who had destroyed him and whom he had destroyed. He cast a retrospective glance over the twisting paths which fate had made each of them follow up to their point of intersection, where it had mercilessly broken them against each other. He thought of the folly of eternals vows, of the vanity of chastity, science, religion and virtue; he thought of the uselessness of God. He plunged wholeheartedly into evil thoughts and the further he went into them the more he felt a satanic laugh rising within him.

And in thus delving into his soul, when he saw what a large place nature had prepared for the passions, he laughed even more bitterly. He stirred up all the hatred and wickedness in the depths of his heart and, with the cold eye of a physician examining a patient, he perceived that it was only corrupted love; that love, the source of all virtue in man, turned into horrible things in a priest's heart and that when a man constituted as he was made himself a priest he also made himself a demon. He laughed hideously, then turned pale again as he considered the most sinister side of his fateful passion, of that corrosive, venomous, hateful and implacable love which had led to the gallows for one person and to hell for the other; she was condemned to death, he was damned.

He laughed once again when he reflected that Phoebus was not dead, that he was still alive, gay and contented, that he had a finer uniform than ever and a new mistress whom he took to see his old one hanged. His laughter redoubled when he thought that, of all the living beings whose death he had desired, the gypsy girl, who was the only one he did not hate, was the only one who had not escaped him.

From the captain his thoughts turned to the people gathered in the square and he was seized with unspeakable jealousy on recalling how the woman he loved had been exposed nearly naked to the eyes of the entire crowd. He wrung his hands in despair when he thought that that woman, whose form glimpsed in the shadows by him alone would have been the supreme happiness for him, had been delivered in broad daylight to the whole populace dressed as for a night of voluptuousness. He wept with rage at all those mysteries of love profaned, defiled and tarnished forever, at the pleasure which that unfastened slip had given to so many base eyes, at how that beautiful girl, that virgin lily, that cup of modesty and delight, had been converted, so to speak, into a public fountain at which the vilest citizens of Paris, thieves, beggars and lackeys, had come to drink with impudent, impure and depraved pleasure.

And when he sought to form an idea of the happiness which he might have found on earth if she had not been a gypsy and he had not been a priest, if Phoebus had not existed and if she had not loved him, when he thought that a life of love and serenity would have been possible for him also, that there were at that moment happy couples talking softly under the trees, beside a brook, in the presence of the setting sun or a starry night, and that, if God had so willed, he and she could have formed one of those blessed couples, his heart almost broke with longing and despair.

The thought of her haunted him incessantly, tortured him, gnawed at his brain and twisted his entrails. He had neither regret nor repentance for what he had done; he preferred to see her in the hands of the executioner than in the arms of Phoebus. Nevertheless he was suffering; he suffered so much that now and then he tore out a handful of his hair to see if it was turning white.

Once it occurred to him that it might be just then that the hideous chain he had seen on the scaffold that morning was tightening its iron noose around that frail, graceful neck. The thought made the sweat stream from every pore of his body.

There was another moment when, as he was laughing diabolically at himself, he recalled La Esmeralda as she had been the first day he saw her, lively, carefree, merry, gaily dressed, dancing and harmonious, and La Esmeralda as she was on her last day, wearing only her slip, a rope around her neck, barefooted, slowly climbing up the steep ladder of the gallows. This double image forced a terrible cry from him.

As this whirlwind of despair was overturning, breaking and uprooting everything in his soul, he looked at nature around him. At his feet were several hens pecking in the underbrush, insects were scurrying around in the sunlight, clusters of dappled gray clouds were scudding along in the blue sky above his head, the spire of the Abbey of Saint-Victor pierced the curve of the hill on the horizon with its slated obelisk, and on the Butte Copeaux the miller was idly watching the revolutions of the laborious sails of his windmill. All that active, peaceful life was painful to him. He began to flee once again.

He ran across the fields until evening. His flight from nature, life, himself, mankind and God lasted all day. Sometimes he would throw himself face downward against the earth and pull up young stalks of wheat with his fingers. Sometimes he would stop in a deserted village street and his thoughts were so unbearable that he would take his head between his hands and try to tear it from his shoulders as if he wanted to throw it down on the pavement and dash it to pieces.

Toward sundown he examined himself once again and found that he was nearly mad. The storm which had been raging in him since he had lost the hope and the will to save the gypsy girl had not left a single healthy idea or coherent thought in his mind. His reason had been almost destroyed. Only two images remained clear to him: La Esmeralda and the gallows. Everything else was black. The more he fixed what little attention he had left on those two images, the more he saw the first grow in beauty and light and the other increase in horror until finally La Esmeralda appeared to him as a star and the gallows as a monstrous fleshless arm.

It is remarkable that, during all that torture, it never occurred to him to think seriously of dying. The wretched man clung tenaciously to life; perhaps he really saw hell waiting for him.

Meanwhile it was growing darker. The living being which still existed in him thought confusedly of going back. He thought he was far away from Paris but when he took his bearings he saw that he had only circled the enclosure of the university. The steeple of Saint-Sulpice and the three sharp spires of Saint-Germain-des-Prés rose above the horizon on his right. He walked toward them. When he heard the challenge of the sentries on the ramparts of Saint-Germain, he turned down a path running between the mill of the abbey and a leper hospital. Several minutes later he found himself at the edge of the Pré-aux-Clercs. This meadow was famous for the fights and disturbances which took place in it night and day, making it a source of great annoyance for the poor monks of Saint-Germain. The archdeacon was afraid of meeting someone there; he shrank from the thought of all human contact. He wanted to enter the streets of the city as late as possible. He walked around the Pré-aux-Clercs, took the deserted path which separated it from the Dieu-Neuf and finally arrived at the river. There he found a boatman who, for a few deniers, agreed to take him to the tip of the Ile de la Cité.

The steady rocking of the boat and the splashing of the

water against its sides lulled the wretched archdeacon to a certain extent. When the boatman had left him he stood on the bank, staring straight ahead in a dazed fashion. It is not rare for the fatigue of a great sorrow to produce such an effect on the mind.

The sun had sunk below the lofty Tour de Nesle and the twilight had begun. The sky and the water were both white. Between them, the left bank of the Seine, on which his eyes were fixed, projected its dark mass. Only the outlines of its houses were visible, standing out sharply against the light background of the sky and the river. Candles were beginning to flicker here and there in windows. The chimneys of the houses, the battlements of the walls, the carved gables of the roofs, the spires of the Augustins and the Tour de Nesle all gave the impression of being part of some complex, fantastic piece of sculpture. In his hallucinatory state, Claude imagined that he was looking at the tower of hell. The countless lights gleaming up and down its sides appeared to him as the openings of the immense furnace inside it; the voices and clamor coming from it sounded like so many shrieks and groans. Terror-stricken, he put his hands over his ears in order not to hear, turned his back in order not to see and fled from the terrible vision. But the vision was within him.

When he entered the streets the passers-by jostling one another in the light coming from the shops looked to him like an endless parade of specters. Strong sound echoed in his ears; extraordinary fantasies troubled his brain. He saw neither the buildings, the pavement, the vehicles nor the people, but a chaos of indeterminate objects merging into one another. On one corner of the Rue de la Barillerie there was a grocer's shop whose awning, following an immemorial custom, was decorated with tin hoops from which hung wooden candles clattering in the wind. The archdeacon imagined that he heard the skeletons at Montfaucon rattling in the darkness. "Oh!" he murmured. "The night wind is driving them against each other and mingling the sound of their chains with the sound of their bones! Perhaps she's there among them now!"

He walked on, bewildered, until he found himself on the Pont Saint-Michel. There was a light in a ground-floor window. He stopped before it. Through a cracked windowpane he saw a squalid room which awakened a confused memory in his mind. In that room, dimly lighted by a lamp, there was a blond young man with a merry face kissing, between bursts of laughter, a very immodestly dressed girl. Near the lamp was an old woman spinning and singing in a quavering voice. It was Falourdel; the girl was a prostitute; the young man was his brother, Jehan.

He watched them for some time—the sight was as good as any other. He saw Jehan go over to the window at the back of the room, open it and look at the lights gleaming along the bank of the river. Then he heard him say, closing the window, "It's dark outside! The citizens are lighting their candles and God His stars."

Jehan came back to his prostitute and smashed a bottle which was on the table. "Empty already, by God!" he cried. "And I don't have any more money! Isabeau, my darling, I won't be satisfied with Jupiter till he changes your white breasts into black bottles from which I can suck wine day and night." As the girl was laughing at this remark, Jehan went out.

Dom Claude scarcely had time to throw himself to the ground in order not to be seen and recognized by his brother. Fortunately the street was dark and Jehan was drunk. He did, however, notice the archdeacon lying on the pavement in the mud. "Aha!" he said, pushing Claude with his foot. "There's a man who had a fine time of it today!" Claude held his breath. "Drunk!" continued Jehan. "Dead drunk, by God! A real souse!" He bent down and added, "Bald, too—an old man." Then Claude heard him walk away, saying to himself, "Just the same, reason is a fine thing and my brother the archdeacon is lucky to be wise and have money too."

The archdeacon stood up and ran headlong toward Notre Dame, whose enormous towers could be seen jutting up in the darkness above the houses. When he arrived at the square, out of breath, he drew back and dared not look up at the fateful edifice. "Oh!" he whispered. "Can it be that such a thing happened here, today, this very morning?"

He finally ventured to look at the church. Its façade was dark. The sky behind it was bright with stars. The crescent-shaped moon, which had just risen above the horizon, was on a level with the top of the right-hand tower and seemed to be perched on the balustrade like a luminous bird. The door of the cloister was locked but he still had the key to the tower in which his laboratory was located. He used it to enter the church. He found the inside of it as dark and silent as a tomb. From the large shadows that fell in broad masses on all sides, he knew that the hangings for the ceremony of that morning had not yet been taken down. The great silver cross glittered in the shadows, dotted with sparkling points,

like the Milky Way of that sepulchral night. The upper ends
of the long pointed windows of the choir were visible above
the black hangings. With the moonlight shining through
them, they had only the doubtful colors of the night, the
shades of violet, white and blue which are found on the face
of a corpse. When he perceived those pale pointed window
tops he imagined them at first to be the miters of bishops in
hell. He closed his eyes and when he opened them again he
seemed to be surrounded by a circle of livid faces looking
down at him.

He began to run wildly through the church. Then it seemed
to him that the church itself shook, stirred and came to life,
that each massive column became an enormous leg pressing
against the earth with its broad stone foot and that the gigantic cathedral was a sort of prodigious elephant which
breathed and walked with its pillars for legs, its two towers
for trunks and the immense black hangings for a caparison.

The archdeacon's frenzy became so intense that for him the
external world was only a sort of Apocalypse, visible, palpable
and terrifying. He felt a surge of relief for a moment when
he perceived a reddish glow behind a cluster of pillars. He
ran toward it as toward a star. It was the dim lamp which day
and night illuminated the public breviary of Notre Dame
under its iron grating. He eagerly rushed up to the holy book
in the hope of finding some consolation or encouragement
in it. It was opened to this passage from the Book of Job:
"And a spirit passed before my face; and I heard a faint
breathing; and the hair of my flesh stood up."

On reading these fearful words his emotions were those of
a blind man who feels himself pricked by the staff he has
picked up. His knees failed him and he sank to the floor,
thinking of the girl who had died that day. He felt so many
monstrous fumes passing through his brain that it seemed to
him his head had became one of the chimneys of hell.

He remained for a long time in that position, unthinking,
helpless and passive in the grip of the demon. When he finally
recovered a little of his strength he thought of taking refuge
in the tower with his faithful Quasimodo. He stood up and,
since he was frightened, he took the lamp of the breviary to
light his way. It was a sacrilege but he was in no state to consider such a detail.

He climbed slowly up the stairs of the tower, filled with
an obscure fear which must have communicated itself to the
rare passers-by in the square by the mysterious light of his

lamp rising toward the top of the tower from loophole to loophole.

Suddenly he felt cool air on his face and found himself beneath the doorway of the uppermost gallery. The night was cold. The sky was streaked with clouds whose broad white masses drifted into one another, like river-ice breaking up in winter. The moon shining through them looked like a celestial ship caught fast in those aerial icebergs.

He looked down for an instant and saw, through a veil of mist and smoke, the silent multitude of roofs below, pointed, innumerable, crowded together and small as the ripples of a calm sea on a summer night. The faint light of the moon gave an ashy tint to the earth and the sky.

Just then the clock of the cathedral raised its harsh, broken voice. Midnight. He thought of noon. The same twelve strokes had returned. "She must be cold by now," he said to himself softly.

Suddenly a gust of wind blew out his lamp and almost at the same moment he saw, on the other side of the town, a shadow, something white, a form, a woman. He started. Beside the woman was a little goat, mingling its bleating with the sound of the last strokes of the clock. He had the strength to look at her. It was she.

She was pale and melancholy. Her hair hung down over her shoulders as it had that morning. But there was no longer a rope around her neck and her hands were no longer tied. She was free; she was dead. She was dressed in white and wore a white veil over her head.

She came toward him, slowly, looking up at the sky. The supernatural goat followed her. He felt as though he were made of stone, too heavy to run away. All he could do was to take one step backward for every step she took forward until he was finally under the dark roof of the staircase. His blood froze at the thought that she might follow him there; if she had done so he would have died of terror. She did walk up to the door of the staircase and stand there looking into the darkness for several moments, but she did not appear to see him. She passed on. She seemed to be taller than when she was alive; he saw the moon shining through her white dress; he heard her breathing.

When she had gone past he began to descend the stairs as slowly as he had seen the specter move, feeling as though he himself were a specter, wild-eyed, his hair erect, his extinguished lamp still in his hand; and, as he walked down the spiral staircase, he distinctly heard a voice laughing and repeating, "And a spirit passed before my face; and I heard a faint breathing; and the hair of my flesh stood up."

CHAPTER TWO

Hunchbacked, One-Eyed and Lame

IN THE MIDDLE AGES EVERY TOWN HAD ITS PLACES OF SANCtuary. In the flood of penal laws and barbarous jurisdiction they rose like islands above the level of human justice. Any criminal who could reach one of them was safe. In each section of town there were almost as many places of sanctuary as places of execution. The abuse of impunity went side by side with the abuse of punishment—two evils striving to correct each other. Royal palaces, the houses of princes and especially churches had the right of sanctuary. Sometimes the right was temporarily bestowed upon an entire city when it stood in need of repopulation. Louis XI made Paris a sanctuary in 1467, for example.

Once he set foot inside a sanctuary, a criminal was sacred; but he had to take care never to leave it. One step outside it and he fell back into the flood. The gallows, the wheel and the rack kept close guard around the place of refuge and ceaselessly lay in wait for their prey like sharks around a ship. Thus there were condemned men and women who grew old in a cloister, on the stairs of a palace, in the garden of an abbey or under the porch of a church; in a sense, the sanctuary was a prison like any other.

A solemn decree of Parliament would sometimes violate the sanctuary and restore the criminal to the executioner, but this was rare. Parliament stood in fear of the bishops and usually came off second best in any clash with them. Occasionally, however, as in the case of the murderers of Petit-Jean, Executioner of Paris, or that of Emery Rousseau, the murderer of Jean Valleret, justice would leap over the Church to carry out its sentences. But woe to anyone who violated a sanctuary without a parliamentary decree! The deaths of Robert de Clermont, Marshal of France, and of Jean de Châlons, Marshal of Champagne, are well known, yet the criminal involved was only a certain Perrin Marc, a money-changer's employee and a wretched murderer. But the two marshals broke down the door of the Church of Saint-Méry—that was the enormity.

There was such an aura of respect around a sanctuary that, according to tradition at least, it sometimes overawed even animals. Aymoin tells us that when a stag, being pursued by Dagobert, took refuge near the tomb of Saint Denis, the hounds stopped short and did nothing but bark.

Most churches had a room prepared especially for fugitives. In Notre Dame it was a cell constructed under the buttresses above one of the side aisles, looking toward the cloister. It was there that, after his wild and triumphant race across the galleries and up the tower, Quasimodo had deposited La Esmeralda. During that race she did not completely return to consciousness; she felt nothing except that something was carrying her upward. Once, hearing Quasimodo's harsh voice and loud laughter in her ear, she opened her eyes a little and saw the slate roofs of Paris below her and his frightening and elated face above her. Her eyes fell shut again; she believed that everything was finished, that she had been executed while she was unconscious, that the misshapen spirit which had presided over her destiny had seized her and was now carrying her off. She dared not look at him and passively resigned herself to her fate.

But when the bellringer, disheveled and panting, set her down in the cell of sanctuary and when she felt his huge hands gently take off the rope that was chafing her neck, she experienced the kind of shock which abruptly awakens the passengers of a ship which has run aground at night. Her thoughts awakened also and came back to her one by one. She saw that she was in Notre Dame, she remembered having been snatched from the hands of the executioner, that Phoebus was still alive and that he no longer loved her. These last two ideas, one of which spread so much bitterness over the other, came to her simultaneously. She turned to Quasimodo, who was standing before her and who frightened her. "Why did you rescue me?" she asked him. He looked at her anxiously, as if he were seeking to guess what she had said. She repeated her question. He looked at her sadly and went away. She was astonished.

He returned a short time later, bringing something which he threw at her feet. It was a bundle of clothes which charitable women had left for her on the threshold of the church. She looked down at herself, saw that she was almost naked and blushed. Life was coming back to her. Quasimodo appeared to feel something of her modesty. He covered his eye with his hand and went away again, but slowly.

She hastened to put on the white dress and veil he had left for her. It was the costume of a novice of the Hôtel-Dieu. She had hardly finished when she saw Quasimodo coming back, this time carrying a basket under one arm and a mattress under the other. In the basket were bread, wine and other provisions. He set it down and said, "Eat." He laid out the mattress on the floor and said, "Sleep." He had just brought her his own meal and his own bed.

She looked up at him to thank him but she could not utter a word. The poor devil was truly horrible. She lowered her eyes with a shudder. Then he said to her, "I frighten you, don't I? I'm very ugly. Don't look at me. Just listen to me: stay here during the day; at night you can go anywhere in the church. But don't ever leave the church, either at night or during the day. You'd be lost. They'd kill you and I'd die."

Touched, she raised her head to answer him. He had disappeared. She found herself alone once more, thinking over the strange words of that almost monstrous man and struck by the sound of his voice, which was so harsh and yet so gentle.

Then she looked around her cell. It was a room some six feet square with a small window and a door cut out into the slightly inclined plane of the roof, which was made of flat stones. Several waterspouts carved into the shapes of animals seemed to be stretching their necks and trying to look in at her through the window. Beyond her roof she perceived the tops of countless chimneys from which the smoke of all the fires of Paris seemed to be rising. It was a sad sight for the unfortunate girl, a foundling, under sentence of death, without country, family or home.

As the thought of her isolation was returning to her, more poignant than ever, she felt a hairy, bearded head slip between her hands. She started (everything frightened her now) and looked down. It was her goat, the nimble Djali, which had escaped along with her when Quasimodo dispersed Charmolue's brigade and which had been affectionately rubbing against her feet for nearly an hour without obtaining any response. "Oh, Djali!" she said. "I'd forgotten you, but you were still thinking of me! You're not ungrateful!" At the same time, as if an invisible hand had lifted the weight which had kept her tears pressed down inside her heart for so long, she began to weep; and as her tears flowed she felt the sharpest and bitterest part of her sorrow flowing out of her with them.

When night came she found it so beautiful and the moon so soft that she walked around the high gallery which encircles the church. This brought her some relief, so peaceful did the earth seem to her, seen from that height.

CHAPTER THREE

Deaf

WHEN SHE AWOKE THE NEXT MORNING SHE WAS SUPRISED TO realize that she had slept—she had been unaccustomed to sleep for so long! The rising sun was shining cheerfully in her face through the window. But when she looked up she saw something else in the window which frightened her: the unfortunate features of Quasimodo. Involuntarily she closed her eyes, but in vain; it seemed to her she could still see that gnomelike face, one-eyed and gap-toothed. Then she heard a rough voice saying, very gently, "Don't be afraid. I'm your friend. I came to watch you sleeping. It's all right for me to be here when your eyes are closed, isn't it? I'll go away now. . . . There, I'm behind the wall. You can open your eyes again."

The tone in which he spoke these words was even more plaintive than the words themselves. La Esmeralda was touched. She opened her eyes; he was gone from the window. She went over to it and saw the poor hunchback crouching in a corner outside with an air of sorrow and resignation.

She struggled to overcome the repugnance he aroused in her. "Come here," she said to him softly. Seeing the movement of her lips, he thought she was telling him to leave. He stood up and began to limp slowly away, head down, not daring even to raise his despairing eye to her. "Come back!" she cried, but he continued on his way. She darted out of the cell, ran up to him and took his arm. He trembled in every limb at her touch. When he looked up and saw that she wanted to draw him toward her, his whole face beamed with joy and tenderness. She tried to make him come into her cell but he stubbornly refused to cross the threshold. "No, no," he said, "the owl never enters the nest of the lark."

She seated herself gracefully on the bed. They both remained silent for a while, he contemplating her beauty and she his ugliness. Each moment she looked at him she discovered another deformity; her eyes wandered from his knockknees to his hunchback, from his hunchback to his single eye. She could not understand how a creature so awkwardly put together could exist. At the same time, he was pervaded by an air of such sadness and gentleness that she began to reconcile herself to his appearance.

He was the first to break the silence: "Were you telling me to come back?"

She nodded and said, "Yes."

He understood the nod. "I'm sorry, but . . ." he began hesitantly, "you see . . . I'm deaf."

"Poor man!" she cried with an expression of tender pity.

He smiled sadly. "You're thinking that's all there was lacking, aren't you? Yes, I'm deaf; and this is how I'm made. It's horrible, isn't it? And you're so beautiful!"

There was such deep misery in his voice that she did not have the strength to say a word—and he would not have heard her if she had. He went on:

"I never realized how ugly I really am till now. When I compare myself to you, I can't help feeling sorry for myself, miserable monster that I am. I must seem like some kind of beast to you. As for you, you're a sunbeam, a dewdrop, the song of a bird! But I'm something hideous, neither a man nor an animal, something harder, more unshapely, more trampled on than a stone!" He gave a heart-rending laugh. "Yes, I'm deaf. But you can speak to me by signs and gestures. I have a master who talks to me like that. Also, I'll know what you want by the movement of your lips and the expression of your eyes."

"Well, then," she said, smiling, "suppose you begin by telling me why you rescued me."

He had been looking at her attentively as she spoke. "I understand," he said. "You asked me why I rescued you. You've already forgotten a wretched scoundrel who tried to abduct you one night, a wretched scoundrel to whom you brought relief the very next day while he was on their infamous pillory. A drink of water and a little pity—it was worth so much to me that I could not repay you for it with my life."

She listened to him with deep emotion. There was a tear in

his eye but it did not fall; he seemed to make it a point of honor to hold it back.

"Listen," he went on when he was no longer afraid the tear would escape him, "there are very high towers here. A man falling from the top would be dead even before he hit the ground. If you should ever want me to fall from one of them, you won't have to say a word; a look will be enough."

He stood up. Despite her own misfortune, the strange creature aroused her compassion. She motioned him to remain.

"No," he said, "I mustn't stay too long. I'm not at ease when you look at me. It's only out of pity that you don't turn your eyes away. I'm going to a place where I can see you but you can't see me. That will be better."

He took a small metal whistle from his pocket. "Here," he said, "if you need me or if you want me to come for any reason and won't be too horrified at the sight of me, blow this. That's one sound I can hear." He laid the whistle on the floor and went away.

CHAPTER FOUR

Earthenware and Crystal

As THE DAYS PASSED, PEACE GRADUALLY RETURNED TO LA ESmeralda's soul. Excessive pain, like excessive joy, is a violent thing which is of short duration. The human heart cannot remain in an extreme for long. Her suffering had been so great that the only thing which remained of it was a feeling of astonishment.

With security came a return of hope. She was outside of society, outside of life, but she had a vague feeling that it might perhaps not be impossible for her to enter into them once more. She was like a dead woman keeping a key to her tomb in reserve.

The terrible images which had obsessed her for so long left her little by little. All the horrible phantoms began to fade from her mind: Pierrat Torterue, Jacques Charmolue, even the priest himself.

And then Phoebus was alive, she was sure of it, she had seen him. His life was everything to her. After the series of fateful shocks which had destroyed almost everything in her soul, only one thing remained intact: her love for Phoebus. Love is like a tree: it grows by itself, roots itself deeply in our being and continues to flourish over a heart in ruin. The inexplicable fact is that the blinder it is, the more tenacious it is. It is never stronger than when it is completely unreasonable.

No doubt La Esmeralda did not think of the captain without pain. No doubt it was terrible that he too had been deceived, that he could think such a thing possible, that he could believe himself to have been stabbed by a woman who would have given her life for him. But, after all, he was not too much to blame. Had she not confessed to the crime? Had she not yielded, weak woman that she was, to the torture? It was all her fault. She ought to have let them tear the nails from her fingers rather than such a confession from her lips. After all, if she could see Phoebus once, for just one minute, it would take only a word, only a look, to dispel his error and bring him back to her. She had no doubt of it. She deceived herself about a number of other things also—about Phoebus' accidental presence on the day of her public penace, for example, and about the young lady who was with him. It was no doubt his sister. An implausible explanation, but she was satisfied with it, for she needed to believe that Phoebus still loved her and no one but her. Had he not sworn it to her? What more could she ask, naïve and credulous as she was? Also, were not appearances in the matter more against her than him? She waited, therefore, and hoped.

We may also add that the church, that immense cathedral which enveloped her on every side, which had saved her and which still protected her, was itself a wonderfully calming influence. The solemn lines of its architecture, the religious aura of all the objects around her and the pious and serene thoughts which oozed, so to speak, from every stone all acted on her without her being aware of it. Also, the edifice had sounds of such majesty and blessedness that they soothed her sick soul. The monotonous chanting of the priests during Mass, the responses of the people, sometimes almost inaudible, sometimes thunderous, the harmonious quivering of the windowpanes, the organ bursting forth like a hundred trumpets, the three belfries buzzing like hives of enormous bees—all this lulled her memory, her imagination and her pain.

Thus each rising sun found her more tranquil, breathing more freely, less pale. As her inner wounds healed, her grace and beauty bloomed again. Her former character began to come back also, including even a certain part of her gaiety, her pretty pout, her love for her goat, her delight in singing and her modesty. In the morning she was careful to dress herself in the corner of her cell, lest some inhabitant of a neighboring attic should see her through the window.

When she was not thinking of Phoebus, she would sometimes think of Quasimodo. He was the only link, the only communication that was left between her and mankind. The poor girl was cut off from the world even more completely than Quasimodo. She understood nothing about the strange friend whom chance had given her. She often reproached herself for not being grateful enough to blind herself to his appearance but, try as she might, she could not accustom herself to him. He was too ugly.

She had not picked up the whistle he gave her but that did not prevent him from reappearing from time to time during the first few days. She did her best not to turn away from him with too much repugnance when he came to bring her food and water; but he always perceived the slightest movement of that kind and would then walk sadly away.

Once he came up to her as she was caressing Djali. He stood thoughtfully for a moment before the two graceful creatures. After a time he shook his heavy, misshapen head and said, "My misfortune is that I still look too much like a man. I wish I were an outright animal, like that goat."

Another time he came to the door of her cell (which he never entered) while she was singing an old Spanish ballad, whose words she did not understand but which had remained in her ears because the gypsies had lulled her to sleep with it when she was a little child. At the sight of that hideous face which appeared abruptly in the middle of her song, she stopped short with an involuntary movement of fright. The unfortunate bellringer dropped to his knees in the doorway and clasped his hand supplicatingly. "Oh!" he said sorrowfully. "Go on, I beg you, and don't send me away!" She did not wish to hurt him, so, trembling, she resumed her ballad. Her alarm gradually subsided and she gave herself up completely to the slow, melancholy air that she was singing. Quasimodo remained on his knees with his hands clasped, as if he were praying, attentive and hardly breathing, looking steadfastly into her shining eyes, in which he seemed to be hearing her song.

Still another time he came to her with a timid, awkward air. "Listen to me," he said with an effort, "I have something to tell you." She made a sign to him that she was listening. He began to sigh, opened his lips, seemed about to speak for a moment, then withdrew slowly, holding his forehead in his hand. She looked after him in amazement.

Among the grotesque figures carved into the wall there was one for which he had a particular affection and with which he often seemed to exchange a fraternal glance. Once she overheard him saying to it, "Would to God I were made of stone like you!"

One morning she was standing at the edge of the roof, looking down into the square. Quasimodo was behind her, where he habitually placed himself in order to spare her as much as possible the displeasure of seeing him. Suddenly she started, a tear and a flash of joy appeared simultaneously in her eyes; she knelt on the edge of the roof, stretched out her arms in anguish toward the square and cried, "Phoebus! Come to me! Come! A word, just one word, in the name of God! Phoebus! Phoebus!" Her voice, her face, her gestures, everything about her had the agonized expression of a shipwrecked voyager making signals of distress to a faraway ship sailing gaily along in the sunshine on the horizon.

Quasimodo looked down into the square and saw that the object of this wild and passionate appeal was a young man, a captain, a handsome cavalier with glittering weapons and a superb uniform, riding along the opposite side of the square and saluting with his plumed helmet a beautiful lady who stood smiling on her balcony. He did not hear the unhappy girl calling to him; he was too far away.

But the poor deaf bellringer heard her. He heaved a deep sigh and turned around. His heart was swollen with repressed tears; he convulsively dashed his fists against his head and when he withdrew them they each held a handful of red hair.

La Esmeralda was not even aware of his presence. She remained kneeling and cried out in extraordinary agitation, "Oh, he's dismounting! He's about to go into that house! Phoebus! . . . He can't hear me . . . Phoebus! . . . How cruel that woman is to talk to him at the same time I do! . . . Phoebus! Phoebus!"

Quasimodo looked at her. He could not hear her words but he understood her gestures. His eye filled with tears but he let none of them fall. Suddenly he tugged gently at her sleeve. She turned around. He had taken on a calm expression. "Would you like me to go bring him to you?" he asked.

She uttered a cry of joy. "Oh, yes!" she said. "Go bring him!

Run! Hurry! That captain, down there! Bring him to me! I'll love you for it!" She embraced his knees. He could not help shaking his head sorrowfully. "I'll bring him to you," he said feebly. Then he turned and rushed down the stairs, choking with sobs.

When he arrived in the square, he saw only the fine horse tied in front of the Gondelaurier mansion. The captain had just gone inside. He looked up toward the top of the tower of Notre Dame. La Esmeralda was still in the same place and in the same posture. He nodded sadly to her, then leaned against one of the pillars of the Gondelaurier porch, determined to wait until the captain came out.

Inside the house it was one of those festive days which precede a wedding. Quasimodo saw many people enter but none come out. From time to time he looked up to the top of the tower; La Esmeralda did not stir any more than he did. A groom came up to the horse, untied it and led it into the stable.

The entire day passed in this way: Quasimodo at the pillar, La Esmeralda looking down from the tower and Phoebus no doubt at Fleur-de-Lys' feet. Night finally fell, a dark, moonless night. Quasimodo kept his eye fixed on La Esmeralda but she was soon only a patch of white in the twilight, then nothing at all. Everything faded into darkness.

He saw the windows of the Gondelaurier mansion lighted up from top to bottom, along with those of the other houses facing the square. Then he saw the latter all become dark again, one by one, for he remained at his post all evening. Still the captain did not come out. When the last passer-by had gone home, when the lights in all the windows of the other houses had been extinguished, Quasimodo was all alone in the darkness. In those days there were no street lights in the square.

Meanwhile the windows of the Gondelaurier mansion remained illuminated, even after midnight. Quasimodo, motionless and attentive, saw a host of lively, dancing shadows pass before the many-colored windowpanes. If he had not been deaf he would have heard, more and more distinctly as the clamor of Paris died down and went to sleep, the sounds of festivity, laughter and music coming from inside the house.

Toward one o'clock in the morning the guests began to leave. Quasimodo, enveloped in darkness, watched them all pass under the porch, which was lighted by torches. None of them was the captain.

He was filled with sad thoughts. He looked up into the air occasionally, like those who are bored. Heavy black clouds hung down like ragged festoons from the starry vault of the night.

At one of those moments he saw the door of the balcony above his head open mysteriously. A man and a woman came through it and shut it noiselessly behind them. It was not without difficulty that Quasimodo succeeded in recognizing the man as the handsome captain and the woman as the young lady he had seen that morning greeting the officer from that same balcony. The square was totally dark and a double crimson curtain, which had fallen in place again behind the glass door as soon as it was closed, allowed almost no light from inside to reach the balcony.

The young man and the young lady, as far as Quasimodo could judge without being able to hear anything they said, appeared to be engaged in a very tender *tête-à-tête*. The girl permitted the officer to put his arm around her waist and gently resisted a kiss.

Quasimodo witnessed this scene from below. The fact that it was not intended to be seen made it all the more charming. He contemplated that happiness and beauty with bitterness. After all, nature was not mute in the poor devil; deformed though he was, he was still as capable of emotion and sensation as any other man. He thought of the wretched lot which Providence had given him: that women, love and sensuality were to pass constantly before his eyes but that he was never to do more than witness the happiness of others. But the most painful part of the spectatcle that he was now watching, the thing that mingled indignation with his anger, was the thought of how La Esmeralda would suffer if she were present. The night was dark, however, and even if she were still at the top of the tower (which he did not doubt) she would be unable to see from that distance, for he himself could scarcely distinguish the lovers on the balcony. This consoled him.

Meanwhile their conversation was becoming more and more animated. The young lady seemed to be begging the officer not to ask anything more of her. Quasimodo could discern her lovely hands clasped together, her smiles mingled with tears, her eyes looking up at the stars and the captain's eyes ardently looking down at her.

Fortunately, for she was beginning to resist only feebly, the door of the balcony opened suddenly, an old lady appeared, the girl seemed embarrassed and the officer annoyed, then all three of them went inside.

A moment later a horse came prancing under the porch. The splendid officer, wrapped in his cloak, went swiftly past Quasimodo. The bellringer waited until he had turned the corner, then ran after him with his monkeylike agility, shouting, "Captain! Captain!"

The captain reined up. "What can that rascal want with me?" he said to himself as he watched the ungainly figure lumbering toward him in the darkness. Quasimodo came up to him and boldly took hold of the bridle of his horse.

"Follow me, captain," he said, "someone wants to talk to you."

"By God!" muttered Phoebus. "I think I've seen this ugly scarecrow somewhere before . . . Hey there! Take your hands off my horse!"

"Are you asking me who it is, captain?" answered the deaf man.

"I'm telling you to let go of the bridle!" retorted Phoebus angrily.

Quasimodo, far from letting go of the horse, was preparing to pull it around in the other direction. Unable to understand the captain's resistance, he hastily said to him, "Come, captain, it's a woman who's waiting for you." He added, with an effort, "A woman who loves you."

"What a strange fellow!" exclaimed Phoebus. "He thinks it's my duty to see all the women who love me—or say they do! What if she looks like you, you owl-faced monster? Go back and tell her I'm going to get married and that she can go to the devil!"

"Listen, sir! It's the gypsy girl!" cried Quasimodo, thinking this would be sure to overcome his reluctance. It had a strong effect on him but not what Quasimodo expected. It will be remembered that our gallant officer had withdrawn with Fleur-de-Lys a few moments before Quasimodo saved La Esmeralda from the gallows. Since then, when he visited the Gondelaurier mansion he was careful not to mention that woman, whose memory, after all, was painful to him. And as for Fleur-de-Lys, she had not deemed it advisable to tell him that the gypsy girl was still alive. Phoebus therefore believed that the poor "Similar" had been dead for a month or two. Also, for several moments he had been thinking of the profound darkness of the night, of the strange messenger's supernatural ugliness and sepulchral voice, of the fact that the street was deserted, as it had been the night the phantom monk accosted him, and that his horse snorted at the sight of Quasimodo.

"The gypsy girl!" he cried, almost frightened. "Have you come from the next world?" He put his hand to the hilt of his dagger.

"Hurry, hurry!" said Quasimodo, trying to pull his horse. "This way!"

Phoebus kicked him violently in the chest. Quasimodo's eye sparkled. He prepared to rush at him, then stopped short and said, "Oh, but you're lucky there's someone who loves you!" He stressed the word "someone." Letting go of the bridle he said, "Go!"

Phoebus swore and spurred his horse. Quasimodo watched him until he had disappeared down the dark street. "Oh!" he said to himself. "To refuse that!"

He went back to Notre Dame, lighted his lamp and climbed up the tower. As he expected, La Esmeralda was still in the same place. She ran toward him as soon as she caught sight of him. "Alone!" she cried, sorrowfully clasping her hands.

"I couldn't find him," said Quasimodo coldly.

"You should have waited all night!" she said indignantly.

He saw her angry gesture and understood the reproach. "I'll watch for him more closely next time," he said, lowering his head.

"Go away!" she said.

He left her. She was dissatisfied with him. He had preferred to incur her anger rather than cause her pain. He had kept all the pain for himself.

From that day on she no longer saw him. He stopped coming to her cell. At most she occasionally saw him looking sadly down at her from the top of a tower but as soon as she perceived him he would vanish. It must be admitted that his voluntary absence was not a source of great affliction to her. At the bottom of her heart she was grateful to him for it. And he had no illusions on the subject.

She no longer saw him but she felt the presence of a watchful protector around her. Her provisions were replenished by an invisible hand while she slept. One morning she found a cage with birds in it on her windowsill. Above her cell was a sculptured figure which frightened her, as she had more than once communicated to Quasimodo. One morning (for all these things happened at night) it was no longer there. It had been broken off. The person who had climbed up to it must have risked his life.

Sometimes, in the evening, she would hear a voice from the belfry singing a strange, sad song, as if to lull her to sleep. The words were verses without rhyme, such as a deaf man might compose.

One morning when she awoke she saw two vases full of flowers in her window. One vase was made of crystal; it was beautiful and clear but cracked. All the water in it had leaked out and the flowers it contained were withered. The other vase was made of clay; it was coarse and common but it had kept all its water and its flowers had remained fresh and bright.

I do not know if it was intentional but La Esmeralda took the withered bouquet and wore it in her bosom all day. That evening she did not hear the voice singing in the tower.

She felt little concern over it. She spent her days caressing Djali, watching the door of the Gondelaurier mansion, talking softly to herself about Phoebus and crumbling her bread for the swallows.

She no longer either heard or saw Quasimodo. He seemed to have vanished from the church. One night, however, as she lay awake thinking of her handsome captain, she heard a sigh just outside her cell. Frightened, she got up and saw by the light of the moon a shapeless mass lying across her threshold. It was Quasimodo sleeping there on the stone floor.

CHAPTER FIVE

The Key to the Red Door

IN THE MEANTIME THE ARCHDEACON HAD BEEN TOLD OF THE miraculous way in which the gypsy girl had been saved. He no longer knew what he felt when he learned of it. He had reconciled himself to the thought of her death; he had touched the bottom of all possible pain. The human heart (Dom Claude had meditated on these matters) can contain only a certain quantity of despair. When a sponge is saturated the whole ocean can pass over it without making one more drop of water enter it.

When he believed La Esmeralda to be dead, the sponge

was saturated; everything was over for him on this earth. But to be aware that she was alive, and Phoebus also, was to begin the torture all over again, to be subject to shock again, to be forced to choose again; in short, to begin to live again. And he was weary of all that.

When he learned the news he shut himself up in his cell in the cloister. He appeared neither at the conferences of the chapter nor at the regular services of the church. He closed his door to everyone, even the bishop. He remained secluded in this way for several weeks. He was believed to be ill; and, in fact, he was.

What was he doing during seclusion? With what thoughts was he wrestling? Was he engaged in one last struggle against his formidable passion? Was he elaborating a final plan of death for La Esmeralda and damnation for himself?

His beloved brother Jehan, his spoiled child, came to his door once, knocked, swore, begged and called out his name ten times, but Claude would not open.

He spent whole days with his face pressed against the window. From there he could see La Esmeralda's cell; he often saw her with her goat and sometimes with Quasimodo. He noticed the hideous hunchback's little attentions, his obedience and the tactful, submissive way in which he behaved toward her. He remembered (for he had a good memory and memory is the tormentor of the jealous) the singular way in which the bellringer had looked at her one evening. He wondered what motive had pushed him to rescue her. He witnessed countless little scenes between her and Quasimodo, whose pantomime, seen from a distance and commented on by his passion, appeared extremely affectionate to him. He thought with mistrust of the unaccountability of women's tastes. Then he felt jealousy begin to awaken confusedly in him, a jealousy which he would never have expected and which made him blush with shame and indignation. "The captain is bad enough," he said to himself, "but *that* creature! . . ." The thought overwhelmed him.

His nights were horrible. Since he had learned that she was still alive the cold ideas of specter and tomb which had obsessed him for a whole day vanished and he began to feel the prickings of the flesh once more. Feeling the dark-haired girl so near to him made him writhe on his bed.

Each night his delirious imagination pictured her in all the attitudes that had most excited him. He saw her stretched out on the wounded captain, with her eyes closed and her lovely bosom covered with his blood. He saw her at that delicious moment when he had imprinted on her lips the kiss whose burning pressure she had felt even in her half-unconscious state. He saw her undressed by the savage hands of the torturers, letting her small foot and shapely leg be squeezed into the iron-clad boot. He saw her smooth white knee uncovered above the horrible apparatus. He pictured her in her slip, with a rope around her neck, almost naked, as he had seen her on the last day. These sensual images made him clench his fists and sent a shiver through his whole body.

One night they so cruelly heated his priestly virgin blood that he bit his pillow, leaped out of bed, threw a surplice over his nightshirt and rushed out of his cell with a lamp in his hand, half-naked, frenzied and fiery-eyed.

He knew where to find the key to the red door which connected the cloister and the church and, as we have seen, he always had a key to the towers with him.

CHAPTER SIX

Sequel to the Key to the Red Door

THAT NIGHT LA ESMERALDA WENT TO SLEEP IN HER CELL forgetful of the past and full of pleasant, hopeful thoughts. She had been asleep for some time, dreaming, as always, of Phoebus, when she seemed to hear a sound near her. She always slept lightly, like a bird; the slightest noise would awaken her. She opened her eyes. It was an extremely dark night but she could distinguish the outline of a face peering in at her through the window, illuminated by a lamp. When the intruder saw that she had perceived him, he blew out the lamp. She nevertheless had time to catch a glimpse of his face. She closed her eyes in terror. "Oh," she cried weakly. "The priest!"

All her past misery flashed back into her mind. She fell back on her bed, chilled. A moment later she felt something touch her all along her body. She shuddered and sat up furiously. The priest had laid down beside her and put his arms around her. She tried to scream but could not. "Get away,

monster, murderer!" she said in a voice which was faint and
trembling with rage and horror.

"Please, please!" murmured the priest, pressing his lips to
her shoulder. She clutched his bald head by the remaining hair
on both sides and strove to thrust back his kisses as though
they were bites. "Please!" repeated the wretched man. "If
you only knew what my love for you is like! It's fire, molten
lead, a thousand knives in my heart!" He gripped her arms
with superhuman force.

Frantic, she cried out, "Let me go or I'll spit in your face!"

He let her go. "Yes, debase me, strike me, be cruel!" he
said. "Do whatever you like to me! But, please, love me!"

She struck him in the face with the fury of a child. "Get
away, demon!"

"Love me! Love me! Mercy!" cried the priest, rolling on
her and answering her blows with caresses.

Suddenly she felt him overpowering her. "It's time to put
an end to this!" he said, gnashing his teeth. She was subju-
gated, trembling in his arms and at his disposal. She felt a
lascivious hand wandering over her body. She made one last
effort and began to scream, "Help! Help! A vampire! A vampire!" No one came, Djali alone was awake, bleating in anguish.

"Silence!" panted the priest.

Then, as she struggled, crawling on the floor, her hand
touched something cold and metallic. It was Quasimodo's
whistle. She seized it with a surge of hope, put it to her lips
and blew into it with all her remaining strength. It gave
forth a shrill, clear sound.

"What's that?" said the priest. At almost the same moment
he felt himself lifted by a vigorous arm. The cell was dark
and he could not see clearly who was holding him but he
heard teeth chattering with rage and there was just enough
light to enable him to see the wide blade of a cutlass glittering
above his head.

He thought he perceived the form of Quasimodo. He supposed that he could be no one else. He remembered having
stumbled against something stretched out in front of the door
on entering. However, since the newcomer did not utter a
word, he did not know what to believe. He clutched the
arm holding the cutlass and shouted, "Quasimodo!" forgetting
in his anxiety, that Quasimodo was deaf.

An instant later the priest was dashed to the floor and felt
a heavy knee pressing against his chest. From the angular

imprint of that knee he recognized Quasimodo. But what was he to do? How was he to make himself known? The night made the deaf man blind.

He was lost. The girl, merciless, like an angry tigress, did not intervene to save him. The cutlass came down toward his head. Then his adversary seemed to hesitate. "No bloodshed in her presence," he said dully. It was Quasimodo's voice.

The priest felt himself being dragged out of the cell by one foot. That was where he was to die. Fortunately for him, the moon had just risen. Its pale rays fell on his face as soon as he was past the threshold. Quasimodo looked at him, began to tremble, let go of him and shrank back.

La Esmeralda, who was standing in the doorway, saw with surprise that the two men had abruptly changed roles. It was now the priest who was threatening and Quasimodo who was supplicating. The priest, after assailing the hunchback with gestures of anger and reproach, motioned him to leave.

Quasimodo bowed his head, then came over and knelt before La Esmeralda's door. "Master," he said in a deep voice full of resignation, "do as you like later but kill me first." He handed his cutlass to the priest, who, beside himself with rage, reached out his hand to take it. But La Esmeralda was quicker than he. She snatched the cutlass from Quasimodo's hands and burst into furious laughter.

"Come here!" she said to the priest.

She raised the cutlass. The priest hesitated. She would certainly have struck him. "You're afraid to come near me, coward!" she cried. Then she added, with a pitiless expression, knowing that she was about to pierce his heart with a red-hot iron, "Ha! I know Phoebus isn't dead!"

The priest kicked Quasimodo to the floor and plunged into the staircase, trembling with rage. When he was gone, Quasimodo picked up the whistle which had just saved the gypsy girl and handed it to her. "It was getting rusty," he said, then he left her alone.

Overwhelmed by this violent scene, she fell exhausted on her bed and began to sob. Her horizon had once again become sinister.

As for the priest, he groped his way back to his cell. It was done: Dom Claude was jealous of Quasimodo! He thoughtfully repeated his fateful words, "No one will have her!"

Book VIII

CHAPTER ONE

Gringoire Has Several Good Ideas in the Rue des Bernardins

As soon as Pierre Gringoire saw the turn this whole affair was taking and realized that hanging and other unpleasant things were in store for the principal protagonists of the drama, he lost all desire to take part in it. His comrades of the Court of Miracles, with whom he had remained after deciding that they were, after all, the best company in Paris, had continued to take an interest in the gypsy girl. This seemed quite natural to him for people who, like her, had no other prospect but Charmolue and Torterue and who did not, as he did, soar off into the realms of imagination between the wings of Pegasus. He had learned from them that his wife had taken sanctuary in Notre Dame, which made him very happy. But he was not even tempted to go to see her there. He sometimes thought of the little goat and that was all. During the day he went on performing his feats of strength to earn a living and at night he lucubrated a dissertation against the Bishop of Paris, for he still remembered being drenched by his mills and bore him a grudge for it. He was also engaged in writing a commentary on *De Cupa Petrarum*, the admirable work by Baudry-le-Rouge, which had given him a keen enthusiasm for architecture, an interest which had replaced his passion for alchemy.

One day he stopped near Saint-Germain-l'Auxerrois before

217

a mansion known as the For-l'Evêque, which had a charming fourteenth-century chapel whose chancel faced the street. He stood before it in reverent contemplation of its outside sculpture. He was in one of those moments of supreme self-contained enjoyment in which the artist sees nothing in the world except art and sees the world through art. Suddenly he felt a heavy hand on his shoulder. He turned around. It was his old friend and former master, the Archdeacon of Josas.

Gringoire was dumfounded. He had not seen him for a long time and the archdeacon was one of those grave, intense men who always disturb the equilibrium of a skeptical philosopher.

The archdeacon remained silent for a few moments, during which Gringoire had time to observe him. He found him drastically changed: pale as a winter morning, hollow-eyed and almost white-haired. It was the priest who finally broke the silence. "How are you, Master Pierre?" he asked calmly but coldly.

"Well, I suppose I'm in fairly good health," answered Gringoire. "I take nothing in excess. As you know, master, the secret of good health, according to Hippocrates, is 'cibi, potus, somni, Venus, omnia moderata sint.'"

"Have you no worries, Master Pierre?" asked the archdeacon, looking at him steadfastly.

"No, not especially."

"What are you doing now?"

"Just what you see: I'm examining the cut of these stones and the way this bas-relief is carved."

The priest smiled, one of those bitter smiles which raise only one corner of the mouth. "And does that amuse you?" he asked.

"It's wonderful!" exclaimed Gringoire. Turning to the sculpture with an ecstatic expression, he said, "For example, don't you think this bas-relief is executed with great skill, delicacy and patience? And look at this column. Have you ever seen more gracefully carved leaves? Here are three sculptures by Jean Maillevin, who was a great genius. They're not his greatest works but the naïveté and sweetness of the faces, the gaiety of their attitudes and garments and that indefinable charm which is mingled in all his faults make his figures extremely lively and delicate, perhaps even too much so. Don't you find it interesting?"

"Yes, of course."

"And if you could only see the inside of the chapel!" went on Gringoire with his garrulous enthusiasm. "Sculpture everywhere! The apse is made in exquisite style and so original that I've never seen anything like it!"

Dom Claude interrupted him: "You're happy, then?"

Gringoire answered spiritedly: "Yes, I really am! First I loved women, then animals and now I love stones. They're just as amusing as women and animals and they're much less treacherous."

The archdeacon put his hand to his forehead, one of his habitual gestures. "That's true," he said.

"I'll show you some of my pleasures," said Gringoire. Taking the archdeacon's arm, he led him under the staircase turret of the For-l'Evêque. "Now there's a staircase for you!" he exclaimed. "It makes me happy every time I look at it. It's the simplest yet the most unusual one in Paris. Each step is rounded underneath. Their beauty and simplicity consist in the way they dovetail into each other in such a firm, harmonious manner."

"And you desire nothing?"

"No."

"Do you regret anything?"

"I have neither regrets nor desires. I've arranged my life."

"Circumstances derange what men arrange," said Claude.

"I'm a Pyrrhonian philosopher," replied Gringoire, "and I keep everything in equilibrium."

"How do you earn your living?"

"I still write epics and tragedies now and then but I make most of my income from the trade which you've already seen me exercise: carrying pyramids of chairs with my teeth."

"That's an ignoble trade for a philosopher."

"Well, at least it has to do with equilibrium. When you get an idea into your head you find it in everything."

"I know," replied the archdeacon. After a silence he said, "Still, you're rather poor, aren't you?"

"Poor, yes; but not unhappy."

Just then the two men heard the sound of horses and saw a company of the King's Archers passing by at the end of the street with their lances raised and an officer at their head. It was a brilliant cavalcade and made the pavement echo with its tread.

"Why are you looking at that officer in such a strange way?" asked Gringoire.

"I think I know him."

"What's his name?"

"I think he's called Phoebus de Châteaupers."

"Phoebus! That's a curious name. There's also a Phoebus Comte de Foix. And I once knew a girl who swore only by Phoebus."

"Come with me," said the archdeacon, "I have something to say to you." A certain agitation had been discernible through his frozen exterior since the company of archers had passed. He began to walk. Gringoire followed, accustomed to obeying him, as was everyone else who had ever had any contact with his commanding personality. They continued in silence until they came to the Rue des Bernardins, which was almost deserted. Dom Claude stopped.

"What did you want to say to me, master?" asked Gringoire.

"Don't you think," replied the archdeacon thoughtfully, "that the costume of those soldiers we just saw is handsomer than yours or mine?"

Gringoire shook his head. "No," he said, "I like my red and yellow coat better than those scales of iron and steel. What's so fine about making a noise like an ironmonger's shop in an earthquake when you walk?"

"Haven't you ever envied those handsome cavaliers in their warlike uniforms?"

"Why should I envy them? For their strength, armor and discipline? I'd much rather have my philosophy and independence in rags. I'd rather be the head of a fly than the tail of a lion."

"That's strange," remarked the archdeacon. "Still, a handsome uniform is a splendid thing."

Gringoire, seeing him lost in thought, left him and went over to admire the porch of a nearby house. He returned a while later and said, "If you were less occupied with the fine uniforms of men of war, master, I'd ask you to take a look at that doorway. I've always said that Sieur Aubry's house has the most superb entrance in the world."

"Pierre," said the archdeacon, "what happened to that little gypsy girl?"

"La Esmeralda? That's a sudden change of subject!"

"Wasn't she your wife?"

"Yes, we were married for four years by a broken jug. . . . By the way," he added, almost banteringly, "are you still thinking about her?"

"What about you, do you still think about her?"

"Not often; I have so many other things to think about. . . . But what a pretty little goat she had!"

"Didn't she once save your life?"

"Yes, she did."

"Well, then, don't you even know what's happened to her? What have you done with her?"

"I couldn't say. I think they hanged her."

"Do you think so?"

"I'm not sure. When I saw they were about to start hanging people, I got out of the way."

"Is that all you know about her?"

"Wait a minute—someone told me she took refuge in Notre Dame, and that she was safe there, and I'm very glad of it, and I couldn't find out if her goat was saved with her, and that's all I know about the matter."

"I'll tell you more about it!" cried Dom Claude, whose voice, which had been soft and low, now became thunderous. "It's true that she took refuge in Notre Dame. But in three days she'll be arrested again and hanged at the Place de Grève. Parliament has issued a decree."

"That's a shame," said Gringoire.

The priest abruptly became cold and calm once more.

"Who the devil took it upon himself to solicit an order of restitution?" asked the poet. "Couldn't they leave Parliament alone? What difference does it make to anyone if a poor girl takes refuge among the swallows' nests under the roof of Notre Dame?"

"There are Satans in this world," replied the archdeacon.

"Well, it was a devilish thing to do."

"She saved your life once, didn't she?" asked the archdeacon after a silence.

"Yes, she saved me from my friends of the Court of Miracles. If it hadn't been for her, they'd have hanged me. But they'd be sorry for it now."

"Aren't you willing to do anything for her?"

"I'd like nothing better, Dom Claude, but I'm not anxious to have a noose around my neck."

"What does that matter?"

"What does that matter! That's very kind of you, master! I'm working on two great books right now!"

The archdeacon struck his forehead. Despite the outward calm he strove to maintain, his inward convulsions were occasionally betrayed by a violent gesture. "How can she be saved?" he asked.

"Master, this is my answer: *Il padelt*, which means, in Turkish, 'God is our hope.'"

"How can she be saved?" repeated Dom Claude thoughtfully.

"Listen, master," said Gringoire, "I have a good imagination. I'll think of a way. . . . Why doesn't someone ask the king to pardon her?"

"What! Ask Louis the Eleventh to pardon someone?"

"Why not?"

"You might as well try to take a bone away from a tiger!"

Gringoire began to cast about for other solutions. "What about this," he said: "suppose we get a midwife to declare that the girl is pregnant."

This brought a malicious gleam to the archdeacon's hollow eyes. "Pregnant!" he exclaimed. "What do you know about it, you scoundrel?"

Gringoire was frightened by his expression and hastened to say, "Oh, no, not I! Our marriage was a real *forismaritagium*. I remained outside. But in any case we'd get her a reprieve that way."

"That's madness! Keep quiet, you foul-minded idiot!"

"You're wrong to be angry about it," muttered Gringoire. "If we get her a reprieve it won't do anyone any harm and it will let the midwives earn a little money, which they need."

The archdeacon was not listening to him. "She must get out of there!" he murmured. "The decree goes into effect three days from now! And even if there were no decree, Quasimodo would still be there! Women have such depraved tastes!" He raised his voice: "Master Pierre, I've thought it over: there's only one way to save her."

"How? I can't see any way to do it."

"Listen—and remember that you owe your life to her. The church is watched night and day. Only people who have been seen going in are allowed to come out. You can go in. I'll bring you to her. You'll exchange clothes with her."

"That's fine so far," remarked the philosopher. "What then?"

"Then she'll come out wearing your clothes and you'll stay behind wearing hers. They may hang you but she'll be safe."

Gringoire scratched his ear with a serious air. "Now that's an idea that would never have occurred to me!" he said.

At Dom Claude's unexpected proposal the poet's open and benign face abruptly darkened, like a smiling Italian countryside when some unfortunate gust of wind pushes a cloud against the sun.

"Well, Gringoire, what do you think of my plan?"

"I say, master, that it's doubtful they won't hang me and certain they will."

"That doesn't concern us."

"What!"

"She saved your life. You'll only be repaying your debt to her."

"I have many other debts that I don't pay."

"You must do it," said the archdeacon imperiously.

"Listen, Dom Claude," said the poet in consternation, "you're wrong to insist on your idea. I don't see why I should get myself hanged in place of someone else."

"What reason do you have to be so strongly attached to life?"

"Ah, a thousand reasons!"

"Would you please tell me what they are?"

"Why, there's the air, the sky, the morning, the evening, moonlight, my friends, women, the beautiful architecture of Paris to study, three big books to write and all sorts of other things. Anaxagoras used to say that he was in the world in order to admire the sun. And then I have the good fortune to be able to spend all my days from morning to night in the company of a man of genius—myself—and it's very pleasant."

"Imbecile!" growled the archdeacon. "Just tell me, who saved that life that you find so charming? Who made it possible for you to go on breathing your air, looking up at your sky and amusing your childish mind with nonsense and folly? Where would you be without her? Do you want her to die, the girl to whom you owe your life, that beautiful, gentle, adorable creature who is necessary to the light of the world and more divine than God Himself? Do you want her to die while you go on living the life you stole from her, you, a rough sketch of something or other, half-wise and half-mad, a kind of vegetable which thinks itself capable of thought, as useless as a candle at noon? Come, Gringoire, have a little pity! It's your turn to be generous. She's already set you an example!"

The archdeacon spoke vehemently. At first Gringoire listened indecisively, then he began to be moved and finally took on a tragic expression which made his face resemble that of a newborn baby with the colic. "I'm deeply touched by what you say," he said, wiping away a tear, "and I'll think it over carefully. . . . It's a strange idea you have there. . . . After all, who knows? Maybe they won't hang me; there's many a slip 'twixt the cup and the lip. When they find me in her cell so ridiculously dressed up in a skirt and a veil, maybe they'll only laugh. And then, even if they do hang me, it's as good a way to die as any. In fact, it's a fitting death for a wise man who has oscillated all his life, a death which is neither fish nor flesh, like the mind of a true skeptic, a death impregnated with Pyrrhonism and hesitation, one which remains midway between heaven and earth and leaves you in suspense. It's a philosopher's death and I was perhaps predestined for it. It's magnificent to die as one has lived."

The archdeacon interrupted him: "Do you agree to do it?"

"What is death, after all?" went on Gringoire in an exalted tone. "A disagreeable moment, a toll-gate, a passage from little to nothing. When someone asked Cercidas of Megalopolis if he was willing to die, he replied, 'Why not? I'll see great men after my death: Pythagoras among the philosophers, Hecataeus among the historians, Homer among the poets and Olympus among the musicians.' "

The archdeacon held out his hand and said, "All right, then, it's settled. Come tomorrow."

This brought Gringoire back to reality. "Oh, no!" he exclaimed like a man who has just awakened. "Get myself hanged? That's ridiculous! I won't do it!"

"Good-by, then," said the archdeacon. He added between his teeth, "I'll see you again!"

"I don't want that diabolical man to see me again," thought Gringoire. He ran after the archdeacon. "Wait, master! Old friends shouldn't leave each other angry! You've taken an interest in that girl—in my wife, I mean. That's very good. You've thought of a stratagem to get her safely out of Notre Dame but your plan is extremely unpleasant for me. I only wish I could think of another one . . . Wait! A brilliant idea just occurred to me! What would you say if I told you I had an idea for rescuing her without the slightest danger of getting a noose around my neck? Is it absolutely necessary for me to be hanged before you're satisfied?"

The archdeacon tore the buttons off his cassock in impatience. "What's your plan, you everlasting stream of chatter?"

"Yes," said Gringoire, talking to himself and touching his nose with his forefinger as a sign of meditation, "that's it! My friends in the Court of Miracles are brave fellows. The Tribe of Egypt loves her. They'll go into action at the drop of a hat. Nothing could be simpler; it will be easy to carry her off in all that disorder. Tomorrow night. They'd like nothing better."

"What's your plan? Talk!" said the priest, shaking him.

Gringoire turned to him majestically: "Leave me alone!

Can't you see I'm thinking?" He reflected for some time longer, then clapped his hands and cried out, "Magnificent! It's sure to succeed!"

"What's your plan?" repeated Claude angrily.

Gringoire was radiant. "Let me whisper it to you," he said. "It's a bold stroke of genius that will keep us all out of trouble. You'll have to admit I'm no imbecile!" He interrupted himself: "Oh yes! Is the little goat with her?"

"Yes. May the devil take you!"

"They wanted to hang the goat too, didn't they?"

"What do I care about that?"

"Yes, they wanted to. They hanged a sow last month. The executioner likes that. He eats the animal afterward. They were going to hang my pretty Djali! Poor little lamb!"

"Damnation!" cried Dom Claude. "What plan have you worked out to save her? Will I have to tear it out of you with pincers?"

"Gently, master; here it is." He leaned close to the archdeacon's ear and whispered to him, looking anxiously up and down the street despite the fact that there was no one in it. When he had finished, Dom Claude took his hand and said coldly, "Very well. Tomorrow."

"Tomorrow," repeated Gringoire. He and the archdeacon walked off in opposite directions. "It will be a splendid affair, Monsieur Pierre Gringoire," said the poet to himself. "There's no reason why a man of humble condition should be afraid to undertake a great exploit. Biton carried a full-grown bull on his shoulders; wagtails, linnets and swallows cross the ocean."

CHAPTER TWO

Turn Vagabond

WHEN THE ARCHDEACON RETURNED TO THE CLOISTER HE found his brother Jehan waiting for him at the door of his cell. He had been whiling away the time by drawing a profile of his elder brother on the wall with a piece of charcoal. He had embellished the portrait with a nose of inordinate size. Dom Claude hardly looked at him; he had other things on his mind. That merry, roguish face which had so often brightened the archdeacon's somber features had lost its power to dispel the gloom which settled more thickly every day over his corrupted, stagnant soul.

"Brother Claude," said Jehan timidly, "I've come to see you."

"Well?" said the archdeacon, not even looking at him.

"You're so good to me," said the hypocrite, "and you give me such good advice that I always come back to you."

"Go on."

"Alas, brother Claude, you've always been right when you've said to me, 'Jehan, be wise; Jehan, be studious; Jehan, don't leave the college at night without permission from your masters; Jehan, don't get into fights; Jehan, submit to your master's punishment; Jehan, go to chapel every evening and sing an anthem to the blessed Virgin Mary.' Alas, it was all very good advice!"

"Go on."

"Brother Claude, you see before you a criminal, a libertine, a wretched, worthless man! My dear brother, I've trampled your advice underfoot. I've been punished for it and God is extremely just. I've squandered all my money on carousing and folly. Oh, how charming debauchery is from the front but how ugly it is behind! Now I have nothing left; I've sold my tablecloth, my shirt and my towel. My joyous life is over. Women mock me. I drink only water. I'm constantly assailed by remorse and creditors."

"Go on."

"I'd like to turn over a new leaf, dear brother. I come to you full of contrition. I confess my sins. I beat my breast. You're right to want to see me on the faculty of Torchi College some day. I now feel strongly attracted to that career. But I have no more ink, I must buy some; I have no more pens, I must buy some; I have no more paper or books, I must buy some. I desperately need money for all that and I come to you, my brother, with a heart full of remorse."

"Is that all you have to say?"

"Yes. A little money."

"I have none."

"Well, then, dear brother," said Jehan gravely and resolutely, "I'm sorry to have to tell you that I've received some good offers and propositions from other quarters. You refuse to give me any money. In that case, I'm going to turn vagabond." As he made this monstrous statement he assumed the look of Ajax expecting the thunderbolt to descend on his head.

"Very well, then, turn vagabond," said the archdeacon coldly.

Jehan made a low bow and walked whistling down the steps of the cloister.

As he was crossing the courtyard beneath his brother's window, he heard it opened, looked up and saw the archdeacon's stern countenance. "Go to the devil!" said Dom Claude. "Here's the last money you'll ever get from me!" So saying he threw down a purse which struck Jehan on the forehead and raised a large bump. He walked away angry and satisfied at the same time, like a dog pelted with bones.

CHAPTER THREE

Vive la Joie!

THE READER HAS PERHAPS NOT FORGOTTEN THAT ONE PART OF the Court of Miracles was enclosed by the ancient wall of the city, many of whose towers were already beginning to fall to ruin at that time. One of these towers had been converted into a place of debauch by the vagabonds. There was a tavern in the basement; the upper stories were devoted to other activities. This tower was the liveliest spot in the Court of Miracles and therefore the most hideous. It was a sort of monstrous hive which was buzzing day and night. At night, when most of the vagabonds were asleep, when not one light was to be seen in any of the dilapidated houses, when no other sound came from that swarm of thieves, prostitutes and stolen or bastard children, then the joyful tower could be recognized by the noise it made and the crimson light which, shining through the windows and the cracks in the walls, escaped, so to speak, from all its pores.

One evening, as curfew was sounding from all the belfries of Paris, the sergeants of the watch, if they had ventured to enter the dreaded Court of Miracles, would have noticed that the vagabonds' tavern was even more tumultuous than usual, that there was even more drinking and swearing going on in it. Outside, there were many clusters of people talking together in low tones as if they were plotting some great undertaking. Ragged scoundrels were squatting here and there, sharpening rusty iron blades on the pavement.

Inside the tavern, however, wine and gambling diverted the vagabonds so strongly from the ideas which occupied them that evening that it would have been difficult to discover what was on foot by listening to the drinkers' conversation. They seemed even gayer than usual, but each one of them had some sort of weapon: a pruning-hook, an ax or a large broadsword.

The round room was very large but the tables were packed so tightly together and the drinkers were so numerous that everything in the tavern—men, women, benches, beer mugs, drinkers, sleepers and gamblers—seemed to be thrown together pell-mell with no more order and harmony than a pile of oyster shells. A few tallow candles were burning on the tables but the fire was the main source of light; it was to the tavern what the chandelier is to the opera house. The basement was so damp that the fire was never allowed to go out, even in the middle of summer. It was a huge fire of wood and peat, blazing in an immense fireplace with a sculptured mantel, bristling with heavy andirons and kitchen utensils. A large dog, sitting solemnly in the ashes, was turning a spit laden with meat.

Despite all this confusion it was possible to distinguish in the multitude three principal groups of people, who were crowded around three persons with whom the reader is already acquainted. The first, grotesquely decked out in Oriental rags, was Mathias Hungadi Spicali, Duke of Egypt and Bohemia. He was seated at a table with his legs crossed and his finger raised, giving lessons in white and black magic to the swarm of gaping faces around him. Another group was clustered around our friend Clopin Trouillefou, the valiant King of the Court of Miracles. Armed to the teeth and speaking in a low, serious voice, he was regulating the distribution of the weapons contained in a barrel which had been broken open before him and from which poured axes, swords, coats of mail, bows, arrows, helmets and spears, like apples and grapes from a horn of plenty. Everyone, down to the small children, took something from the pile; between the legs of the drinkers, even legless cripples were scuttling like huge beetles wearing armor and holding some weapon in their hands.

A third group, finally, the largest, noisiest and merriest of all, was gathered around a heavy suit of armor from which a shrill voice could be heard declaiming and swearing. All that could be seen of the person inside it was a red snub nose, a

lock of blond hair, a mouth and a pair of mischievous eyes. He
had his belt stuck full of daggers, a huge sword on one side,
a rusty crossbow on the other and an enormous jug of wine
in front of him, not to mention a hefty, half-naked wench beside him. Everyone around him was laughing, swearing and
drinking.

Add to all this twenty or so secondary groups, the waiters
and waitresses running back and forth, the gamblers crouched
over their games, the quarrels in one corner, the kisses in another, and you will have some idea of the whole scene, illuminated by the flickering light of a great fire which cast a host
of enormous, grotesque, dancing shadows on the walls.

As for the noise, it was like the inside of a great bell ringing
at full peal. Amid all the uproar there was a philosopher seated
on the bench inside the fireplace, meditating with his feet
in the ashes and his eyes fixed on the flames. It was Pierre
Gringoire.

"Come on, hurry up! Take your weapons! We're going to
march in one hour!" said King Clopin Trouillefou to his subjects.

"Ouf!" roared a Norman, recognizable by his nasal accent.
"We're packed in here like the saints at Caillouville!"

"My sons," said the Duke of Egypt to his listeners, "the
witches of France go to their sabbaths without broomsticks or
anything else to ride on, only with a few magic words. The
witches of Italy always have a goat waiting for them at their
door. They must all go out through the chimney."

The voice of the young man in the suit of armor dominated
the hubbub: "Hurrah! Hurrah!" he shouted. "My first feat of
arms today! Vagabond! I'm a vagabond, by the belly of Christ!
Pour me out some more wine! . . . My friends, my name is
Jehan Frollo and I'm a gentleman. In my opinion, if God were
a soldier, He wouldn't miss a chance to pillage. Brethren, we're
going on a noble expedition. We are valiant men. Besiege the
church, break down the doors, take out the pretty girl, save
her from the judges, save her from the priests, tear down the
cloister, burn the bishop in his house—we'll do all that in less
time than it takes a burgomaster to swallow a spoonful of
soup! Our cause is just; we'll pillage Notre Dame and that's
that. We'll hang Quasimodo. Do you know Quasimodo,
ladies? Have you ever seen him work himself out of breath on
the great bell on a holiday? It's a fine sight—like the devil riding a gaping monster!

"Listen to me, my friends: I'm a vagabond in my soul. I

was once very rich but I squandered it all. My mother wanted me to be an officer; my father, a subdeacon; my aunt, an inquest counselor; my grandmother, a head notary. But I became a vagabond. When I told my father about it, he spat his curses in my face and my mother, poor old lady, began to cry and sputter like that log on the fire over there. *Vive la joie!* Bring on more wine! I can still pay for it."

The crowd applauded him with bursts of laughter and, seeing that the tumult was redoubling around him, he cried out, "What a magnificent uproar!" Then he began to sing in Latin with an ecstatic expression on his face and in the tone of a canon leading the vesper chant; but he soon stopped short and shouted, "Hey there, you barmaid of the devil, give me something for supper!"

There was a moment of relative silence during which the shrill voice of the Duke of Egypt could be heard teaching his gypsies: "The weasel is called Aduine; the fox, Bluefoot or the Woods-Runner; the wolf, Grayfoot or Goldenfoot; the bear, the Old Man or the Grandfather. . . . A gnome's cap makes a person invisible and enables him to see invisible things. . . . Every toad which is baptized must be dressed in red or black velvet with bells on its head and feet. The godfather holds its head, the godmother its behind. . . . It's the demon Sidragasum who has the power to make girls dance naked."

"By the Mass!" interrupted Jehan. "I'd love to be the demon Sidragasum!"

Meanwhile the vagabonds continued to arm themselves and whisper to one another on the opposite side of the tavern.

"Poor La Esmeralda!" said a gypsy. "She's our sister. We must save her."

"Is she still in Notre Dame?" asked a peddler.

"Yes."

"Well, then, comrades," cried the peddler, "let's go to Notre Dame! Especially since in the Chapel of Saint Féréol there are two statues, one of John the Baptist and the other of Saint Anthony, both of gold, and together they weigh more than seventeen marks; their pedestals are made of silver gilt and also weigh over seventeen marks. I know—I'm a goldsmith."

Meanwhile Clopin Trouillefou had finished distributing the weapons. He walked over to Gringoire, who appeared to be absorbed in a profound reverie with his feet on one of the andirons. "Friend Pierre," said the king, "what the devil are you thinking about?"

Gringoire turned to him with a melancholy smile. "I love the fire, your majesty," he said. "Not for the trivial reason that it warms our feet and cooks our soup, but because it has sparks. Sometimes I spend hours looking at the sparks. I discover all sorts of things in those stars which sprinkle the dark background of the fireplace. Those stars, too, are worlds in themselves."

"I'll be damned if I understand you!" said the king. "Do you know what time it is?"

"I don't know," replied Gringoire.

Trouillefou walked over to the Duke of Egypt and said, "Comrade Mathias, we've chosen a bad time: they say King Louis is in Paris now."

"All the more reason to get our sister out of his clutches," answered the old gypsy.

"Spoken like a man, Mathias!" said the king. "Besides, we'll have no trouble. We won't meet any resistance in the church. The canons are as cowardly as rabbits and we'll have a big army. The officers of Parliament will get a big surprise tomorrow when they come for her; We won't let them hang such a pretty girl, by God!" He then went out of the tavern.

During this time Jehan was shouting hoarsely, "I'm eating, I'm drinking, I'm drunk, I'm Jupiter! . . . Pierre l'Assommeur, if you look at me like that once more I'll knock the dirt off your nose!"

Gringoire, distracted from his meditations, gazed on the wild, uproarious scene around him and muttered to himself, "I'm so right not to drink!"

Just then Clopin Trouillefou came back in and cried out in a thunderous voice, "Midnight!" At this word all the vagabonds, men, women and children, rushed out of the tavern with a great clatter of weapons and iron instruments.

The moon was behind a cloud and the Court of Miracles was in total darkness. Not one light was showing in it but it was far from being deserted. A crowd of men and women could be distinguished, talking in low tones. All sorts of weapons gleamed in the shadows. Clopin Trouillefou stood up on a large stone and shouted, "Fall in!" There was agitated movement in the darkness. The immense multitude formed itself into a single column. After several minutes the king raised his voice again: "Now, silence in crossing the city! The password is 'Petite flambe en baguenaud.' Don't light the torches till we get to Notre Dame. Forward march!"

Ten minutes later the horsemen of the watch fled in terror

before a long black procession of silent men heading toward the Pont-au-Change through the winding streets in the neighborhood of Les Halles.

CHAPTER FOUR

A Blundering Friend

THAT SAME NIGHT, QUASIMODO WAS NOT ASLEEP. HE HAD JUST finished making his last round through the church. He did not notice, as he was closing the doors, that the archdeacon had passed by and manifested a certain irritation at seeing him carefully bolt and lock the enormous iron bars which gave the wide doors the solidity of a city wall. Dom Claude had an even more preoccupied air than usual. And ever since his nocturnal adventure in La Esmeralda's cell he had treated Quasimodo very harshly, sometimes going so far as to strike him; but nothing could shake the faithful bellringer's submission, patience and devoted resignation. He would submit to anything from the archdeacon—insults, threats or blows— without uttering a single word of reproach or complaint. At most he would watch him with anxiety when he climbed up the staircase of the tower; but the archdeacon voluntarily refrained from appearing in the gypsy girl's presence again.

That night, after glancing at his poor forsaken bells, Quasimodo climbed to the top of the northern tower, set down his shaded lantern and stood looking out over Paris. It was a dark night, as we have already mentioned. In those days the city was scarcely lighted at all; at night it presented to the eye only a jumble of black masses cut here and there by the whitish curve of the Seine. Quasimodo saw no light anywhere except in one window of a faraway building whose vague outline could be discerned above the rooftops in the direction of the Saint-Antoine Gate. There, too, someone was awake.

As his eye ranged over that horizon of mist and shadow, an unaccountable feeling of anxiety came over him. For several days he had been on his guard. He had seen sinister-looking men constantly prowling around the church, looking up at the gypsy girl's refuge, and it occurred to him that perhaps some plot against her was being hatched. He supposed that the people hated her as they did him and that something might well be about to happen. He therefore kept a careful watch from his tower, looking first at her cell and then down at the city, with his mind full of mistrust.

As he was scrutinizing the city with that eye which nature, as a sort of compensation, had made so sharp-sighted that it almost made up for the other organs he lacked, it suddenly seemed to him that there was something strange about one of the streets running along the river, that there was some kind of movement there, that the black line of the street standing out against the whiteness of the water was not straight and still as it should have been, but that it was undulating like the waves of a river or the heads of a walking crowd.

He looked more attentively. The movement seemed to be coming toward him. It lasted awhile longer, then faded away little by little and finally stopped entirely. The line of the street became straight and motionless once again.

He was absorbed in conjectures when it seemed to him that the movement reappeared in the Rue du Parvis, which runs at right angles to the façade of Notre Dame. Finally, despite the thick darkness, he saw the head of a column in that street. An instant later a crowd had spread itself over the square. He could tell nothing about it except that it was a crowd.

The sight was not without terror. It is probable that the singular procession, which seemed so anxious to remain hidden in the darkness, was also equally anxious to keep silence. Nevertheless some noise must have escaped from it, if only the sound of footsteps. But no sound whatever reached the deaf bellringer; and that great multitude, of which, despite its nearness, he saw scarcely anything and heard nothing, seemed to him like a legion of the dead, mute, impalpable and lost in the mist. He saw a fog full of men advancing toward him; he saw shadows stirring within shadows.

His fears returned to him; the idea of an attempt against the gypsy girl flashed back into his mind. He had a vague foreboding that something violent was about to happen. At that critical moment he reflected on what course of action to take with clearer and quicker reasoning than one would have expected from such a badly organized brain. Should he awaken La Esmeralda? Get her out of the church? How? The streets were occupied and the church was on the edge of the river. There was no boat. No way out! There was only one course to follow: fight to the death on the threshold of Notre Dame,

resist at least until help came—if it ever did—and not disturb
La Esmeralda. The poor girl would be awakened soon enough
to die. Once he had made this resolution he set about examining the enemy with greater calm.

The crowd in the square seemed to be growing constantly
larger. He supposed that it was making very little noise, for all
the windows facing the square remained closed. Suddenly a
light flared up. An instant later seven or eight torches were
shaking their tufts of flame in the darkness. Quasimodo then
distinctly saw a frightful troop of men and women in rags,
armed with sickles, pikes, pruning-hooks and halberds, whose
myriad points sparkled in the glare of the torches. Here and
there black pitchforks made horns above hideous faces. He
remembered those faces vaguely and thought he recognized
them as those who had hailed him as Pope of Fools several
months before. One man, holding a torch in one hand and
a whip in the other, stood up on a post and appeared to be
making a speech. At the same time the strange army began to
maneuver as if it were taking up positions around the church.
Quasimodo picked up his lantern and went down to the platform between the two towers in order to have a closer look
and begin to plan his defenses.

When he arrived before the central doorway of Notre
Dame, Trouillefou had, in fact, arrayed his troops in battle
order. Although he expected no resistance, he had decided to
be prudent and maintain an order which would enable him to
repulse a sudden attack from the soldiers of the watch if
necessary. He therefore formed his brigade into a triangle
with the base at the far end of the square in order to block
off the Rue du Parvis. He placed himself at the apex of the
triangle, along with the Duke of Egypt, our friend Jehan and
the boldest of the vagabonds.

Undertakings like the one they were about to attempt were
not rare in the cities of the Middle Ages. What we of today call
the police did not exist then. In the large cities, in the capitals especially, there was no single regulating power. The feudal
system had constructed these great communities in a strange
fashion. A city was an assemblage of countless feudal domains
which divided it into compartments of all shapes and sizes.
There were therefore countless conflicting police forces; in
other words, no police at all. In Paris, for example, besides the
one hundred and forty-one lords who claimed manorial rights,
there were twenty-five who had the right to administer
justice, from the Bishop of Paris, who had one hundred and

five streets under his jurisdiction, to the Prior of Notre-Dame-des-Champs, who had four. None of these feudal justiciaries gave more than nominal recognition to the sovereign authority of the king. Each of them was the undisputed master of his own domain.

Louis XI, that indefatigable worker who so largely began the demolition of the feudal edifice—continued by Richelieu and Louis XIV in the interest of the royalty and finished by Mirabeau in the interest of the people—had tried to break this web of feudal domains spread out over Paris by hurling two or three general police ordinances through it. Thus in 1465 the inhabitants of Paris were ordered to keep lighted candles in their windows at night and lock up their dogs, under penalty of the gallows. In the same year there was an order to close off the streets with chains at night and it was forbidden to carry daggers and other dangerous weapons in the street at night. But all these attempts at municipal legislation fell into neglect a short time later. The citizens let the wind blow out the candles in their windows and allowed their dogs to run loose; the chains were put across the streets only when the city was under siege; the prohibition against carrying weapons in the street was almost universally ignored. The old structure of feudal jurisdiction was left standing. The city was still cut up into a tangle of separate and discordant domains; there was a useless profusion of watches, sub-watches and counter-watches, through which theft, armed robbery and sedition were constantly passing.

In all this disorder, therefore, it was not at all unheard-of for a part of the populace to make an attack on a palace, a mansion or an ordinary dwelling, even in the center of the city. In most cases, the neighbors did not interfere unless the pillage extended to their own houses. They closed their shutters, barricaded their doors and waited for the fighting to come to an end, with or without the aid of the watch. The next day people would tell each other, "Etienne Barbette's house was broken into last night"; "Maréchal de Clermont was attacked," et cetera. Therefore, not only did the royal habitations—the Louvre, the Palace, the Bastille, and the Tournelles—have their battlements and portcullises, but lesser noble residences as well, such as the Petit-Bourbon, the Hôtel de Sens and the Hôtel d'Angoulême. The churches protected themselves with their holiness but some of them (Notre Dame was not of their number) were also fortified. The Abbey of Saint-Germain-des-Prés was embattled like a baronial castle and there was more brass in its cannons than in its bells.

But let us return to Notre Dame. When the first arrangements were completed—and we must say, to the credit of the vagabonds' discipline, that Clopin Trouillefou's orders were carried out in silence and with admirable precision—the worthy king climbed up to the parapet and raised his husky voice, facing Notre Dame and waving his torch, whose flame, agitated by the wind and periodically veiled by its own smoke, made the reddish façade of the cathedral appear and disappear at intervals.

"To you, Louis de Beaumont, Bishop of Paris and Counselor of the Court of Parliament," he shouted, "I, Clopin Trouillefou, King of the Court of Miracles and Bishop of Fools, proclaim the following: that one of our sisters, falsely accused of witchcraft, has taken refuge in your church; you owe her sanctuary and safekeeping. The Court of Parliament wishes to come and arrest her and you have consented; she would be hanged tomorrow if God and the vagabonds were not here. We therefore come to you, bishop. If your church is sacred, so is our sister; if our sister is not sacred, neither is your church. We order you to surrender her to us if you want to save your church; otherwise we will take her and pillage the church, in testimony of which I here plant my banner. God have mercy on you, Bishop of Paris!"

Quasimodo unfortunately could not hear these words, which were uttered with a kind of somber and savage majesty. A vagabond handed the king's banner to him and he planted it solemnly between two cobblestones. It was a pitchfork from whose tines hung a lump of bleeding carrion. Then he turned around and glanced over his army, a ferocious multitude whose eyes gleamed almost as brightly as their weapons. He paused for a moment, then cried out, "Forward, brethren!"

Thirty robust men stepped out of the ranks with hammers, pincers and crowbars over their shoulders. They walked toward the central door of the church, climbed up the steps and were soon crouching before the door, working at it with their tools. A crowd of vagabonds followed them to help them and look on.

But the door held firm. "Damnation, but it's hard and stubborn!" said one. "It's old and stiff in the joints," said another. "Courage, comrades," said Trouillefou. "I'll bet my head against a slipper that you'll get the door open, take the girl and strip the high altar before a single beadle wakes up. There! I think the lock's giving way!"

He was interrupted by an uproar behind him. He turned around. An enormous beam had just fallen from the sky, crushed a dozen vagabonds on the steps of the church and bounced into the square with the noise of a cannon shot, breaking legs here and there among the vagabonds and making them scatter in terror. In the twinkling of an eye the space in front of the church was empty. Those working on the lock, although protected by the porch, abandoned the door and even Trouillefou withdrew to a respectful distance from the church.

"I had a close call!" cried Jehan. "I felt the wind from it, by God! But Pierre l'Assommeur is dead."

It would be impossible to describe the fear and consternation which fell upon the bandits with the beam. They stood for several minutes looking up into the air, more panic-stricken by that piece of wood than they would have been by twenty thousand soldiers of the watch. "Satan!" muttered the Duke of Egypt. "It smells like magic to me!"

"The moon threw down that log at us," said Andry-le-Rouge.

"Yet they say the moon is a friend of the Virgin!" said François Chante-Prune.

"By a thousand popes!" cried Trouillefou. "You're all a pack of fools!" But he could not explain the falling beam.

Meanwhile nothing could be seen on the façade. The light from the torches did not reach to the top of it. The heavy beam lay in the middle of the square. Groans were heard from those who had been crushed against the stone steps by it.

Once he recovered from his first astonishment, Trouillefou found an explanation which seemed plausible to his companions: "By the snout of God! The canons are defending themselves! Forward!"

"Forward!" repeated the mob with a thunderous roar. And they opened fire on the church with crossbows and arquebuses. This woke up the peaceful inhabitants of the surrounding houses. Several windows were opened and nightcaps and hands holding candles appeared in them. "Shoot at the windows!" cried Trouillefou. The windows were hastily closed and the poor citizens, who had scarcely had time to cast a frightened glance over the tumultuous scene, drew back to sweat beside their wives and wonder if a witches' sabbath was now being held in the square or if the Burgundians were attacking again as they had in '64. The husbands thought of robbery, the wives thought of rape and they all trembled.

"Forward!" repeated the vagabonds. But they dared not advance. They looked at the church, then at the beam. The beam did not move. The cathedral kept its calm and deserted air but there was something about it that chilled the vagabonds' hearts.

"To work!" cried Trouillefou. "Break open the door!" No one took a step. "Are you afraid of a beam?" he asked angrily.

An old vagabond spoke to him: "Your majesty, it's not the beam that's bothering us. It's that the door is bolted with heavy iron bars; the pincers are useless."

"What do you need to break it open, then?"

"It will take a battering-ram."

The king strode bravely over to the formidable beam and placed his foot on it. "Here's one!" he cried. "The canons have sent it to us. Thank you, canons," he added, making a derisive bow toward the church.

His bravado had a good effect: the spell of the beam was broken. The vagabonds plucked up their courage and soon the massive beam, picked up like a feather by two hundred vigorous arms, was crashing furiously against the great door. Seen in the half-light which the vagabonds' scattered torches shed on the square, it looked like a monstrous thousand-footed animal attacking the stone giant with lowered head.

At the first impact the half-metal door resounded like an immense drum. It did not give way but a tremor ran through the entire cathedral. Just then a shower of large stones began to fall on the attackers from the top of the façade. "Are the towers shaking their balustrades down on our heads?" asked Jehan. But the impulse was given; the king was right: it was the bishop defending himself. They went on battering the door even more furiously, despite the stones that were breaking skulls on all sides.

Strangely enough, the stones fell one at a time, but they followed one another at short intervals. The vagabonds always felt two of them at once: one against their legs and one on their heads. There were few of them which missed their mark and soon there was a layer of dead and wounded bleeding and quivering beneath the feet of the attackers; but they were replaced as soon as they fell. The long beam continued to crash against the door at regular intervals, the stones continued to rain down and the door continued to groan.

The reader has no doubt guessed that this unexpected resistance was coming from Quasimodo. Chance had unfortunately favored the brave hunchback. When he came down to the platform between the towers his mind was in a whirl. For several minutes he ran wildly back and forth along the gallery, looking down at the compact mass of vagabonds ready to hurl themselves against the church, and asking God or the devil to save the gypsy girl. He considered climbing up into the southern tower and ringing the alarm bell. But in the time it would take him to arrive there and set the bell in motion, would not the vagabonds have more than enough time to break open the door? It was just at that moment that he saw them advancing with their pincers and crowbars. What was he to do?

Suddenly he remembered that workmen had been busy all day repairing the wall, woodwork and roof of the southern tower. The thought was like a flash of light to him. The wall was made of stone, the roof of lead. Then there was the prodigious woodwork, so thickly clustered that it was called "the forest."

He ran to the tower. The lower rooms were indeed full of building material. There were piles of rough-hewn stones, rolls of sheet-lead, bundles of laths and heaps of debris: a complete arsenal.

There was no time to lose. The hammers and crowbars were busily at work below. With a strength increased tenfold by the sense of danger, he picked up the heaviest and longest of the beams, pushed it out through a window, then took hold of it from outside the tower, slid it over the balustrade of the platform and sent it hurtling downward. It fell for one hundred and sixty feet, scraping the wall, breaking off sculpture and turning over several times like the arm of a windmill revolving by itself in space. Horrible shrieks arose when it finally hit the ground; the black beam looked like a writhing serpent as it bounced on the pavement.

Quasimodo saw the vagabonds scatter like ashes before the wind. He took advantage of their terror. While they were staring superstitiously at the log that had fallen from the sky and while they were putting out the eyes of the stone saints of the façade with their crossbows and arquebuses, he was silently heaping up rubbish, stones and even workmen's tools at the edge of the balustrade from which he had dropped the beam. Thus when they began to batter the great door, the hail of stones began to fall and it seemed to them that the church was falling to pieces over their heads.

Anyone who could have seen Quasimodo at that time would have been frightened. Besides the projectiles he had heaped up on the balustrade, he had carried a pile of stones to the platform itself. As soon as he had used up the stones lying near the outer edge, he began to take those which he had placed further back on the platform. He stooped and rose, stooped and rose again with incredible activity. His huge gnomelike head would lean over the balustrade, an enormous stone would fall, then another, then another. Now and then he would follow the fall of a particularly heavy stone with his eye, and if it killed well he would grunt loudly and ferociously.

Meanwhile the vagabonds were not losing courage. The thick door had already trembled more than twenty times under their massive oaken battering-ram. The panels cracked, the carvings flew off in splinters, the hinges leaped up on their pivots at every blow and the wood was reduced to powder, ground between the iron reinforcements. Fortunately for Quasimodo, there was more iron than wood.

Nevertheless he knew that the door could not hold out much longer. Although he could hear nothing, each blow from the battering-ram reverberated in his entrails as well as in the depths of the church. As he looked down at the vagabonds he saw them shaking their fists at the dark façade, full of rage and triumph, and he envied, for the gypsy girl's sake as well as his own, the wings of the owls which were flying away in panic above his head.

This rain of stones was not enough to repulse the attackers. At that moment of anguish he happened to notice two long stone waterspouts which were placed slightly below his balustrade and directly over the central doorway. Their inside opening began in the floor of the platform. An idea occured to him. He ran to his cell to get a fagot, placed it over the openings of the two waterspouts, piled a great number of laths and sheets of lead on top of it and set fire to it with his lantern.

During that time the stones no longer fell and the vagabonds stopped looking up. Panting like a pack of dogs holding a wild boar at bay, they thronged tumultuously around the great door, which had been shattered by the battering-ram but was still standing. They were eagerly awaiting the great blow, the blow which would finally break it open. Each man strove to push himself as far forward as possible, in order to be the first to rush into the church, an immense treasure-house in which the riches of three centuries had been accumulating.

With roars of joy and cupidity they reminded one another of the beautiful silver crucifixes, the brocade copes, the silver-gilt monuments and all the magnificent religious celebrations in which chandeliers, shrines, tabernacles and reliquaries covered the altars with a crust of gold and diamonds. At that superb moment the vagabonds were thinking much less of rescuing La Esmeralda than of pillaging Notre Dame. We would say that La Esmeralda was only a pretext for many of them, if thieves needed a pretext.

As they were grouping themselves around the battering-ram for one last effort, each man holding his breath and stiffening his muscles in order to give all this strength to the decisive blow, a shriek suddenly rang out, even more frightful than the one which had arisen and expired under the beam. Those who were not shrieking, those who were still alive, saw two streams of molten lead falling from the top of the church into the thickest part of the crowd, making two black, smoking holes in it, like hot water poured onto snow. Dying men, half burned to ashes, were writhing and groaning in agony. Around the two main streams there were drops of horrible rain which scattered over the attackers and pierced their skulls like gimlets of flame.

The outcry was heartrending. They fled in wild disorder, dropping the battering-ram on the corpses, the brave along with the fearful, and the space in front of the church was emptied a second time.

All eyes were raised toward the top of the church. What they saw was extraordinary. On the highest gallery, above the central rose window, a great flame was rising up between the two towers in a whirlwind of sparks; a turbulent, furious flame, tongues of which were now and then carried off by the wind along with the smoke. Below it two waterspouts carved into the shape of monsters were incessantly vomiting that burning rain, whose silvery streams stood out against the dark background of the lower part of the façade. As they approached the ground, the two jets of liquid lead spread out into a spray. The innumerable sculptured demons and dragons of the two towers rising above the flames took on a formidable aspect. The flickering light made them move their eyes. There seemed to be dragons laughing, gargoyles yelping, salamanders blowing into the fire and griffins sneezing in the smoke. And among those monsters awakened from their stony sleep by the flames and the noise, there was one which could be seen passing before the fire from time to time like a bat before a candle.

This strange beacon light must have awakened the wood-cutters in the faraway Bicêtre Hills, startled to see the gigantic shadows of the towers of Notre Dame wavering in the darkness.

A terrified silence fell over the vagabonds. Nothing could be heard except the cries of alarm of the canons enclosed in their cloisters and more frantic than horses in a burning stable, the furtive sound of windows being hastily opened and even more hastily closed again, the wind in the flames, the last moans of the dying and the continuous crackling of the leaden rain on the pavement.

Meanwhile the leaders of the vagabonds had withdrawn under the porch of the Gondelaurier mansion to hold a council of war. The Duke of Egypt, sitting on a post, contemplated with religious awe the resplendent blaze two hundred feet up in the air. Trouillefou bit his huge fists in rage. "Impossible to get inside!" he muttered between his teeth.

"An enchanted old church!" grumbled the duke.

"By the pope's mustache!" exclaimed a gray-haired scoundrel who had once been a soldier. "The waterspouts of that church spit out molten lead better than the portcullis of Lectoure!"

"Look at that demon walking up and down in front of the fire!" said the Duke of Egypt.

"It's that damned bellringer, Quasimodo!" said Trouillefou.

The duke shook his head. "No," he said, "it's the spirit Sabnac, the demon of fortifications. He has the body of an armed soldier and the head of a lion. Sometimes he rides a hideous horse. He changes men into stones and builds towers out of them. He has fifty legions under his command. That's who it is, all right. I recognize him."

"Where's Bellevigne de l'Etoile?" asked Trouillefou.

"He's dead," replied one of the vagabonds.

"There must be some way to break open that door!" cried the king, stamping his foot.

The Duke of Egypt sadly pointed to the two long streams of molten lead which were still streaking the dark façade and said, "There have been other churches that defended themselves like that. Forty years ago the Church of St. Sophia in Constantinople threw back the crescent of Mohammed by shaking her domes, which are her heads. And William of Paris, who built Notre Dame, was a magician."

"Shall we just slink away, then, like a pack of pitiful cowards?" said Trouillefou. "Shall we leave our sister to be hanged by those hooded wolves?"

"And there are cartloads of gold in the sacristy!" added a vagabond whose name we unfortunately do not know.

"Damnation!" cried Trouillefou. "Who'll go with me? . . . By the way, where's that little student, Jehan, who was dressed in steel up to his ears?"

"He must be dead," replied someone. "I don't hear him laughing any more."

The king frowned and said, "That's a shame; he had a brave heart under all that hardware. . . . And what about Master Pierre Gringoire?"

"He slipped away before we got to the Pont-aux-Changeurs," said Andry-le-Rouge.

Trouillefou stamped his foot. "This was all his idea, by God!" he roared. "And then he leaves us in the lurch! The babbling coward!"

"Look, Captain Clopin," said Andry-le-Rouge, "here comes Jehan!"

"Thank God!" said Trouillefou. "But what the devil is he dragging behind him?"

Jehan was running toward them as fast as he could with his heavy iron clothing and the long ladder which he was dragging along the pavement. "Victory! *Te Deum!*" he cried.

Trouillefou walked out to meet him. "What are you doing with that ladder?" he asked.

"I got it!" panted Jehan. "I knew where it was: under the shed of the lieutenant's house. I know one of the maids there who thinks I'm as handsome as a god. I used her to get the ladder and I got it! And she came to the door in nothing but her slip!"

"Very good," said Trouillefou, "but what are you going to do with that ladder?"

Jehan gave him a smug, knowing look and snapped his fingers like castanets. At that moment he was sublime. He had on his head one of those overloaded helmets of the fifteenth century which were intended to frighten the enemy with their monstrous crests. The one he was wearing bristled with ten steel beaks. "I'll tell you what I'm going to do with it, your majesty," he said. "Do you see that row of statues with idiotic faces up there above the three doorways?"

"Yes."

"That's the Gallery of the Kings of France."

"What of it?"

"Just wait! At the end of that gallery there's a door which is kept closed only by a latch. With this ladder I climb up there and I'm inside the church!"

"Let me be the first to climb up, my boy."

"No, comrade. It's my ladder. Come on, you can be second."

"May the devil strangle you!" cried Trouillefou angrily. "I won't be second to any man!"

"Then go find yourself another ladder," said Jehan. He began to run across the square, dragging his ladder behind him and shouting, "Follow me, men!"

An instant later the ladder was leaning against the balustrade of the lower gallery above one of the side doorways. The vagabonds, cheering loudly, crowded around the bottom of it, but Jehan defended his rights and was the first to set foot on its rungs. It was a long climb. The Gallery of the Kings of France is about sixty feet above the pavement. Jehan mounted slowly, impeded by his heavy armor, holding a rung in one hand and his crossbow in the other. Halfway up, he cast a melancholy glance at the dead vagabonds scattered over the steps below. "Alas," he said, "there's a pile of corpses worthy of the fifth book of the *Iliad*." Then he resumed his climb. The vagabonds followed him. There was one of them on each rung of the ladder. The line formed by their armored backs was like a serpent with steel scales climbing up the front of the church.

Jehan finally reached the gallery and strode across it to the applause of all the vagabonds. He let out a shout of joy at being thus master of the citadel but a moment later he stopped short, petrified. He had just caught a glimpse of Quasimodo standing behind a statue, glaring at him.

Before a second attacker was able to gain a foothold on the gallery, the formidable hunchback sprang to the top of the ladder, gripped it between his powerful hands, pushed it back from the wall amid cries of anguish, then, with superhuman strength, sent the long ladder, covered with vagabonds from top to bottom, crashing into the square below. For an instant it stood upright and seemed to hesitate, then it plummeted toward the pavement with its load of bandits more rapidly than a drawbridge whose chains have broken. There was a frightful uproar of screams and curses, then it died down and a few wretched, mutilated men crawled out from under the heap of corpses.

The attackers' first shouts of triumph gave way to a clamor of pain and anger. Quasimodo looked on impassively with his elbows leaning on the balustrade.

As for Jehan, he was in a critical situation. He was alone in the gallery with the terrifying hunchback, separated from his companions by a vertical wall sixty feet high. While Quasimodo was occupied with the ladder, he ran over to the door, which he believed to be unlocked. It was not. Quasimodo had locked it behind him when he entered the gallery. Jehan then hid behind the statue of a king, not daring to breathe and looking out at the monstrous hunchback in dread.

At first Quasimodo paid no attention to him but he finally turned around and straightened up; he had just caught sight of the student. Jehan prepared himself to meet an attack but Quasimodo merely stared at him.

"Ha!" said Jehan. "Why are you giving me such a melancholy look?" So saying, he stealthily adjusted his crossbow. "Quasimodo the Deaf," he cried, "you're about to become Quasimodo the Blind!"

He shot. The arrow whizzed through the air and planted itself in Quasimodo's left arm. It seemed to affect him no more than a pin-prick. He took hold of it with his right hand, pulled it out of his arm, calmly broke it over his thick knee and dropped the two pieces to the floor. But Jehan did not have time to shoot a second time. When he had broken the arrow, Quasimodo snorted loudly, rushed at Jehan and pinned him against the wall, flattening his armor.

Then a horrible thing happened. Quasimodo took both of Jehan's arms in his left hand. The student was so terror-stricken that he put up no resistance. In silence and with sinister slowness, the hunchback then pulled off all his armor: sword, dagger, helmet, arm-pieces and breastplate, dropping Jehan's iron shell piece by piece at his feet.

When he found himself disarmed, unprotected and weak between those formidable hands, he did not try to speak to the deaf man but laughed insolently in his face with the carefree boldness of a boy of sixteen.

He did not laugh long. The vagabonds saw Quasimodo standing at the edge of the gallery, holding him by the feet with one hand and swinging him over his head like a sling. Then they heard a sound like that of something hard being smashed against a wall and saw something falling. It was stopped a third of the way down by a projection of the façade.

It was a dead body which remained suspended there, bent double, its back broken, its skull empty.

A cry of horror went up from the vagabonds. "Vengeance!" shouted Trouillefou. "Attack! Attack!" replied the multitude. Then followed a prodigious outcry in which all languages, dialects and accents were mingled. The death of the poor student fired the crowd with fury. They were overcome with shame and anger at having been held off so long in front of a church by a hunchback. Driven by their rage, they found more ladders and torches and several minutes later the frantic Quasimodo saw them swarming up on all sides. Those who had no ladder had knotted ropes; those who had no ropes were climbing up the façade with the aid of the projecting sculpture. There was no way to push back that rising tide of grim-faced men with sweat streaming down their grimy foreheads and lightning flashing from their eyes. All these hideous figures were closing in on Quasimodo. It was as though some other church had sent its most fantastic gargoyles and demons to attack Notre Dame. The stone monsters of the façade were covered with a layer of living monsters.

Meanwhile the square was glittering with the light of a thousand torches. Plunged in darkness until then, the tumultuous scene was suddenly flooded with light. The fire on the topmost platform was still burning, lighting up the surrounding houses. The whole city seemed to have been aroused. Distant bells were clanging in alarm. The vagabonds continued to shout, swear and climb; and Quasimodo, powerless in the face of so many enemies, trembling for the gypsy girl as he saw their furious faces coming closer and closer to his gallery, prayed for a miracle and wrung his hands in despair.

CHAPTER FIVE

The Retreat in Which King Louis Says His Prayers

THE READER HAS PERHAPS NOT FORGOTTEN THAT WHEN QUASI-modo was looking over Paris from the top of his tower, just before he perceived the nocturnal band of vagabonds, the only light he saw was one shining from the uppermost story of a high and forbidding edifice near the Saint-Antoine Gate. That edifice was the Bastille; the light was coming from the candle of King Louis XI.

The king had arrived in Paris two days before. He was to leave again two days later for his fortress of Montilz-lès-Tours. He never stayed in Paris for long, not feeling the presence of enough trap doors, gibbets and Scottish archers around him there.

He had come to sleep in the Bastille that night. He disliked his great bedroom in the Louvre with its large mantelpiece laden with twelve big beasts and thirteen great prophets and its enormous bed, twelve feet long and eleven feet wide. He felt himself lost amid all that grandeur. He preferred the Bastille, with its smaller room and more modest bed. And then the Bastille was stronger than the Louvre.

The chamber which the king had reserved for himself in the famous state prison was nevertheless rather large and occupied the top story of a tower which began with a dungeon. It was a round room with gleaming straw matting on the floor and gilded fleurs-de-lis on the rafters of the ceiling. There was only one window; it was long and pointed, latticed with brass wire and iron bars and darkened by beautiful stained-glass panes bearing the coats of arms of the king and queen.

The only furniture in the room was a magnificent folding armchair. Its woodwork was adorned with roses painted on a red background and its seat was made of scarlet morocco leather, decorated with a silk fringe and studded with an abundance of gold nails. The solitude of this chair made it plain that only one person had the right to sit down in the room. Between the chair and the window was a table on which were scrolls of parchment, pens, an inkpot and a silver mug. Farther on, there was a prayer stool covered with crimson velvet and embossed with gold studs. Finally, at the other end of the room there was a simple bed without any lace or trimming except a plain fringe.

Such was the room which was called "the retreat in which King Louis says his prayers."

This retreat was now dark. Curfew had sounded an hour before and there was only one flickering candle on the table to serve as a light for the five persons who were variously grouped in the room.

The first was a nobleman splendidly arrayed in a doublet and hose of scarlet with silver stripes and a fur-trimmed coat made of gold cloth with black designs. This splendid costume glittered at every fold as the light played on it. The man who wore it carried his head high and had a haughty, ill-tempered expression. His face was at once crafty and arrogant.

He was standing, with a long scroll in his hand, behind the armchair, in which an extremely badly dressed personage was sitting, with his body ungracefully bent double, his knees crossed over each other and his elbows propped on the table. Imagine, on the opulent seat of moroccan leather, a pair of bony thighs poorly attired in black knitted wool, a torso wrapped in a loose coat of linsey-woolsey with a fur trimming which showed more leather than hair, and crowned by an old greasy hat of coarse black cloth adorned with a band of leaden figures. Along with a dirty skullcap beneath which hardly a single hair was visible, this was all that could be seen of the seated personage. His head was bent down so far over his chest that his face was completely hidden in the shadows, except for the tip of his nose, which was evidently quite long. The thinness of his wrinkled hand indicated that he was old. It was Louis XI.

Some distance behind him, two men dressed in the Flemish fashion were talking together in low tones. Anyone who had attended the performance of Gringoire's play would have recognized them as the two principal Flemish ambassadors: Guillaume Rym, the sagacious pensionary of Ghent, and Jacques Coppenole, the popular hosier.

In the darkness near the door, finally, stood a stocky, muscular man in military attire. His square face, with its eyes set near the top, its wide mouth, its lack of forehead and its ears hidden under two eaves of straight hair resembled that of both a dog and a tiger.

All these men were uncovered, except the king. The nobleman standing near the king was reading what was apparently a long report, to which his majesty was listening attentively. The two Flemings were whispering to each other.

"My God, but I'm tired of standing up!" grumbled Jacques Coppenole. "Aren't there any chairs here?"

Rym shook his head and smiled nervously.

"By God!" exclaimed Coppenole once again, unhappy at being obliged to lower his voice. "I've got half a mind to sit down on the floor and cross my legs, the way I do in my shop in Ghent!"

"You'd better not, Master Jacques!"

"Yes, I know, Master Guillaume . . . In this room a man can be only on his feet."

"Or on his knees," added Rym.

Just then the king raised his voice: "What! Fifty sols for robes for our valets and twelve livres for cloaks for our clerks! That's right, throw away gold by the ton! Are you mad, Olivier?"

The old man raised his head as he said this. The golden shells of the Collar of Saint Michael were seen glittering around his neck. The candlelight shone full on his thin, morose profile. He snatched the paper from Olivier's hands.

"You're ruining me!" he cried, looking over the scroll. "What is all this? Do we need such a prodigious household? Two chaplains at ten livres per month each and a chapel clerk at a hundred sols! A roast cook, a vegetable cook, a sauce cook, a chief cook and a butler at ten livres a month each! A porter, a pastry cook, a baker and two carters at sixty livres a year each! And on and on and on! It's a crime! The wages of our servants are ruining France. All the treasures of the Louvre will melt away in such a blaze of expense! We'll have to sell everything! And next year, if God and the Holy Virgin [here he raised his hat] still grant us life, we'll be drinking our camomile tea from a pewter pot!"

He glanced at the silver mug sparkling on the table, coughed and went on: "Master Olivier, kings and emperors must not allow extravagance to take root in their households, for from there the infection spreads to the provinces. Therefore, Master Olivier, remember that this displeases us. Our expenses have been rising every year. They've more than doubled in the last four years! That's monstrous!"

He stopped to catch his breath, then went on angrily: "I see nothing around me but people who are growing fat on my leanness! You all suck money out of me from every pore!"

Everyone kept silent. It was one of those fits of anger which one lets run its course. He continued: "It's like that petition in Latin from the noblemen asking that we re-establish what they call the 'great obligations of the crown.' Obligations indeed! Crushing obligations! Ah, gentlemen, you say we are not a king to reign *dapifero nullo, buticulario nullo!* We'll show you, by God, whether or not we are a king!" Here he smiled at the consciousness of his power, which softened his anger.

Turning to the Flemings, he said, "You see, gentlemen, a grand butler, a grand baker, a grand chamberlain and a grand seneschal are not worth as much as the humblest lackey. Remember this, my dear Coppenole: they're worth nothing at all. Standing uselessly around the king, they remind me of the four evangelists around the dial of the great clock of the palace which Philippe Brille has just renovated: they're gilded, but they don't tell the time and the hands of the clock could get along very well without them."

He remained thoughtful for a moment, then added, shaking his aged head, "Oh, no, by Our Lady! I'm not Philippe Brille and I'm not going to regild the great vassals! I agree with King Edward: save the people and kill the lords. . . . Go on, Olivier."

The man whom he designated by this name took back the scroll and began to read aloud once more:

"To Adam Tenon, Keeper of the Seals of the Provostry of Paris, for the silver, making and engraving of the said seals, which have been made anew because the former ones were so old and worn out that they could no longer be used, the sum of twelve livres.

"To Guillaume Frère, the sum of four livres and four sols for his work and expense in caring for and feeding the pigeons of the Hôtel des Tournelles during the months of January, February and March of this year.

"To a Gray Friar, for receiving the confession of a criminal, the sum of four sols."

The king listened in silence. From time to time he coughed, then raised the silver mug to his lips and drank a mouthful, making a wry grimace.

"Fifty-six public proclamations to the sound of trumpets have been made this year by judicial order. The account remains to be settled.

"For having searched and excavated in certain places, both in Paris and elsewhere, in order to find the money which was said to be hidden there, but of which nothing has been found, the sum of forty-five livres.

"For two new sleeves for the king's old doublet, the sum of twenty sols.

"For a box of grease with which to grease the king's boots, twenty deniers.

"For a new sty for the king's black hogs, thirty livres.

"For various partitions, planks and trap doors made to enclose the lions of the Hôtel Saint-Paul, twenty-two livres."

"Those are very costly animals," said Louis XI. "But no matter, it's a fitting piece of royal magnificence. There's one big red lion that I like especially—have you seen him, Master Guillaume? We kings need to have impressive animals. Our dogs must be lions and our cats tigers. Great things befit the crown. In the time of the pagans, when the people gave a hundred oxen and a hundred sheep to the temple, the emperors would give a hundred lions and a hundred eagles, proud and magnificent creatures. The kings of France have always had roarings around their thrones. Nevertheless, it must be admitted that I spend less money on lions, bears, elephants and leopards than my predecessors did . . . .Go on, Master Olivier; we only wanted to tell our Flemish friends that."

Guillaume Rym made a deep bow, while Coppenole, with his sullen face, looked like one of the bears his majesty had been talking about. The king paid no attention. He had just taken another sip of camomile tea. "Bah! What a disgusting drink!" he exclaimed. His reader continued:

"For feeding a vagabond criminal locked up in a cell in the slaughterhouse, pending decision on what to do with him, the sum of six livres and four sols."

"What's that?" interrupted the king. "Feed a man who ought to be hanged? I won't give a single sol for that food! Olivier, take the matter up with Monsieur d'Estouteville. By tonight I want preparations made for wedding that gentleman to the gallows."

Olivier made a mark with his thumbnail at the item of the "vagabond criminal" and went on.

"To Henriet Cousin, Master Executioner of Paris, the sum of sixty sols, adjudged to him by the Provost of Paris, for having bought, by order of the said Provost of Paris, a large sword to be used in executing and decapitating persons condemned for their misdeeds and for having furnished this sword with a scabbard and everything pertaining thereto; also, for having repaired and reconditioned the old sword, which had been broken and notched in executing justice upon Monsieur Louis de Luxembourg, as may be made to appear more clearly . . ."

The king interrupted: "That will do. I authorize the payment gladly. I don't quibble about that kind of expense. I've never begrudged money spent for such purposes. Go on."

"For making a large cage . . ."

"Ah!" said the king, gripping the arms of his chair with both hands. "I knew there was a reason why I came to this Bastille. Just a moment, Master Olivier; I want to see that cage for myself. You can read over the expenses of it while I examine it. Come with me and look at it, gentlemen of Flanders; I think you'll find it interesting."

He stood up, leaned on Master Olivier's arm, motioned the silent man by the door to precede him and the two Flemings to follow him, then walked out of the room.

Outside the door the royal procession was reinforced by men of arms encumbered with iron and by slender pages carrying torches. They all pursued their way for some time inside the dark dungeon. The captain of the Bastille walked ahead of them, having the doors opened before the sickly old king, who coughed as he walked along. At each door everyone was obliged to stoop in order to pass through, except for the king, who was already bent with age.

Finally, after going through one last door which was so laden with locks that it took a quarter of an hour to open it, they entered a large room with a pointed ceiling. In the center of it they saw by the light of the torches a massive cube of masonry, iron and wood. It was hollow inside. It was one of those famous cages for prisoners of state which were known as the "king's daughters." In the sides were two or three small windows, so thickly latticed with heavy iron bars that no glass was visible. The door was a large slab of stone, like those laid on graves—one of those doors which are used for entrance only. Here, however, the corpse was alive.

The king walked slowly around the small edifice, examining it closely while Master Olivier read aloud from the report:

"For making a large cage of heavy wooden beams and planks, measuring nine feet long by eight feet wide by seven feet high, planed and bolted together with heavy iron bolts, the said cage having been placed in a room in one of the towers of the Bastille Saint-Antoine, for the purpose of detaining, by order of Our Lord the King, a prisoner who previously inhabited an old, dilapidated cage. There were used in making this new cage ninety-six horizontal beams, fifty-two perpendicular beams and ten joists three fathoms long. Nineteen carpenters were employed in squaring, planing and fitting this wood in the courtyard of the Bastille for twenty days . . ."

"Excellent heart of oak," said the king, rapping the wood with his knuckles.

"Also used in this cage," continued Master Olivier, "were two hundred and twenty large iron bolts, some nine feet long, others eight and the rest of medium length. The weight of these bolts, together with their plates and nuts, is three thousand, seven hundred and thirty-five pounds; besides eight large iron clamps weighing two hundred and eighteen pounds, without counting the iron bars for the windows and door of the room in which the cage has been placed, and several other items . . ."

"What a lot of iron to repress the levity of one mind!" said the king.

"The total cost comes to three hundred and seventeen livres, five sols and seven deniers."

"My God!" cried the king. This exclamation seemed to awaken someone inside the cage. There was a sound of chains scraping along its floor and a feeble voice, which seemed to come from the tomb: "Sire! Sire! Mercy!" The man who said these words could not be seen.

"Three hundred and seventeen livres, five sols and seven deniers!" said Louis XI.

The pitiful voice which had come out of the cage had chilled everyone else present, even Master Olivier. Only the king seemed not to have heard it. At his command, Master Olivier resumed his reading and his majesty coldly continued his inspection of the cage.

"Furthermore, a mason was paid twenty-seven livres to make the holes for the window grates and to reinforce the floor of the room containing the cage because otherwise the floor would not have been able to support the cage, due to its great weight . . ."

The voice began to moan once again: "Mercy, sire! I swear it was Cardinal d'Angers who committed the treason, not I!"

"The mason is expensive," said the king. "Go on, Olivier."

"To a carpenter, for window frames, bedsteads, toilet seats and other items, the sum of twenty livres and two sols . . ."

The voice continued: "Alas, sire! Won't you listen to me? I insist it wasn't I who wrote to Monseigneur de Guyenne, but Cardinal La Balue!"

"The carpenter is also expensive," remarked the king. "Is that all?"

"No, sire. . . . To a glazier, for the windowpanes of the said room, forty-six sols and eight deniers . . ."

"Have mercy, sire! I'm innocent! I've been shivering in an iron cage for fourteen years! Have mercy, sire! You'll be rewarded for it in heaven."

"What's the total, Master Olivier?" asked the king.

"Three hundred and sixty-seven livres, eight sols and three deniers."

"Holy Virgin!" cried the king. "What an outrageously expensive cage!" He snatched the scroll from Master Olivier's hands and began to count on his fingers, looking from the

paper to the cage and back again. Meanwhile the prisoner was
still sobbing. In the gloomy shadows it produced an appalling
effect; the listeners looked at one another and turned pale.

"Fourteen years, sire! It's been fourteen years! Ever since
April, 1469! In the name of the Holy Mother of God, sire,
listen to me! You've enjoyed the heat of the sun during all
that time. I'm a sick man; won't I ever see the sun again?
Mercy, sire! Clemency is a beautiful royal virtue which stems
the tide of rage. Does your majesty believe that the knowledge
of never having let an offense go unpunished is a great satisfaction to a king when he's about to die? Besides, sire, I did
not betray you. It was Cardinal d'Angers. And I have a heavy
chain on my foot with a big iron ball at the end of it, much
heavier than it needs to be. Sire! Sire! Have mercy on me!"

"Olivier," said the king, shaking his head, "I notice they've
charged twenty sols a load for plaster. It's worth only twelve.
You'll have to correct this report."

He turned his back to the cage and began to walk out of
the room. The wretched prisoner, noticing that the light and
the voices were growing fainter, judged that the king was
leaving. "Sire! Sire!" he cried in despair. The door closed. He
saw and heard nothing more.

The king walked silently back to his retreat, followed by
the members of his train, who were still horrified by the last
groans of the prisoner. His majesty turned to the captain of
the Bastille. "By the way," he said, "wasn't there someone in
that cage?"

"Of course, sire!" replied the captain, astounded at the
question.

"Who is it?"

"The Bishop of Verdun."

The king knew this better than anyone else but it was a
little game he liked to play. "Really?" he said with an air of
simplicity, as though he had just thought of it for the first
time. "Oh, yes, Guillaume de Harancourt, the friend of Cardinal La Balue. A likable bishop!"

Several minutes later the door of the retreat had opened
and closed again behind the five men whom the reader saw
there at the beginning of this chapter. They all resumed the
same places, postures and whispered conversations.

During the king's absence several dispatches had been
placed on the table. He broke open their seals and began to
read them quickly one after the other. He motioned Master
Olivier, who seemed to act as his minister, to take a pen

and, without revealing the contents of the dispatches, began to dictate their replies to him. Master Olivier knelt uncomfortably before the table as he wrote.

Guillaume Rym looked on. The king spoke so softly that the Flemings were unable to hear what he was dictating, except for a few isolated and almost unintelligible scraps here and there, like the following: " . . . maintain the fertile places by commerce and the barren ones by manufacturing . . . show our four cannons to the English lords. . . . Due to artillery, war is waged more judiciously nowadays. . . . Armies cannot be maintained without taxes . . ."

Suddenly the door opened and a man rushed into the room shouting, "Sire! Sire! The people of Paris are in revolt!"

The king's stern features contracted but all visible signs of his emotion vanished with the speed of lightning. He controlled himself and said with tranquil severity, "You've entered rather abruptly, Master Jacques."

"Sire! Sire! There's a revolt!"

The king, who had stood up, seized him roughly by the arm and, with concentrated anger and a sidelong glance at the Flemings, whispered in his ear, "Either keep quiet or talk more softly!"

The newcomer understood and began to relate something to him in a terrified whisper. The king listened to him calmly, while Guillaume Rym pointed out his clothing to Coppenole: his furred hood, short cloak and black velvet robe indicated a President of the Court of Accounts.

This personage had not been speaking long when the king laughed and exclaimed, "Is that all? Speak louder, Monsieur Coictier! Why are you whispering? We have nothing to hide from our Flemish friends."

"But sire . . ."

"Speak louder!"

Monsieur Coictier was speechless with surprise.

"Go on, speak!" said the king. "You were saying there's some sort of commotion among the inhabitants of our good city of Paris?"

"Yes, sire."

"And you say it's directed against the bailiff of the Palace of Justice?"

"So it seems," said the messenger, still disconcerted by the king's abrupt and inexplicable change of attitude.

"Where did the soldiers of the watch encounter the mob?"

"On the way from the Grande-Truanderie to the Pont-aux-

Changeurs. I saw it myself as I was coming here in obedience to your majesty's orders. I heard some of them shouting, 'Down with the bailiff of the Palace!'"

"And what complaint do they have against the bailiff?"

"It's because he's their lord."

"What!"

"Yes, sire. They're all scoundrels from the Court of Miracles. For years they've been complaining about the bailiff, whose vassals they are. They won't acknowledge his authority in either criminal or civil matters."

"Aha!" exclaimed the king, with a smile of satisfaction which he vainly tried to disguise.

"In all their petitions to Parliament," went on Coictier, "they claim to have only two masters: your majesty and their God, who is, I believe, the devil."

"I see!" said the king. He rubbed his hands together and laughed an inward laugh that made his face beam. He could not conceal his joy, despite his efforts to control himself. Everyone present was puzzled by his behavior, even Master Olivier. He remained silent for a moment, with a thoughtful but satisfied expression. "Are there many of them?" he asked abruptly.

"Yes, sire," replied Coictier.

"How many?"

"At least six thousand."

The king could not help exclaiming, "Good!" Then he asked, "Are they armed?"

"Yes, with sickles, pikes, arquebuses, pickaxes—all sorts of dangerous weapons."

The king did not appear to be at all disturbed. Coictier thought it his duty to add, "If your majesty does not send help to the bailiff immediately, he is lost."

"We will send help," said the king, with an air of affected gravity. "The bailiff is our friend. Six thousand! They're certainly determined rascals! Their impudence is outrageous and has greatly aroused our wrath. But we have few soldiers around us tonight. Tomorrow morning will be soon enough."

"But sire!" cried Coictier. "By tomorrow morning they'll have had time to tear down the bailiff's house and hang him twenty times! For the love of God, sire, send help immediately!"

The king looked him in the eye and said, "I told you tomorrow morning." It was one of those looks to which there is no reply. After a silence he spoke again: "You no doubt know this, Master Jacques: what was . . . what is the bailiff's feudal domain?"

"Sire, the bailiff of the Palace has the Rue de la Calandre as far as the Rue de l'Herberie, the Place Saint-Michel and the territory commonly known as Les Mureaux, located near the Church of Notre-Dame-des-Champs [Louis XI raised his hat] and including thirteen houses, plus the Court of Miracles, the lazar-house known as La Banlieue and all the pavement between there and the Saint-Jacques Gate. He is the lord of all these places, with complete and total jurisdiction."

"Yes indeed," said the king, scratching his left ear with his right hand, "that makes a sizable part of my city! Well, the bailiff was the king of all that!" He continued, thoughtfully and as though talking to himself, "Very good, bailiff; you had a fine piece of my city between your teeth."

Suddenly he exclaimed angrily, "My God! Who do these people think they are, claiming to be judges, lords and masters in our territory! With their toll-gates at the end of every street and their scaffolds on every corner! The Greeks thought they had as many gods as they had fountains, the Persians as many as there were stars and the French think they have as many kings as there are hangmen! It's a terrible state of affairs and all that confusion displeases me! By the faith of my soul, the day must come when there's only one king, one lord, one judge and one executioner in France, just as there's only one God in heaven!"

He raised his hat once again and went on in the tone of a hunter urging on his dogs: "Good, my people! Well done! Cut down those false lords! After them! Plunder them! Hang them! So you wanted to be kings, did you, gentlemen? After them, my people, after them!"

He stopped short and bit his lip as though his thoughts were running away with him and he wished to restrain them. He gazed piercingly at each of the five men around him, then, glancing around again with the cautious, anxious look of a fox slinking back into its den, he said, "Just the same, we will send help to the bailiff. Just now, however, we unfortunately have only a small number of troops to send against such a great number of rebels. We must wait till tomorrow. Then we'll restore order and hang everyone who's arrested."

"That reminds me," said Coictier, "I was so upset that I forgot to tell your majesty that two stragglers have already been captured. If you wish to see these men, sire, they are here."

"How could you forget such a thing?" cried the king. "Quickly, Olivier! Have them brought in!"

Master Olivier went out and came back a moment later with the two prisoners, surrounded by soldiers. The first one had a fat, drunken, astonished and stupid-looking face. He was dressed in rags and dragged his feet as he walked. The second had a pale, smiling face with which the reader is already familiar.

The king looked them over in silence for a moment, then abruptly addressed the first one:

"What's your name?"

"Geoffroy Pincebourde."

"Your profession?"

"Vagabond."

"What were you doing in that abominable revolt?"

The vagabond stared at the king with his arms dangling stupidly. "I don't know," he said. "Everyone else was going, so I went along too."

"Weren't you about to make an outrageous attack on your lord, the bailiff of the Palace?"

"We were going to take something from somebody's house, that's all I know."

A soldier showed the king a pruning-hook which had been taken away from the vagabond.

"Do you recognize this weapon?" asked the king.

"Yes, that's my pruning-hook. I'm a vine-grower."

"And do you recognize this man as your companion?" asked the king, pointing to the other prisoner.

"No. I don't know him."

"That will do," said the king. Motioning to the silent man standing beside the door, he said, "Master Tristan, here's a man for you."

Tristan l'Hermite bowed and gave a low-toned order to two archers, who led the poor vagabond away.

The king approached the second prisoner, who was sweating profusely. "What's your name?" he asked.

"Pierre Gringoire, sire."

"Your profession?"

"Philosopher, sire."

"How dare you go to assault our friend the bailiff of the Palace, scoundrel? And what do you have to say about the revolt?"

"I had no part in it, sire."

"What! You were arrested on the scene, weren't you?"

"No, sire. It's all a mistake. I'm a playwright. I beg your majesty to listen to me. I'm a poet. It's a melancholy habit of men of my profession to walk the streets at night. It was only by chance that I passed by there tonight. I was arrested by mistake. I had nothing to do with the uprising. Your majesty has already seen that the vagabond didn't recognize me. I beg your majesty . . ."

"Silence!" said the king between two swallows of camomile tea. "You're giving us a headache with all your chatter."

Tristan l'Hermite stepped forward, pointed to Gringoire and said, "Shall I take this one also, sire?"

"I see no reason why you shouldn't," said the king casually.

"I see a lot of reasons why he shouldn't!" cried Gringoire.

Our philosopher had turned greener than an olive. He could see from the king's cold and indifferent expression that his only chance lay in some dramatic gesture. He therefore threw himself desperately at his feet and cried out, "Deign to listen to me, your majesty! Don't expend your wrath on such an humble object as I! God doesn't hurl his thunderbolts against a cabbage. You're an august, powerful monarch, sire; have mercy on a poor honorable man who could no more stir up a revolt than an icicle could give off sparks! Most gracious lord, clemency is a kingly virtue. Severity, alas, only exasperates: the icy blasts of the north wind cannot make the traveler take off his coat, but the sun, gently warming him with its rays, makes him glad to walk in his shirt sleeves. Sire, you are the sun. I insist, my sovereign lord and master, that I am neither a vagabond, a thief nor a rebel. I am a loyal subject of your majesty. A good subject must be as jealous of his king's glory as a good husband is jealous of his wife's honor. Any other passion can be only an irrational fury. Such, sire, is my political creed. Do not think me seditious, therefore, simply because my clothes are worn out at the elbows. If you take mercy on me, sire, I will wear them out at the knees by praying for you morning and night! I'm not extremely rich, it's true; in fact, I'm rather poor. But I'm not vicious because of that. It's not my fault.

"It's well known that the pursuit of literature doesn't bring great wealth and those who are most passionately devoted to good books don't always have a big fire in winter. The lawyers take all the grain and leave nothing but the straw for the other learned professions. There are countless good proverbs concerning the threadbare coat of the philosopher. Oh, sire, clemency is the only light which can illuminate the interior of a great soul! It carries the torch before all other virtues. Without it they are blind and can only search God by groping in the darkness. Mercy, which is the same as clemency, nourishes the love of a king's subjects for him and forms his most powerful bodyguard. What difference does it make to your majesty, before whom all eyes are dazzled, if there is one more poor man on earth? A poor innocent philosopher, floundering in the darkness of calamity with an empty purse and a hollow stomach?

"Besides, sire, I'm a writer. A great king adds another pearl to his crown by patronizing literature. But hanging a writer is a bad way to patronize literature. What a stain there would be on Alexander the Great's memory if he had hanged Aristotle! Sire, I've written a very appropriate play for the Princess of Flanders. That's certainly not an act of rebellion. Your majesty can see that I'm not an ignorant clod, that I'm a learned man and have a great deal of natural eloquence. Have pity on me, sire! Such a merciful action will be pleasing to the Holy Virgin and I assure you I'm extremely frightened by the idea of being hanged!"

Gringoire finally stopped, out of breath. He fearfully looked up at the king, who was scratching a spot on the knee of his breeches with his fingernail. His majesty took a sip of camomile tea, but he still said nothing. His silence was a torture to Gringoire. Finally the king looked at him and said, "What a long-winded babbler!" Then, turning to Tristan l'Hermite, he said, "We might as well let him go."

Gringoire fell backward, overcome with joy.

"Let him go!" grumbled Tristan. "Doesn't your majesty want him to be kept in a cage for a while?"

"Do you think it's for birds like this that we make cages costing three hundred and sixty-seven livres, eight sols and three deniers? Release the scoundrel immediately and throw him outside with a sound thrashing."

"Oh, what a great king!" exclaimed Gringoire. Then, fearing a counter-order, he rushed toward the door, which Tristan l'Hermite opened for him with rather bad grace. The soldiers went out with him, pushing him before them with forceful blows, which Gringoire bore patiently like a true philosopher.

Since the revolt against the bailiff had been announced to him, the king's good humor showed itself in everything he did. This unusual clemency was no small sign of it. Tristan l'Hermite looked as surly as a dog which has had a bone snatched from between its jaws.

Meanwhile the king was gaily tapping his fingers on the arms of his chair to the rhythm of a march. He was a crafty monarch, but he was much more skillful at concealing his sorrow than his joy. He sometimes went to extremes in his manifestations of joy on hearing some piece of good news. At the death of Charles the Bold, for example, he vowed a silver balustrade to Saint Martin of Tours, and when he took over the throne he forgot to make arrangements for his father's funeral.

"Tell me, sire," said Jacques Coictier, "what became of the acute attack of illness for which your majesty sent for me?"

"Oh!" said the king. "I'm really in great pain. I have a buzzing in my ears and my chest feels as though it were being scraped with a rake of fire."

Coictier took hold of the king's wrist and began to take his pulse with a competent air. His face took on an expression of greater and greater alarm. The king eyed him uneasily. Coictier frowned gloomily. The king's ill health was the good man's only estate; he therefore cultivated it as industriously as he could.

"This is very serious indeed!" he finally murmured.

"Is it?" asked the king anxiously.

"*Pulsus creber, anhelans, crepitans, irregularis,*" said the doctor.

"My God!"

"It's been known to be fatal in less than three days."

"Holy Virgin!" cried the king. "What's the remedy?"

"I'm thinking about it, sire."

He made the king put out his tongue, shook his head and made a wry face. Then, in the midst of his grimaces, he said abruptly, "Oh, yes, sire, I forgot to tell you that there's a receivership of episcopal revenues vacant and that I have a nephew."

"I'll give your nephew the receivership, Master Jacques," replied the king, "but first put out this fire in my chest."

"Since your majesty is so kind," said the doctor, "he will no doubt not refuse to aid me in the construction of my house."

"What?" said the king.

"I've come to the end of my financial resources," continued

the doctor, "and it would be a great pity if the house should lack a roof."

"Leech!" grumbled the king. "Come to the point!"

"I need a roof for my house, sire, and although the cost is trifling, I have no more money."

"How much is your roof going to cost?"

"Well, for a copper roof, gilded and embellished . . . no more than two thousand livres."

"Assassin!" cried the king. "Every time you pull out one of my teeth you turn it into a diamond for yourself!"

"Will I have my roof, sire?"

"Yes! And you can go to the devil, but cure me first!"

Coictier made a deep bow and said, "Sire, nothing but a repellent can save you. We will apply to your loins that great specific composed of cerate, bole armoniac, egg whites, oil and vinegar. Continue to drink your camomile tea and I will answer for your majesty's health."

A burning candle never attracts one moth only. Master Olivier, seeing the king in a generous mood and deciding that it was a good opportunity, approached him and said, "Sire . . ."

"What now?"

"Sire, is your majesty aware that Master Simon Radin is dead?"

"Yes, what of it?"

"He was Counselor of Justice to the Exchequer."

"Well?"

"Sire, his position is vacant."

As he spoke, Master Olivier's haughty face abandoned its arrogant expression for one of servility. This is the only change which ever comes over a courtier's face.

The king looked him in the eye and said dryly, "I understand. Master Olivier, Marshal de Boucicaut used to say, 'All good fish come from the sea, all good gifts come from the king.' I see that you are also of that opinion. Now listen to this, we have a good memory: in '68 we made you groom of our chamber; in '69, Keeper of the Castle of the Saint-Cloud Bridge, at a salary of a hundred livres; in '73, Keeper of the Vincennes Forest; in '79, Keeper of the Forest of Senart, then Governor of the Castle of Loches, then Captain of the Meulan Bridge, for which honor you have given yourself the title of Count. Out of the fine of five sols paid by every barber who shaves a customer on a holiday, three go to you and we get your leavings. In '74, to the great displeasure of our nobility, we granted you a coat of arms of a dozen different colors, which you wear spread out on your chest like a peacock. My God! Aren't you satisfied yet? Haven't you already had miraculous fishing in the royal sea? And aren't you afraid one more salmon may capsize your boat? Pride will be your downfall, my friend. Pride always has shame and ruin at its heels. Think it over and keep quiet."

These words, uttered in a tone of severity, caused Master Olivier's angry face to resume its customary insolent expression. "Very well," he murmured. "It's easy to see the king is ill today: he gives everything to the doctor."

The king, far from being angered by this impertinent remark, said gently, "Oh, yes, I was forgetting that I made you my ambassador to Madame Marie at Ghent." Turning to the Flemings, he added, "Yes, gentlemen, this man was my ambassador." Then he addressed Master Olivier once again: "Let's not be angry with each other; we're old friends. It's late and we've finished our work. Shave me now."

Our readers may already have recognized "Master Olivier" as the terrible Figaro whom Providence so skillfully worked into the long, bloody drama of the reign of Louis XI. We shall not attempt to describe his curious personality here. This king's barber had three names: at court he was politely called Olivier le Daim; among the people he was known as Olivier the Devil; his real name was Olivier le Mauvais.

Olivier le Mauvais, then, stood looking sullenly at the king and glancing at Jacques Coictier out of the corner of his eye. "That's right, the doctor!" he said between his teeth.

"Of course," said the king with singular good humor. "The doctor has even more influence than you do. It's very simple: he holds us by the entire body, while you hold us only by the chin. Don't worry, my poor barber, you'll still do quite well for yourself. What would become of you if I were like King Chilperic, whose favorite gesture was to hold his beard in one hand? Do your duty, my friend, shave me. Go get your equipment."

Olivier, seeing that the king was taking the whole thing as a joke, went out, grumbling, to execute his orders. The king walked over to the window, then suddenly opened it with extraordinary agitation. "Look!" he cried, clapping his hands. "There's a red glow in the sky! It must be the bailiff's house burning! Well done, my people! At last you're helping me to destroy the feudal domains!" Turning to the Flemings, he said, "Come here, gentlemen, and tell me if that isn't the glow of a fire in the sky." They walked over to the window.

"Yes, a big fire," said Rym.

Coppenole's eyes sparkled. "That reminds me of the burning of Seigneur d'Hymbercourt's house," he said. "There must be a serious revolt over there."

"Do you think so, Master Coppenole?" asked the king, whose eyes were almost as joyous as those of the hosier. "It would be difficult to quell such a revolt, wouldn't it?"

"My God, yes! It will thin the ranks of a great many companies of your majesty's soldiers!"

"Not at all! If I chose to, I could . . ."

Coppenole interrupted boldly: "If that revolt is like I think it is, it will take more than choosing, sire!"

"My friend," said the king, "with two companies of my guards and a few cannon shots I can crush any mob of common people."

Despite Guillaume Rym's frantic signals to him, Coppenole seemed determined to contradict the king. "Sire," he said, "the Swiss also were common people. The Duke of Burgundy was a great nobleman and he had nothing but contempt for that rabble. At the Battle of Grandson he cried, 'Gunners, fire on those low-born scoundrels!' But their leader, Scharnachtal, charged the noble duke with his mace and his army of common people. At the first onslaught of those peasants dressed in buffalo-hides, the shining Burgundian army was shattered like a windowpane by a stone. A great many knights were killed by 'low-born scoundrels' and Monsieur de Château-Guyon, the greatest lord of Burgundy, was found dead with his big gray horse in a little marshy field."

"My friend," said the king, "you're talking about a battle but we have only a mutiny on our hands now. I can stop it whenever I choose to lift a finger."

"Perhaps you can, sire," replied Coppenole indifferently. "If so, it only means that the people's hour hasn't come yet in France."

At this point Guillaume Rym felt obliged to intervene. "Master Coppenole," he said, "you're speaking to a powerful king."

"I know it," replied the hosier gravely.

"Let him speak," replied the king. "I like his frankness. Have you ever seen a revolt, Master Jacques?"

"I've made them," replied Coppenole.

"How do you go about making one?"

"Oh, it's not hard. There are dozens of ways to do it. First of all, the people of the city must be dissatisfied, which isn't rare. Then there's the character of the inhabitants to be considered. The people of Ghent are easy to arouse. They always like a ruler's son but never the ruler himself. Well, let's say someone comes into my shop one morning and says to me, 'Coppenole, this, that or the other has happened; the Princess of Flanders is determined to save her ministers, the bailiff has doubled the price of grinding grain,' and so on and on. I drop my work, walk out of my shop into the street and begin to shout, 'To arms!' There's always some old barrel lying around. I stand up on it and begin to say whatever comes into my head, whatever I've got on my chest—and a common man, sire, always has something on his chest. Then people begin flocking around, pretty soon they're shouting, the alarm bells are ringing, the people arm themselves with weapons taken away from soldiers and off we go! And that's how it will always be as long as there are lords in the castles, citizens in the towns and peasants in the country."

"And against whom do you rebel?" asked the king. "Against your bailiffs? Against your lords?"

"That depends. Sometimes it's against the duke, too."

The king sat down and said, smiling, "Well, in France they haven't yet gone any further than the bailiffs."

Just then Olivier le Daim came back into the room. He was followed by two pages who were carrying the king's toilet articles. But what struck his majesty particularly was that he was also accompanied by the Provost of Paris and the officer of the watch, who both seemed greatly alarmed. The surly barber also wore an air of alarm but satisfaction was visible beneath it. It was he who spoke first: "Sire, I beg you to forgive me for the disastrous news I bring you."

The king, turning abruptly around, ripped the matting on the floor with the legs of his chair. "What news?" he asked.

"Sire," began Olivier, with the malicious expression of a man who rejoices in the opportunity of striking a hard blow, "the revolt is not directed against the bailiff of the Palace of Justice."

"Against whom, then?"

"Against you, sire."

The old king stood up erect like a young man. "Explain yourself, Olivier!" he thundered. "Explain yourself! And be careful, my friend, for I swear by the cross of Saint-Lô that if you're lying to us now, the sword that cut off Monsieur de Luxembourg's head still isn't so jagged that it can't saw off yours!" It was a formidable oath. Louis XI had sworn by the cross of Saint-Lô only twice before in his life.

Olivier opened his mouth to reply. "Sire . . ." he began.

"On your knees!" interrupted the king violently. "Tristan, keep an eye on this man."

Oliver knelt and said coldly, "Sire, a witch condemned to death by your Court of Parliament has taken refuge in Notre Dame. The people are trying to take her out by force. The Provost of Paris and the officer of the watch, who have just come from there, are here to contradict me if I'm not telling the truth. It's Notre Dame that the people are attacking."

"Aha!" said the king softly, pale and trembling with rage. "Notre Dame! They're attacking Our Lady in her own cathedral! Stand up, Olivier. You're right. I give you Simon Radin's position. You're right. It's myself they're attacking. The witch is under the safeguard of the church and the church is under my safeguard. And I thought the revolt was against the bailiff! It's against me!"

Rejuvenated by his fury, he began to stride up and down the floor. He was no longer smiling. His face was terrible to see and he seemed to be choking with rage; his lips twitched and he clenched his bony fists. Suddenly he raised his head, his hollow eyes glowed and his voice burst forth like a trumpet: "After them, Tristan! Cut the scoundrels to pieces! Kill, Tristan! Kill!"

When this explosion had passed, he sat down again and said with cold, concentrated anger, "Here, Tristan! In this Bastille we have the Viscount of Gif's fifty lances, making a total of three hundred horsemen. Take them. There's also a company of our archers commanded by Monsieur de Châteaupers. Take them. You're the Provost Marshal and you have the men of your provostry. Take them. At the Hôtel Saint-Pol you'll find forty archers of Monsieur le Dauphin's new guard. Take them. Then hurry to Notre Dame as fast as you can with all your men. . . . So, citizens of Paris, you've defied the Crown of France, the sanctity of Notre Dame and the peace of this kingdom! Exterminate them, Tristan! Don't spare any of them except to send them to the gallows!"

Tristan bowed and said, "Very well, sire." Then, after a silence, he added, "And what shall I do with the witch, sire?"

"Ah, yes, the witch; Monsieur d'Estouteville, what did the people want to do with her?"

"Sire," answered the Provost of Paris, "since they're trying to take her from her sanctuary in Notre Dame, I imagine they're offended that she escaped the gallows and intend to hang her themselves."

The king appeared to reflect profoundly for a moment, then he addressed Tristan l'Hermite: "Very well, my friend, exterminate the people and hang the witch."

"That's right," whispered Rym to Coppenole, "punish the people for wanting to do something, then do it yourself."

"Yes, sire," replied Tristan. "But if the witch is still in Notre Dame, shall I seize her in spite of the sanctuary?"

"Oh, yes, the sanctuary!" said the king, scratching his ear. "And yet the woman must be hanged." Then, as if an idea had suddenly occurred to him, he knelt on the floor, took off his hat and, devoutly looking at one of the leaden figures with which his chair was decorated, joined his hands and began to pray: "Forgive me, Our Lady of Paris, my gracious patroness! I will do it only this once. That criminal must be punished. I assure you, Holy Virgin, that she is a witch who is unworthy of your loving protection. As you know, many very pious kings have transgressed the privileges of churches for the glory of God and the necessity of the state. Saint Hugh, an English bishop, allowed King Edward to take a sorcerer from his church. Saint Louis of France did likewise in the church of Monsieur Saint-Paul, as did Monsieur Alphonse, son of the King of Jerusalem, in the Church of the Holy Sepulcher itself. I will never do it again and I will give you a beautiful silver statue like the one I gave to Notre-Dame d'Ecouys last year. So be it."

He crossed himself, stood up, put on his hat and said to Tristan, "Hurry, my friend. Take Monsieur de Châteaupers with you. Sound the alarm. Crush the people and hang the witch. I hold you personally responsible for seeing that my orders are thoroughly carried out. . . . Olivier, I won't go to bed tonight. Shave me."

Tristan l'Hermite bowed and went out. Then the king motioned Rym and Coppenole to leave. "God keep you, my good Flemish friends," he said. "Go take a little rest. It's almost dawn."

They both withdrew. As they were being conducted to their lodgings by the captain of the Bastille, Coppenole said to Rym, "I've had enough of that coughing king! I've seen Charles of Burgundy drunk and he's not as cruel as King Louis is when he's sick."

"That's right, Master Jacques," replied Rym. "Wine makes a king less cruel than camomile tea."

CHAPTER SIX

The Password

AS SOON AS HE WAS OUT OF THE BASTILLE, GRINGOIRE RACED down the Rue Saint-Antoine with the speed of a runaway horse. When he reached the Baudoyer Gate, he went straight to the stone cross standing in the middle of the square as if he were able to distinguish in the darkness the figure of a man dressed in black and sitting on the steps of the cross. "Is that you, master?" asked Gringoire.

The man in black stood up and said, "You make my blood boil, Gringoire! The watchman on Saint-Gervais Tower just called out half-past one!"

"It wasn't my fault!" said Gringoire. "You can blame the king and the soldiers of the watch. I've had a narrow escape! I always just miss being hanged. It's my destiny."

"You always miss everything," said the other man. "But let's hurry. Do you know the password?"

"Think of it, master—I saw the king himself! He wears linsey-woolsey breeches. What an adventure!"

"You and your everlasting chatter! What do I care about your adventure? Just tell me if you know the vagabonds' password!"

"Yes, don't worry. It's 'Petite flambe en baguenaud.'"

"Good. Otherwise we wouldn't be able to get through to the church. They've blocked off the streets. Fortunately they seem to have met with some resistance. We may still be able to get there in time."

"But how will we get into the church?"

"I have a key to the towers."

"And how will we get out?"

"Behind the cloister there's a little door that leads to the river. I took a key to it and tied up a boat there this morning."

"I just missed being hanged!" exclaimed Gringoire.

"Come on, hurry!"

They both began to walk rapidly toward Notre Dame.

CHAPTER SEVEN

Châteaupers to the Rescue!

THE READER WILL NO DOUBT REMEMBER THE CRITICAL SITUA-
tion in which we left Quasimodo. The brave hunchback,
assailed from all sides, remained undaunted but he had lost
all hope of saving the gypsy girl. As for his own safety, he
had not once given it a thought.

Notre Dame was about to fall into the hands of the vagabonds. Quasimodo was running frantically back and forth
along the gallery. Suddenly the clatter of horses in full gallop filled the neighboring streets; then, with a long file of
torches and a thick column of horsemen with lowered lances,
these furious sounds burst into the square like a hurricane:
"France! France! Châteaupers to the rescue! Cut the traitors
to pieces!"

The vagabonds turned around in terror. Quasimodo, who
heard nothing, saw the drawn swords, the torches, the spear-
heads and the whole column of cavalry, at the head of which
he recognized Captain Phoebus. He saw the vagabonds' confusion—the alarm of the bravest and the panic of the rest—
and this unexpected help gave him such strength that he
threw back the first attackers, who had already reached the
gallery.

The vagabonds defended themselves with desperate courage. Attacked from the side and from the rear, backed up
against Notre Dame, which they continued to assail and which
Quasimodo continued to defend, they found themselves both
besiegers and besieged.

The fight was furious. The king's soldiers, among whom
Phoebus de Châteaupers bore himself bravely, gave no quarter.
Those who escaped the lance were cut down by the sword.
The vagabonds, badly armed, struck, kicked and bit. Men,
women and children threw themselves on the horses and clung
to them like cats with their teeth and fingernails. Others
thrust lighted torches into the soldiers' faces. Still others tried
to pull the riders off their horses; those who fell were torn to
pieces.

One vagabond had a huge gleaming scythe with which he mowed away at the legs of the horses. He was frightening to watch. Singing in a nasal voice, he never stopped swinging his deadly scythe. At each stroke he described a circle of slashed limbs around himself. He cut his way into the thickest part of the cavalry in this way, with the tranquil slowness, the swaying head and the regular breathing of a mower cutting down a field of wheat. It was Clopin Trouillefou. An arquebus shot finally laid him low.

Meanwhile the windows of the houses facing the square had been opened again. The neighbors, hearing the war cries of the king's soldiers, had taken a hand in the affair and bullets rained down on the vagabonds from every story. The square was filled with dense smoke which was streaked with flame now and then by the firing of arquebuses.

Finally the vagabonds gave up the fight, overwhelmed by fatigue, the lack of good weapons, the panic of the surprise attack, the arquebus fire from the windows and the vigorous assault of the king's soldiers. They broke through their attackers' lines and began to flee in all directions, leaving heaps of their dead and wounded behind them in the square.

When Quasimodo, who had not stopped fighting for a moment, saw their defeat, he fell to his knees and raised his arms to heaven. Then, intoxicated with joy, he ran up to the cell which he had defended so bravely. He now had only one thought: to kneel before the girl he had just saved for the second time.

When he reached the cell he found it empty.

Book IX

CHAPTER ONE

The Little Shoe

LA ESMERALDA WAS ASLEEP WHEN THE VAGABONDS ATTACKED the church but she was soon awakened by the growing tumult and the anxious bleating of her goat. She sat up, listened and looked around; then, frightened by the light and the noise, she rushed out of her cell and looked down into the square. The disorder of the nocturnal assault, the hideous crowd hopping around like a mass of frogs in the shadows, her hoarse croaking and the torches scurrying back and forth in the darkness like will-o'-the-wisps in the murky air of a marsh—all this gave her the impression that a mysterious battle was being fought between the phantoms of a witches' sabbath and the stone monsters of the church. Imbued from childhood with gypsy superstitions, her first thought was that she was witnessing some unholy revel of beings proper to the night. She ran back to her cell, where she cowered in terror and prayed for a less horrible nightmare.

Little by little, her first fears were dispelled. From the constantly increasing tumult and from several other signs of reality, she finally became aware that she was being besieged not by specters but by human beings. Then her terror, without increasing, became transformed. She had already thought of the possibility that the people might rise up and try to take her from her sanctuary by force. Once again she was overwhelmed at the thought of losing her life, of never seeing her

271

Phoebus, whom she always pictured in her future. She was painfully aware of her weakness and of the impossibility of escape or rescue. She fell to her knees and laid her head, with her hands clasped behind it, on her bed; and although she was a pagan gypsy, she sobbingly begged the Christian God to have mercy on her and began to pray to the Holy Virgin. Even if one believes in nothing at all, there are moments in life when one is of the same religion as that of the temple which happens to be nearest at hand.

She remained in this posture for a long time, frozen with fear as the uproar of the furious multitude drew closer and closer, completely bewildered but feeling that something terrible was about to happen. Then in the midst of her anguish she heard someone walking toward her. She looked up. Two men, one of whom was carrying a lantern, had just entered her cell. She uttered a feeble cry.

"Don't be afraid," said a voice which sounded familiar to her. "It's I."

"Who are you?" she asked.

"Pierre Gringoire."

This name reassured her. Peering into the darkness, she recognized the poet. But she was stricken speechless by the sight of a black figure standing beside him, muffled from head to foot.

"Djali recognized me before you did!" said Gringoire reproachfully. The little goat had not waited for him to give his name. As soon as he entered the cell, Djali had affectionately rubbed up against him, covering him with caresses and white hairs, for she was shedding her coat. He warmly returned the caresses.

"Who's that with you?" whispered La Esmeralda.

"Don't worry," replied Gringoire. "He's a friend of mine." Then, setting his lantern down on the floor, he stooped down, put his arms around Djali and cried out enthusiastically, "Oh, what a graceful animal! More remarkable for beauty and cleanliness than for size, to be sure, but intelligent, sensitive and as literate as a grammarian! Tell me, Djali, do you still remember all your pretty little tricks? Show me how Master Jacques Charmolue . . ."

The man in black did not let him finish. He stepped over to Gringoire and roughly pushed him on the shoulder. Gringoire stood up and said, "Excuse me, I was forgetting we're in a hurry. But that's still no reason to shove people around that way. . . . My dear girl, your life is in danger and so is

Djali's. They're trying to violate your sanctuary. We're your friends and we've come to save you. Follow us."

"Is it true?" she cried in amazement.

"Yes, it's true. Come quickly."

"Gladly," she stammered. "But why doesn't your friend say anything?"

"Well, you see, his parents were whimsical people who made him of a silent disposition."

She had to content herself with this explanation. Gringoire took her by the hand. His companion picked up the lantern and walked ahead of them. Dazed by fear, the girl let herself be led along. Djali trotted along behind them, so overjoyed at seeing Gringoire again that she constantly made him stumble by affectionately putting her horns between his legs. "That's life," said the philosopher each time he narrowly escaped falling flat on his face. "It's often our best friends who cause our downfall."

They walked rapidly down the staircase of the tower, through the dark, solitary church resounding with the noise of the fighting outside and out into the courtyard of the cloister. The cloister was deserted, for the canons had all fled to the bishop's residence to offer up their prayers in common. The courtyard was also empty except for a few terrified servants crouching in dark corners.

The man in black opened the door of the courtyard and they went outside. They saw no one. The noise of the vagabonds' assault still reached their ears but it was already softened by distance. The buildings nearest to them were the bishop's residence and the church. There was clearly great disorder inside the bishop's residence. Its dark mass was streaked with lights darting from window to window. Beside it, the enormous towers of Notre Dame, outlined against the red glare which filled the square, looked like the gigantic andirons of some Cyclopean fire.

The man with the lantern walked straight to the bank of the river. Along the water's edge ran a dilapidated fence made of posts and laths, over which a low vine spread its meagre branches like the fingers of an open hand. A small boat was hidden behind this fence. The man motioned Gringoire and the girl to step into it. The goat followed them. The man climbed in last, cut the rope, pushed off from shore with a long boathook and rowed out toward midstream with all his might. The Seine flows swiftly at that point and he had considerable difficulty in clearing the point of the island.

Gringoire's first care on entering the boat was to hold the goat on his lap. He seated himself in the stern and the girl, whom the sight of the stranger filled with some indefinable uneasiness, sat down beside him and pressed up close to him.

When our philosopher felt the boat in motion he clapped his hands and gave Djali a kiss between the horns. "Aha!" he said. "Now all four of us are saved!" He added, with the look of a profound thinker, "We are sometimes indebted to luck and sometimes to strategy for the success of a great undertaking."

The boat moved slowly toward the right bank. The girl watched the stranger with secret terror. He had carefully covered his lantern and now looked like a specter in the darkness. His cowl made him a sort of mask and each time he rowed, his arms, with their wide, hanging sleeves, looked like the wings of a huge bat. He had not yet spoken a single word. The only sound to be heard in the boat was the periodic splash of the oars and the rippling of the water against the sides.

"My God!" cried Gringoire suddenly. "We're about as merry as a bunch of owls! I wish someone would talk to me. The human voice is music to the human ear. I didn't invent that saying: it belongs to Didymus of Alexandria and he was no mean philosopher. Just one word, my lovely La Esmeralda, I beg you to speak just one word to me. . . . By the way, you used to have a funny little pout: do you still have it? Do you know that Parliament has complete jurisdiction over places of sanctuary and that you were in great danger in your cell in Notre Dame? . . . The moon is coming out now, master. If only no one sees us! We're doing an admirable thing in saving this young lady, yet they'd hang us in the name of the king if they caught us. Alas, every human action has two handles and can be picked up by either one of them. What's condemned in one man is applauded in another. Isn't that right, master? What do you think of that philosophy? As for me, I have an instinct for philosophy. . . . What! Isn't anyone going to answer me? You're both in such a surly mood! This is what we playwrights call a soliloquy. . . . They're still making a tremendous uproar in front of the cathedral . . . Louis the Eleventh is a cruel, stingy old king. He still owes me money for my play and he came very close to hanging me tonight, which would have annoyed me greatly. He behaves in a very narrow-minded way toward men of letters and he performs acts of barbarous cruelty. He's like a sponge sucking up money from the people. Under the reign of that gentle, pious monarch the scaffolds are cracking from the weight of the corpses, the chopping-blocks are streaming with blood and the dungeons are bursting with prisoners. He takes money with one hand and hangs people with the other. The great noblemen are stripped of their dignities and the common people are continually having new burdens laid on them. I don't like that king. What about you, master?"

The man in black let the garrulous poet ramble on. He continued to struggle with the current and said nothing.

"By the way, master," went on Gringoire, "as we were pushing our way across the square through that crowd of enraged vagabonds, did you see your deaf bellringer smashing some poor devil's head against the balustrade of the gallery? My eyes aren't too good and I couldn't recognize him. Do you have any idea who it was?"

The stranger said nothing but he abruptly stopped rowing, his arms sank as if they were broken, his head dropped down to his chest and La Esmeralda heard him sigh convulsively. She shuddered. She had heard those sighs before.

The boat drifted with the current for a few moments, then the man in black sat up and began to row again. He passed the tip of the Isle of Notre Dame and headed for the landing at the Port-au-Foin.

"Ah, there's the Barbeau mansion!" said Gringoire. "Look at that cluster of black rooftops forming such strange angles, over there, beneath that mass of low, dirty-looking clouds on which the moon is crushed and spread out like the yolk of a broken egg. It's a beautiful house. It has a chapel with a vaulted roof and a great deal of excellent sculpture. Above it you can see the exquisitely made belfry. There's also a pleasant garden containing a fishpond, an aviary, a mall, a labyrinth, a menagerie and a number of shady lanes which are particularly well suited to amorous activities. There's still an old rascal of a tree that's called 'The Lecher' because it once favored the pleasures of a famous princess and a certain gallant Constable of France. Alas, we poor philosophers are to a Constable of France what a bed of cabbages is to the Louvre Gardens. But what does it matter, after all? For men of high and low rank alike, human life is a mixture of good and evil. Sorrow and joy always go hand in hand. . . . Master, you must let me tell you the story of the Barbeau mansion. It has a tragic ending. It was in 1319, during the reign of Philippe V, the most durable king France has ever had. The moral of the story is that the temptations of the flesh are pernicious and malignant. We must not look too intently at our neighbor's wife, no matter how much our senses may be aroused by her beauty. The thought of fornication is extremely lascivious. Adultery consists of curiosity about another man's amorous pleasures. . . . Listen! the noise is getting louder over there!"

The tumult around Notre Dame was, in fact, raging with increased violence. They listened and clearly heard shouts of victory. Then dozens of torches, whose light was reflected by the helmets of soldiers, appeared all over the church from top to bottom. These torches seemed to be searching for something. Soon the fugitives could distinctly hear these distant shouts: "The gypsy girl! The witch! Death to the gypsy girl!"

The poor girl let her head fall between her hands and the stranger began to row furiously toward shore. Meanwhile our philosopher was meditating. He hugged the goat in his arms and gently moved away from the girl, who was pressing up against him as the only refuge now left to her.

Gringoire was in a cruel dilemma. He reflected that the goat would also be hanged if it were recaptured and that it would be a great pity. Poor Djali! He reflected further that two fugitives clinging to him would be more than he could manage and that his companion would like nothing better than to take charge of La Esmeralda. A violent struggle was taking place in his mind; he considered the girl and the goat and looked at them one after the other. "I can't save them both," he thought.

A jolt announced that the boat had reached shore. The sinister clamor was still coming from Notre Dame. The stranger stood up, came over to the gypsy girl and tried to take her arm to help her out of the boat. She repulsed him and clung to Gringoire's sleeve. For his part, Gringoire, occupied with the goat, almost pushed her away. She climbed out of the boat unassisted. She was so agitated that she did not know what she was doing or where she was going. She stood stupefied for a moment, staring down at the water. When she came back to her senses a little she was alone with the stranger on the landing. Gringoire had apparently slipped away with the goat into the cluster of houses along the Rue Grenier-sur-l'Eau.

The poor girl shuddered at finding herself alone with the man in black. She tried to speak, to cry out, to call to Gringoire, but her tongue would not move and no sound came

from her lips. Suddenly she felt the stranger's hand in hers.
It was a strong, cold hand. Her teeth chattered and she became paler than the moon's rays falling on her. The man said
nothing. He began to walk rapidly toward the Place de Grève,
pulling her along with him. At that moment she was dimly
aware that destiny was an irresistible force. She let herself
be dragged helplessly along, running as he walked. The street
was uphill but it seemed to her that she was going down a
steep slope.

She looked around her. No one in sight; the street was
completely deserted. She heard no sound except the uproar
coming from Notre Dame, from which she was separated
only by a branch of the Seine and from which her name
reached her ears mingled with shouts of death. The rest of
Paris lay spread out around her in vast masses of shadows.

Meanwhile the stranger was pulling her along with the
same silence and the same swiftness. She recognized none of
the places through which they walked. As they were passing
in front of a lighted window, she made a sudden effort, pulled
back and shouted, "Help! Help!" A man wearing a nightshirt
and holding a lamp appeared in the window, looked down at
the street with a stupefied expression, muttered something
which she could not hear, then closed the shutters. She felt
her last glimmer of hope extinguished.

The man in black still said nothing, held her firmly and
began to walk even more swiftly. She no longer resisted. She
was out of breath but from time to time she gathered the
strength to ask him, "Who are you? Who are you?" He did
not answer.

They finally came to a rather large square. The moon shone
faintly. It was the Place de Grève. She could see a sort of black
cross standing in the middle of the square. It was the gibbet.
She recognized everything and knew where she was.

The man stopped, turned to her and raised his cowl.

"Oh!" she stammered, petrified with fear. "I knew it was
you again."

It was the priest. He looked like a phantom. It was an effect
of the moonlight, which seems to reveal only the ghosts of
things to us.

"Listen," he said to her. She shuddered at the sound of that
sinister voice which she had not heard for so long. He spoke
in short gasps which betrayed deep inward agitation: "Listen. We're here. I want to talk to you. This is the Place de
Grève. We've come to the end. Fate has delivered us to each

other. Your life is in my hands and my soul is in yours. Listen
to me and I'll tell you. . . . First of all don't speak to me of
your Phoebus." (He walked back and forth as he spoke, like
a man who finds it impossible to stand still, pulling her along
with him.) "Don't talk about him. Do you understand? If
you utter his name, I don't know what I'll do but it will be
terrible."

When he said this he stood still, like a body which has
found its center of gravity. But his words betrayed no less
agitation. His voice became lower and lower. "Don't turn
away like that!" he said. "Listen to me! This is a serious matter. First, here's what happened: They won't laugh about this,
I can assure you. . . . What was I going to say? Remind me—
oh, yes—Parliament has issued a decree delivering you to the
scaffold again. I've just saved you from them but they're still
pursuing you. Look."

He pointed toward Notre Dame. It was obvious that the
search was still going on. The clamor was drawing closer.
Soldiers could be seen running through the streets carrying
torches and shouting, "The gypsy girl! Where is she? Death
to the gypsy girl!"

"You can see they're after you and that I'm not lying to
you. As for me, I love you. Don't open your mouth! Don't
speak to me if it's only to tell me you hate me; I'm determined
never to hear that again. I've just helped you to escape. . . .
Let me finish first. . . . I can save you completely. I've prepared everything. It's up to you to decide. I can do whatever
you want." He interrupted himself violently: "No! That's not
what I mean!" Then he pulled her over to the gibbet, pointed
at it and said coldly, "Choose between us."

She pulled away from him, threw herself at the foot of the
gibbet and embraced it. Then she turned her head and looked
at him over her shoulder. He was still standing with his finger
pointing at the gibbet, conserving his gesture like a statue.
"I feel less horror of this than of you," she said.

He slowly lowered his arm and looked at the pavement in
deep dejection. "If these stones could speak," he murmured,
"they would say, 'Here is the most wretched of men.'"

Then he began to speak aloud. The girl, kneeling at the
foot of the gibbet, covered by her long, flowing hair, let him
continue without interrupting him. He now spoke in a gentle,
plaintive tone which contrasted sharply with the lofty sternness of his face. "I love you," he began. "Yes, it's true! Can't
you see anything of the fire burning in my heart? Alas, it

burns unceasingly, night and day! Doesn't it deserve at least
a little pity? My love tortures me night and day! Oh, my
suffering is unbearable! I assure you it's something worthy of
your compassion. You can see how gently I'm speaking to you.
I want you to stop having such a horror of me. When a man
loves a woman, it's not his fault . . . Oh, my God! Won't you
ever forgive me? Will you always hate me? Can't you see that's
what makes me malicious and horrifying, even to myself?
You're not even looking at me! You're thinking of something
else, perhaps, while I'm speaking to you standing on the
brink of eternity for both of us! . . . Above all, don't speak
to me of your officer! . . . Even if I threw myself at your
knees, if I kissed—not your feet, for you wouldn't want me to
—but the ground beneath your feet, if I sobbed like a child
and tore out my heart and my entrails to tell you how much
I love you, it would all be in vain! Everything is useless!
And yet you have nothing but tenderness and clemency in
your soul, you're radiant with the most beautiful sweetness in
the world, you're completely gentle, kind, merciful and charming. Alas, you're cruel only to me! Oh, what a terrible fate!"

He hid his face in his hands. She heard him weeping. It was
the first time. Standing up and shaken by sobs, he was more
miserable and supplicating than he had been on his knees.
He continued to weep for some time.

"I'm at a loss for words!" he went on when his first outburst of tears had passed. "I thought very carefully of what I
wanted to say to you but now I'm trembling, I falter at the
decisive moment; I feel something supremely powerful about
to overwhelm us and I stammer. Oh! I'll fall to the ground if
you don't take pity on me, pity on yourself! Don't condemn
us both. If you only knew how much I love you! If you only
knew what's in my heart! Oh, what a desertion of all virtue!
What a desperate abandonment of myself! I'm a learned man,
yet I scoff at science; I'm a nobleman, yet I dishonor my
name; I'm a priest, yet I make my missal a pillow of lust and
spit in the face of my God! And all for you, enchantress; to
be more worthy of your hell! And you'll have nothing to do
with the man whose soul you've damned! Oh! I'll tell you
everything! There's still more, something even more horrible!
Yes, more horrible!"

As he spoke these last words his expression became even
wilder. He was silent for a moment, then he went on, as if
thinking aloud, "Cain, what hast thou done with thy brother?
What have I done with him, Lord? I took him into my care,

raised him, fed him, loved him, worshiped him—and now
I've killed him! Yes, Lord, I've just seen his head crushed
against the stones of Thy house, and it was because of me,
because of this woman. . . ." His voice died down and he
repeated several times, mechanically and at rather long intervals, like a clock prolonging its last vibrations: "Because of
her . . . because of her . . . because of her . . ." Then, although
his lips continued to move, no audible sound came from them.
Suddenly he sank to the pavement and sat there motionless,
with his head on his knees.

A slight movement by the girl as she drew her foot out
from under him brought him back to his senses. He slowly
passed his hand over his hollow cheeks and stared at his wet
fingers. "What!" he exclaimed. "Have I been weeping?"

He turned to her with unspeakable anguish in his eyes and
said, "Alas, you've been coldly watching me weep! My child,
don't you know these are tears of molten lead? Can you hate
me so much that nothing I do will arouse your pity? If you saw
me dying, you'd laugh. But I don't want to see you die! One
word! One single word of forgiveness! Don't tell me you
love me, just tell me you're willing to love me—that will be
enough and I'll save you. Otherwise . . . Oh! Time is passing!
I beg you, don't wait till I've turned to stone again, like this
gibbet, which also claims you! Remember that both our lives
are in your hands, that I'm mad—oh, it's terrible!—that I can
let everything drop, that beneath us is a bottomless abyss in
which my fall will follow yours for all eternity! One word of
kindness! Say a word! Nothing but a word!"

She opened her mouth to reply. He eagerly knelt before
her to receive in adoration the words, perhaps words of tenderness, which were about to come from her lips. She said to him,
"You're a murderer."

He clasped her furiously in his arms and burst into abominable laughter. "Yes, that's right!" he cried. "A murderer! And
you'll be mine! If you won't have me for a slave, you'll have
me for a master! I have a secret hiding-place and I'll drag you
there. You'll have to come with me or I'll turn you over to
the hangman. You must either die or belong to me! Belong
to the priest! To the apostate! To the murderer! Beginning
this very night, do you understand? And now, let's be happy!
Kiss me! Either the grave or my bed!"

His eyes flashed with lust and rage. His lascivious mouth
reddened her neck. She struggled in his arms as he covered
her with furious kisses.

"Don't bite me, you monster!" she cried out. "Oh! What a filthy, disgusting priest! Let me go! I'll tear out your ugly gray hair by handfuls and throw it in your face!"

He flushed, turned pale, then let go of her and looked at her gloomily. She believed herself victorious and went on: "I tell you I belong to my Phoebus, that it's Phoebus I love, that it's Phoebus who's handsome! You, priest, you're old! You're ugly! Go away!"

He let out a violent shriek, like a prisoner who has been branded with a red-hot iron. "Then die!" he said between clenched teeth. She saw his frightful expression and tried to flee. He caught her, threw her to the pavement and dragged her roughly toward Roland Tower.

When they reached the tower he turned to her and said, "For the last time, will you be mine?"

"No!" she answered forcefully.

"Gudule! Gudule!" he called out loudly. "Here's the gypsy girl! Take your vengeance!"

The girl felt something grasp her elbow. She looked and saw a bony arm reaching out of the window of the cell and gripping her with a hand of iron.

"Hold tight!" said the priest. "It's the gypsy girl who escaped. Don't let her go. I'll go bring the sergeants. You'll see her hanged."

These deadly words were answered by a guttural laugh from inside the cell. La Esmeralda saw the priest run off toward the Pont Notre-Dame; the sound of horses could be heard from that direction.

She recognized the malicious recluse. Panting with terror, she struggled to free herself from her grip. She twisted and jerked in agony and despair but the recluse held her with incredible strength. The bony fingers gripped her so tightly that the hand seemed to be riveted to her arm. It was more than a chain, more than an iron ring: it was a pair of living pincers protruding from a wall.

She finally fell against the wall, exhausted. Then she was overwhelmed by the fear of death. She thought of the beauty of life, of youth, of the sight of the blue sky, of love, of Phoebus; of everything in the past and everything which was yet to come; of the priest who was denouncing her, of the hangman who would soon arrive and of the gibbet which was already there. She felt horror rising up to the roots of her hair and heard the sinister laugh of the recluse as she muttered, "They're going to hang you!"

She turned weakly toward the window and saw the recluse's savage face behind the bars. "What have I done to you?" she asked almost inaudibly.

The recluse did not answer; instead, she began to chant, in an angry, mocking tone, "Daughter of Egypt! Daughter of Egypt! Daughter of Egypt!"

The wretched girl bowed her head in despair, realizing that she was not dealing with a human being. Suddenly the recluse cried out, as if La Esmeralda's question had taken all that time to reach her understanding, "What have you done to me! Ah, what you've done to me, gypsy girl! Listen and I'll tell you: I once had a child, do you understand, I once had a child! A lovely little girl . . ." She kissed something in the darkness and murmured gently, "My Agnès . . . Well, gypsy girl, they took my child from me, stole her, ate her! That's what you've done to me!"

"But I probably wasn't even born then!"

"Oh, yes! You must have been born already. You were one of them. She'd be about your age now. . . . I've been here for fifteen years, suffering and praying for fifteen years, beating my head against the wall for fifteen years! I tell you it was the gypsies who stole her from me, do you understand that? And they ate her! Do you have a heart? If you do, imagine what it's like to have a child who plays, who suckles, who sleeps . . . She was so innocent! But they took her away from me and killed her! And now it's my turn—I'm going to eat gypsy flesh! Oh, how I'd bite you if I could get my head through these bars! The poor little baby! While she was asleep! And if they woke her up when they took her, all her cries were in vain, for I wasn't there. Ah, you gypsy mothers, you killed my child—now come and see yours die!"

Dawn was beginning to break. The scene was faintly illuminated by a gray light and the gibbet was standing out more and more distinctly in the middle of the square. From the direction of the Pont Notre-Dame the poor condemned girl seemed to hear the sound of approaching cavalry.

"Madame!" she cried, clasping her hands and falling to her knees, disheveled, frantic and maddened with fear. "Madame! Have mercy on me! They're coming! I've done nothing to you. Do you want to see me die a horrible death before your eyes? You have some pity in your heart, I'm sure of it! It's too horrible! Let me escape! Let me go! Mercy! I can't die like that!"

"Give me back my child!" said the recluse.

"Mercy! Mercy!"

"Give me back my child!"

"In the name of God, let me go!"

"Give me back my child!"

Once again the girl fell back, exhausted. Her spirit was broken and her eyes had the glassy stare of someone who is already in the grave. "Alas!" she stammered. "You're looking for your child and I'm looking for my parents."

"Give me back my little Agnès!" went on Gudule. "You don't know where she is? Then die! . . . I'll tell you more about it. I was a sinful woman. I had a child and they took my child away from me. It was the gypsies. You can see why you must die. When your gypsy mother comes looking for you I'll tell her to look at the gibbet. Or else give me back my child. Do you know where my little girl is? Let me show you —here's her little shoe, everything I have left of her. Do you know where its mate is? If you know where it is, tell me, and even if it's at the other end of the earth I'll walk there on my knees to get it!"

With her free arm she held out the little embroidered shoe to the gypsy girl. It was already light enough to distinguish its form and color.

"Let me see that shoe!" cried La Esmeralda, trembling. "Oh, my God!" She hurriedly opened the little green bag which she wore around her neck.

"That's right, finger your devilish amulet!" muttered Gudule. Then she stopped short, shook in all her limbs and cried out, "My daughter!"

La Esmeralda had just pulled out a little shoe which was exactly like the other one. An instant later the recluse had compared the two shoes, pressed her face, shining with celestial joy, against the bars and cried out once more, "My daughter! My daughter!"

"My mother!" answered the gypsy girl.

The wall and the iron bars were between them. "Oh, the wall!" cried the recluse. "To see her and not be able to embrace her! Your hand! Give me your hand!"

The girl put her hand in between the bars, the recluse seized it, pressed her lips to it and remained lost in that kiss, giving no other sign of life than the sobs which broke from her now and then. The tears streamed down her cheeks in silence, in the darkness, like rain in the night. The poor mother poured out over that adored hand the deep, black well of tears which was inside her and into which all her sorrow had been filtering, drop by drop, for fifteen years.

Suddenly she straightened up, pushed her long gray hair back from her forehead and, without saying a word, began to shake the bars of her cell with the fury of a lioness. Then she went over to a corner of her cell and picked up the large stone which served as her pillow and threw it against the bars with such violence that they cracked. A second blow completely shattered the old iron cross barricading the window. With her hands she finished breaking off and pushing aside the rusty ends of the bars. There are times when a woman's hands have superhuman strength.

When she had cleared a passage—and it took her less than a minute to do so—she took her daughter by the waist and drew her into the cell. "Come, let me save you!" she murmured.

When her daughter was inside the cell she set her down gently on the floor, then picked her up again and, carrying her in her arms as though she were still a baby, walked back and forth in the narrow cell, intoxicated with joy, frenzied, shouting, singing, kissing her daughter, speaking to her, laughing, weeping, all at once and all in ecstatic rapture.

"My daughter! My daughter!" she cried. "I have my daughter! God has given her back to me! He made me wait for fifteen years but it was to give her back to me beautiful. . . . So the gypsies didn't eat her after all! Who told me that? Those good gypsies! I love gypsies! . . . It's really you! That's why my heart leaped up every time you passed. And I took it for hatred! Forgive me, my Agnès, forgive me! You found me very cruel, didn't you? I love you. Oh, you're so beautiful! You got those big eyes from me, young lady. Look at her neck, her hair, her eyes, her hands! I defy anyone to find anything else so beautiful! Oh, she'll have plenty of suitors, I can tell you that! . . . I wept for fifteen years; all my beauty flowed out with my tears and into her!"

A thousand other extravagant things came rushing from her lips. She deranged her daughter's clothes until the girl blushed, stroked her silky hair, kissed her feet, her knees, her forehead and her eyes and went into raptures over everything. The girl let her do as she pleased and softly repeated at intervals, with infinite tenderness, "My mother!"

"Oh, my little girl!" said the recluse, cutting short each word with a kiss. "How I love you! We'll go far away from here. We're going to be so happy! I've inherited a little property in Reims. Do you remember Reims? Oh, no, you were too young. If you only knew how pretty you were when you were four months old! Little feet that people came from miles around to see! We'll have a house to ourselves. We'll sleep in the same bed. My God! My God! Who would have believed it? I have my daughter!"

"Oh, my mother!" said the girl, finally finding the strength to speak despite her emotion. "There was a good gypsy woman who took care of me. She died last year. She was the one who gave me this little bag to wear around my neck. She always told me, 'Keep this with you, my girl. It's a treasure. It will lead you back to your mother. You wear your mother around your neck.' She was right!"

The recluse once again hugged her daughter to her breast. "When we're home again," she said, "we'll put your little shoes on the feet of an Infant Jesus in a church. We owe that to the kind Holy Virgin. Oh, what a lovely voice you have! When you spoke to me just now it was like music! Dear God, I've found my child again! How can such a wonderful thing be true? Surely nothing can kill me, for I haven't died of joy." She laughed, clapped her hands and cried, "We're going to be so happy!"

Just then the cell rang with the clanging of weapons and the sound of galloping horses, which seemed to be coming from the Pont Notre-Dame. The girl threw herself into her mother's arms in anguish. "Save me!" she cried. "Save me, Mother! They're coming after me!"

The recluse turned pale. "God in heaven!" she exclaimed. "I forgot: they're pursuing you! What have you done?"

"I don't know; but I've been sentenced to death!"

"Death!" said Gudule, staggering as if she had been struck by lightning. "Death!" she repeated slowly, looking steadfastly at her daughter.

"Yes, Mother. They want to kill me. There they are, coming for me. That gibbet out there is for me! Save me! Save me! They're coming! Save me!"

The recluse remained motionless for several moments, then shook her head in doubt and laughed. "Oh, no!" she said. "What you're telling me is only a dream! How could I lose her for fifteen years, then find her again for only a minute! And have her taken away from me again! Especially now that she's beautiful and grown up and able to speak to me and love me! How could they come and kill her before my eyes? Oh, no! Such things aren't possible! God wouldn't allow it!"

The horses stopped and a faraway voice was heard saying, "This way, Master Tristan. The priest says we'll find her at the Trou-aux-Rats." The sound of the horses began again.

The recluse leaped to her feet with a shriek of despair. "Run away, my child, run away! It's all coming back to me. You're right,-they want to kill you! Oh, the horror of it! Run away!"

She looked out the window and drew back her head instantly. "No, stay here!" she whispered, convulsively squeezing her daughter's hand. "Stay here! Don't breathe! There are soldiers everywhere. You can't go out. It's too light outside."

Her eyes were hard and dry. She walked silently up and down the floor of the cell for a time, stopping occasionally to tear out a handful of gray hair. Suddenly she said, "They're coming here. I'm going to talk to them. Hide in that corner, they won't see you. I'll tell them you've escaped."

She pushed her daughter into a corner of the cell which could not be seen from the outside. She made her squat down and carefully arranged her so that she was completely hidden in the shadows, then put her jug and her stone, her only furniture, in front of her, imagining that they would conceal her. When she had done all this, she knelt and prayed. The light of dawn, which had broken only a short time before, still left a great many shadows inside the cell.

Just then the priest's voice was heard outside the cell: "This way, Captain Phoebus de Châteaupers!"

At that name and the sound of that voice, La Esmeralda, huddled in her corner, made a movement. "Keep still!" said the recluse.

She had hardly finished saying these words when a tumultuous array of men, swords and horses drew up around the cell. The recluse quickly stood up and ran over to the window to block it. She saw a large troop of armed men, on foot and on horseback. Their leader dismounted and come up to her. "Old woman," he said, "we're looking for a witch. We're going to hang her. We were told you had her."

The poor mother tried to take on an indifferent expression and replied, "I don't understand very well what you mean."

"What kind of a story was that crazy archdeacon telling us, then?" exclaimed the man. "Where is he?"

"He's gone," said a soldier.

"Listen, you old lunatic," said the commander, "don't lie to me. The archdeacon gave you a witch to keep. Where is she?"

She decided not to deny everything, for fear of arousing their suspicion, so she answered in a sincere but sullen tone, "If you're talking about that girl he shoved into my hands awhile ago, she bit me and I let go of her. That's all. Now leave me alone."

The commander made a disappointed grimace. "Don't lie to me, you old hag!" he said. "My name is Tristan l'Hermite and I'm a close friend of the king. Tristan l'Hermite, do you hear?" Looking at the Place de Grève around him, he added, "It's a name that's often been heard here."

"If your name were Satan l'Hermite," said the recluse, whose hopes were beginning to rise, "I still wouldn't have anything else to tell you and I still wouldn't be afraid of you."

"My God, what a shrew!" said Tristan. "So, the witch escaped, did she? Which way did she go?"

"I think she went down the Rue du Mouton," replied Gudule casually.

Tristan turned around and motioned his troop to get ready to start. The recluse began to breathe more easily.

"Sir," said a soldier, "why don't you ask the old hag why the bars of her window are broken that way?"

This question filled her heart with anguish once again but she did not lose her presence of mind. "They've always been like that," she stammered.

"What!" exclaimed the soldier. "Only yesterday they still formed a fine black cross to inspire pious thoughts."

Tristan looked at the recluse out of the corner of his eye. "I think she's worried about something," he said.

The poor woman felt that everything depended on the expression of her face and, with cold despair clutching at her heart, she began to laugh. "Why, that man must be drunk!" she said. "It was over a year ago that a cart full of stones backed into my windows and broke the bars. You can be sure I gave the driver a piece of my mind!"

"That's right," said another soldier. "I was there when it happened."

In any situation there is sure to be someone who has seen everything. This unexpected testimony reassured the recluse, who felt as though she were walking above a bottomless pit on the edge of a knife.

But she was doomed to alternate between hope and alarm. "If it had been done by a cart," said the first soldier, "the bars would be pushed inward but they're turned outward."

"That's right!" said Tristan to the soldier. "You've got a

nose like an inquisitor of the Châtelet. What do you have to say to that, old woman?"

"Oh, my God!" she cried tearfully, at her wit's end. "I swear to you, sir, that it was a cart that broke the bars of my window! You heard that man say he saw it happen! And besides, what does that have to do with your gypsy girl?"

"Look!" said the soldier, flattered by the praise of his superior. "It's easy to see the iron was broken quite recently."

Tristan nodded. "How long ago did you say it happened?" he asked.

"A month ago, maybe two weeks. I don't remember."

"The first time she said it was a year ago," remarked the soldier.

"The whole thing sounds suspicious," said Tristan.

"Sir!" cried the recluse, trembling at the thought that they might become suspicious enough to look in through the window. "I swear it was a cart that did it! I swear by all the saints and angels in heaven! If it wasn't a cart I hope to be damned for all eternity and I deny God to His face!"

"You put a lot of emotion into that oath," observed Tristan, looking at her searchingly.

The poor woman felt all her self-assurance slipping away from her. She was beginning to make awkward blunders and she realized with terror that she was not saying what she ought to.

At this point another soldier ran up shouting, "Sir, the old hag is lying! The witch didn't run down the Rue du Mouton. The chain has been stretched across the street all night and the chain-keeper hasn't seen anyone go by."

Tristan, whose countenance was growing more and more sinister, said to the recluse, "What do you have to say to that?"

She made one more effort to cope with this new development: "I don't know, sir," she said. "I may have been mistaken. She may actually have gone across the river."

"That's in the opposite direction," said Tristan. "And it's hard to believe she'd go back toward where they were looking for her. You're lying, old woman!"

"Also," added the first soldier, "there's no boat on either side of the river here."

"She must have swum across," said the recluse, defending her ground inch by inch.

"Who ever heard of a woman swimming?" asked the soldier.

"You're lying, by God!" exclaimed Tristan angrily. "I've got half a mind to let the witch go and hang you instead." To the woman he said, "A quarter of an hour of torture will pull the truth out of you. Come on, we're taking you with us."

"As you like, sir. Go ahead, torture me! I'm willing!" she said eagerly. "Take me with you. Hurry! Let's go right away!" ("Meanwhile," she thought, "my daughter will have time to escape.")

"Good God!" exclaimed Tristan. "What an appetite for torture! The woman is really a lunatic!"

An old, gray-haired sergeant of the watch stepped out of the ranks and spoke to Tristan: "She's a lunatic, all right, sir. If she let the gypsy girl go, I'm sure it wasn't her fault, because she hates gypsies. I've been on watch in this neighborhood for fifteen years and every night I've heard her cursing gypsies with all her might. And she especially hates the one we're after, the little dancing girl with the goat."

Gudule made an effort and said, "Yes, especially that one."

The other soldiers of the watch unanimously confirmed the old sergeant's words. Tristan l'Hermite, deciding that he would not be able to extract any information from the recluse, turned his back to her. With unspeakable anxiety she watched him slowly walk over to his horse. "All right," he said sullenly, "we'll go on with the search. I won't sleep until that gypsy girl is hanged."

But he hesitated some time before mounting his horse again. The recluse wavered between life and death as she watched him look around the square with the uneasy expression of a hunting dog feeling itself near the hiding place of its prey and reluctant to go away. Finally he shook his head and leaped into the saddle. The mother's horribly contracted heart relaxed; glancing at her daughter, at whom she had not dared to look while the soldiers were there, she whispered, "Saved!"

The poor girl had been in her corner all that time, breathless and motionless, with the specter of death standing before her. Not one word of the conversation had escaped her and she had shared all her mother's anguish. She had heard the successive crackings of the thread by which she was suspended over the abyss and had thought a dozen times that it was about to break; but at last she was beginning to breathe more freely and feel solid ground beneath her feet.

Just then she heard a voice saying to Tristan: "Look, Master Tristan, I'm a soldier and it's not my business to hang witches. The revolt has been put down, so my work is finished; I'll leave you to carry on yours alone. My company is without a captain, so please excuse me if I go to rejoin them." The voice was that of Phoebus de Châteaupers. Its effect on the girl was indescribable. He was there, her friend, her protector, her refuge, her Phoebus! She stood up and, before her mother could stop her, rushed over to the window and shouted, "Phoebus! Here I am, Phoebus!"

Phoebus was gone. He had just turned the corner and was galloping down the Rue de la Coutellerie. But Tristan was still there.

The recluse threw herself at her daughter with a shriek. She pulled her violently backward, sinking her fingernails into her neck. A mother tigress is not gentle. But it was too late. Tristan had seen her.

"Aha!" he cried with a laugh which revealed all his teeth and made his face look like the muzzle of a wolf. "Two mice in the same trap!"

"I thought so," said the soldier.

"You're a good bloodhound," said Tristan, tapping him on the shoulder. "Where's Henriet Cousin?"

A man who had neither the uniform nor the bearing of a soldier stepped out of the ranks. He wore a gray and brown costume with leather sleeves and he held a coil of rope in one of his large hands. This man always accompanied Tristan, who always accompanied Louis XI.

"My friend," said Tristan, "I assume this is the witch we've been looking for. Hang her for me. Do you have your ladder?"

"There's one in the shed of the Maison-aux-Piliers," replied the man. "Shall I do it here?" he added, pointing to the stone gibbet.

"Yes."

"Fine!" said the hangman with a laugh that was even more bestial than Tristan's. "We won't have far to go!"

"Hurry up!" said Tristan. "You'll have time to laugh later."

Meanwhile, since Tristan had seen her daughter and all hope was lost, the recluse had not said a word. She had shoved the poor girl into a corner of the cell and taken her place at the window, with her hands clutching the edge of it like two claws. She glared at the soldiers with eyes which had once again become wild and fierce. When Henriet Cousin stepped up to her she made such a savage grimace at him that he shrank back.

"Sir," he said, turning to Tristan, "which one shall I hang?"

"The young one."

"Good; the old one looks hard to handle!"

"Poor little dancing girl!" said the old sergeant of the watch.

Henriet Cousin turned back to the window. The mother's eyes made him lower his own. "Madame . . ." he began timidly.

She interrupted him in a low, furious voice: "What do you want?"

"I want the other one, not you."

"What other one?"

"The young one."

She shook her head and cried out, "There's no one else here! No one! No one!"

"Yes there is!" said the hangman. "You know very well there is. Let me take the young one. I won't hurt you."

"Oh, so you won't hurt me!" she said with a strange laugh.

"Let me have the young one, madame; it's the provost who wants her."

"There's no one here!" she repeated frantically.

"I tell you there is!" replied the hangman. "We all saw there were two of you."

"Take a look, then," sneered the recluse. "Stick your head in through the window."

He looked at her fingernails and remained motionless.

"Hurry up!" said Tristan, who had just ranged his men in a circle around the cell and posted himself on horseback beside the gibbet.

The hangman turned to him once again, full of embarrassment. He had laid his rope on the ground and was awkwardly fingering his hat. "How shall I go in, sir?" he asked.

"Through the door."

"There isn't any door."

"Through the window, then."

"It's too narrow."

"Then make it wider!" said Tristan angrily. "Don't you have any pickaxes?"

The mother watched them from her den. She had lost all hope and she did not know what to do; she only knew that she did not want them to take her daughter.

Henriet Cousin went to the shed of the Maison-aux-Piliers to get his tools. He also took out the ladder, which he propped

up against the gibbet. Five or six of the provost's men took up
pickaxes and crowbars. Tristan went up to the window with
them.

"Old woman," he said sternly, "this is your last chance to
hand over that girl without any trouble."

She looked at him as if she had not understood.

"Good God!" exclaimed Tristan. "What reason do you
have to try to prevent that witch from being hanged according
to the king's orders?"

The wretched woman laughed savagely. "What reason?"
she said. "She's my daughter."

The way she spoke these words made Henriet Cousin himself shudder.

"I'm sorry," said Tristan, "but the king has ordered her to
be hanged."

She cried out, redoubling her terrible laughter: "What do
I care about your king? I tell you she's my daughter!"

"Break down the wall," said Tristan.

All that was necessary to enlarge the opening was to remove
one large stone from under the window. When the mother
heard the pickaxes and crowbars sapping her fortress she let
out a frightful shriek and began to run around her cell with
amazing swiftness—one of the habits of a wild animal which
her cage had given her. She said nothing but her eyes were
flaming. The soldiers felt their blood run cold.

Suddenly she picked up her stone, laughed madly and
hurled it at the soldiers. Her aim was bad, for her hands were
trembling, and she struck no one. The stone rolled to a stop
under the feet of Tristan's horse. She gnashed her teeth.

Meanwhile, although the sun had not yet risen, it was broad
daylight and the dilapidated chimneys of the Maison-aux-
Piliers were tinged with a lovely pink glow. It was the hour
when the early-rising citizens of the great city cheerfully
opened their windows. A few of them were already crossing
the Place de Grève on their way to the markets, riding on
their donkeys. They stopped for a moment before the soldiers
clustered around the Trou-aux-Rats, looked at them in surprise, then went on their way.

The recluse had gone over to sit in front of her daughter,
covering her with her body. The poor girl sat stock-still but
she murmured softly, "Phoebus! Phoebus!" As the invaders
made progress in their work of demolition, the mother shrank
back, pressing her daughter more and more tightly against the

wall. Suddenly she saw the stone shake and heard Tristan's voice urging on the workers. This roused her from the stupor in which she had been plunged for several minutes and she began to cry out: "Oh! Oh! Oh! It's horrible! You're bandits! Are you really going to hang my daughter? I tell you she's my daughter! Cowards! Murderers! Help! Help! How can they take my daughter away from me like this? How can God let them do it?"

Then foaming at the mouth, wild-eyed and down on all fours like a panther, she addressed Tristan: "Come a little closer and try to take my daughter! Do you know what it is to have a child, you wolf? Haven't you ever made love with your she-wolf? Haven't you ever had a wolf-cub? If you have, isn't there something in your belly that stirs when your little ones cry?"

"Take the stone out of there," said Tristan. "It's loose now."

The crowbars raised the heavy mass. It was, as we have said, the mother's last rampart. She threw herself on it to try to hold it back and scratched at it with her fingernails, but the massive block, set in motion by six men, slipped away from her and fell to the ground.

Seeing that an entrance had been made, she fell across it, blocking the breach with her body, flailing her arms, striking her head against the floor and shouting in a voice so hoarse from fatigue that it was scarcely audible: "Help! Help! Help!"

"Now take the girl," said Tristan impassively.

The mother looked at the soldiers in such a formidable way that they were more inclined to go backward than forward.

"Come here, Henriet Cousin," said Tristan.

No one moved.

Tristan swore: "By the head of Christ! What kind of soldiers do I have? Afraid of a woman!"

"Sir," said the hangman, "do you call that a woman?"

"Go on!" said Tristan. "The breach is wide enough. Go in three abreast and I'll cut down the first man who steps back."

Standing between Tristan and the mother, both of them threatening, the soldiers hesitated for a moment, then made up their minds and went toward the cell.

When the recluse saw them coming, she abruptly raised herself to her knees, pushed back her hair from her face and dropped her lacerated hands to her thighs. Big tears welled up in her eyes and trickled one by one down a wrinkle in her cheek, like a stream flowing along a channel it has hollowed out for itself. At the same time she began to speak in a voice which was so supplicating, gentle, submissive and poignant that more than one old trooper who would have eaten human flesh had to wipe his eyes.

"Please let me speak, gentlemen!" she said. "There's something I must tell you. This is my daughter. Do you understand? My dear little girl that I'd lost! Listen. I know sergeants of the watch very well. They were always good to me in the days when little boys threw stones at me because I was a loose woman. You'll let me keep my child when I've told you everything. You see, I'm only a poor streetwalker. The gypsies stole my little girl. I kept her shoe for fifteen years. Look, here it is. Her feet were that small. In Reims. My name was Paquette la Chantefleurie. Maybe you knew me then, in your youth. You'll take pity on me, won't you gentlemen? The gypsies stole her and kept her for fifteen years. I thought she was dead. Imagine that, my friends, I thought she was dead! I lived here in this cell for fifteen years, with no fire in winter. Poor little shoe! I cried out so much that God finally listened to me. Tonight He gave me back my daughter. It's one of God's miracles. She wasn't dead. You won't take her away from me, I'm sure you won't. If you wanted to take me, I wouldn't say anything, but she's only a girl of sixteen! Let her have time to see the sun! You didn't know she was my daughter but now you know. Oh, how I love her! Monsieur l'Hermite, I'd rather see a hole in my entrails than a scratch on her finger! You look like a kindhearted gentleman. What I've told you explains everything, doesn't it? Remember your own mother, my lord! Let me keep my child! I'm begging you on my knees, the way we all pray to Jesus Christ! She's my daughter, my own daughter! I only want to go away, we want to go away together. Let us go! Oh, you're so kind, gentlemen, and I love you all! You won't take my daughter away from me, that would be impossible! Wouldn't it be completely impossible? My child! My child!"

We shall not attempt to give an idea of her gestures, her intonations, the tears which flowed into her mouth as she spoke, the way she wrung her hands, her heartbreaking smiles, her moans, her sighs and the piercing, agonized cries which she mingled with her wild, rambling and incoherent words. When she had finished, Tristan l'Hermite frowned but it was in order to hide a tear which welled up in his tigerlike eye.

Overcoming his weakness, however, he said dryly, "It's the king's will."

Then he leaned near the hangman's ear and said in a low voice, "Get it over with quickly!" Perhaps even the redoubtable provost felt his heart failing.

The hangman and the soldiers entered the cell. The mother made no resistance but she dragged herself to her daughter and threw herself over her. When the girl saw the soldiers coming toward her the horror of death roused her from her stupor. "Mother!" she cried out in unspeakable despair. "They're coming! Keep them away from me!"

"Yes, my darling, I'll keep them away," answered the mother dully, holding her in her arms and covering her with kisses.

Henriet Cousin seized the girl under the shoulders. When she felt his touch she uttered a cry and fainted. The hangman, whose tears were falling on her, made an effort to pick her up in his arms. He tried to pull away her mother, who had clasped her hands around her daughter's waist, but she clung so tightly to her child that it was impossible to separate them. He therefore dragged them both out of the cell together. They both had their eyes closed.

The sun had just risen and there was already a rather large crowd of people in the square looking on from a distance. It was the provost's custom to prevent curious onlookers from standing too close during an execution.

The hangman stopped at the foot of the fateful ladder and, so overcome with pity that he was scarcely breathing, placed the rope around the girl's lovely neck. When she felt the horrible contact of the hemp she opened her eyes, looked up and saw the fleshless arm of the stone gibbet above her head. A tremor ran through her and she cried out in a piercing voice, "No! No! I don't want to die!"

The mother, whose face was buried in her daughter's clothes, said nothing but the hangman saw her tremble in every limb. He took advantage of the opportunity to pull her away from the girl. Whether from exhaustion or despair, she did not resist. He threw the girl over his shoulder and put his foot on the bottom rung of the ladder.

Then the mother, crouching on the pavement, opened her eyes wide. Without a sound, she stood up, glaring terribly, rushed at the hangman like a wild animal and sank her teeth into his hand. He screamed in pain. Soldiers came running up, pulled her away with great difficulty and pushed her back violently. She fell and her head struck the pavement. They picked her up. She was dead.

The hangman, who had not let go of the girl, began to climb up the ladder.

CHAPTER TWO

La Creatura Bella Bianca Vestita

WHEN QUASIMODO SAW THAT THE CELL WAS EMPTY, THAT the gypsy girl was no longer there, that while he had been defending her she had been carried off, he grasped his hair with both hands and stamped with surprise and grief. Then he began to run all over the church, looking for her, uttering strange cries and strewing his red hair over the floor. When the king's soldiers victoriously entered Notre Dame, also looking for the gypsy girl, poor Quasimodo, deaf as he was, helped them in their search, ignorant of their sinister intentions; he thought the vagabonds were her enemies. He himself led Tristan l'Hermite to every possible hiding place in the church, opening for him all the secret doors, the false backs of the altars and the inner sacristies. If the unfortunate girl had still been there, he would have unwittingly delivered her to her executioners. When Tristan finally became discouraged (and he was not easily discouraged), Quasimodo continued the search alone.

When he was thoroughly convinced that she was no longer in the church, he walked slowly up the stairs of the tower, those same stairs which he had mounted so swiftly and triumphantly the day he saved her life. This time he went up them with bowed head, in a daze. The church was once again deserted and silent. The soldiers had left it to track down the witch in the city. Quasimodo, left alone in the vast cathedral, which had been so tumultuously besieged a short time before, headed for the cell in which the gypsy girl had slept for so many weeks under his protection. Perhaps he still believed he might find her there. When he reached the little room, nestled under a huge buttress like a bird's nest under a branch, his heart failed him and he leaned against a pillar to keep from

falling. He pretended she had come back; he told himself
that the little room was too quiet, too safe and too charming
for her not to be there. He dared not take another step,
for fear of shattering his illusion. "Yes," he thought, "she
may be asleep or perhaps she's praying. I won't disturb her."

At length he summoned up his courage, tiptoed up to the
door and looked in. Empty! He walked slowly around the cell,
lifted up the bed and looked under it, as if she might be
hiding between the floor and the mattress, then shook his
head and stood still for several minutes. Suddenly he furiously
stamped out his torch, dashed his head against the wall with
all his might and fell to the floor unconscious.

When he came back to his senses, he threw himself on
the bed and frenziedly kissed the place where she had slept.
He lay there for several minutes in deathlike immobility;
then he stood up, streaming with perspiration, panting and
wild-eyed, and began to strike his head against the walls with
frightful regularity, as though he were determined to break it.
He finally fell to the floor again, exhausted. He crawled out
of the cell and crouched in front of the door. He remained
there for more than an hour without stirring, gloomier and
more thoughtful than a mother sitting between an empty
cradle and a full coffin. From time to time his whole body was
shaken by a violent sob but a sob without tears, like those
distant flashes of summer lightning which bring no rain.

Then, seeking in the depths of his melancholy reflections
to discover who might have been her unexpected abductor,
he thought of the archdeacon. He remembered that he alone
had a key to the staircase leading to her cell; he remembered
the nocturnal attempts against her, the first of which he,
Quasimodo, had assisted, the second of which he had fore-
stalled. He recalled a thousand details and soon he no longer
had any doubt that it was the archdeacon who had taken her
away from him. His respect for Dom Claude was so great, however, his gratitude, devotion and love for him had such deep
roots in his heart that they withstood even the claws of
jealousy and despair. The bloodthirsty hatred which he would
have felt for any other man was only turned into increased
sorrow.

Just then, as dawn was beginning to whiten the flying
buttresses, he saw a figure walking along an upper gallery of
the cathedral. It was the archdeacon. He was walking slowly
toward the northern tower but his face was turned aside,
toward the right bank of the Seine, and he held his head

high, as though he were trying to see something over the rooftops. He passed above Quasimodo without seeing him.

Quasimodo stood up and started after him. He did not know what he would do or say when he caught up with him. He was filled with both fury and fear. His heart was torn between the archdeacon and the gypsy girl.

When he reached the top of the tower he carefully looked around to see where the archdeacon was before stepping out of the darkness of the staircase and onto the platform. Dom Claude had his back to him. He was leaning against a balustrade, looking down into the city. Quasimodo walked stealthily up behind him to see what he was looking at. The archdeacon's attention was so completely absorbed that he did not hear Quasimodo's approach.

Down in the square, several housewives, milk pots in hand, were pointing in amazement at the shattered condition of the great door of the cathedral and at the two streams of lead hardened in the cracks between the stones. This was all that remained of the tumult of the night before. The fire which Quasimodo had started between the towers had gone out. Tristan had already cleaned up the square and had the corpses thrown into the river. Kings like Louis XI are careful to have the pavement washed immediately after a massacre.

Just below the point of the balustrade at which the archdeacon was standing there was one of those fantastically carved waterspouts with which Gothic buildings bristle and in a crack in that waterspout two pretty wallflowers were bowing animatedly to each other as they were shaken by the morning breeze. The chirping and twittering of birds could be heard high in the sky above the towers.

But the archdeacon neither heard nor saw any of this. He was one of those men for whom there are no mornings, no birds and no flowers. In that vast horizon which wore so many aspects around him, his gaze was concentrated on a single point.

Quasimodo burned with impatience to ask him what he had done with the gypsy girl. But the archdeacon was obviously passing through one of those violent moments of life in which one would not feel the earth crumbling beneath one's feet. He stood motionless and silent, staring straight ahead, and there was something so formidable about his silence and immobility that the savage hunchback shuddered before them and dared not disturb them.

He followed the archdeacon's line of vision until he was

looking at the Place de Grève, where he saw what was absorbing Dom Claude's attention. A ladder had been set up against the permanent gibbet. There were several onlookers and many soldiers standing around it. A man was dragging across the pavement something white to which something black was attached. He stopped at the foot of the gibbet.

Then Quasimodo could not see what happened; not that his eye had lost its keen-sightedness, but because a cluster of soldiers partly cut off his view. Also the sun appeared just then and such a brilliant flood of light overflowed the horizon that all the points of Paris—spires, chimneys and gables— seemed to catch fire at the same time.

Meanwhile the man began to climb up the ladder. Quasimodo could now see him distinctly. He was carrying a woman over his shoulder, a young girl dressed in white with a rope around her neck. Quasimodo recognized her. It was she.

The man reached the top of the ladder. There he arranged the rope. The archdeacon knelt on top of the balustrade in order to see better.

Suddenly the man kicked the ladder away and Quasimodo, who had stopped breathing several moments before, saw the poor girl swing at the end of the rope with the man crouching on her shoulders. The rope twisted around several times and Quasimodo saw her body writhe in horrible convulsions.

At this moment of supreme horror, a fiendish laugh—a laugh which could come only from a man who is no longer a man—burst from the archdeacon's livid lips. Quasimodo did not hear the laugh but he saw it. He furiously rushed at the archdeacon and pushed him off the balustrade.

The waterspout above which he had been leaning stopped his fall and he clung to it desperately. He was about to cry out for help when he saw Quasimodo's vengeful face appear over the side of the balustrade above him. He remained silent.

The abyss was beneath him—a fall of more than two hundred feet, then the pavement. In this terrible situation he did not say a word, did not utter a groan. Hanging from the waterspout, he made incredible efforts to climb up to it but his hands had no hold on the granite and his feet slipped along the blackened wall without finding the slightest support. Those who have climbed to the top of Notre Dame know that the towers bulge immediately below the balustrade. It was against this retreating slope that the wretched archdeacon exhausted himself. He was not struggling against even a vertical wall but against one which receded from him.

Quasimodo could have saved him by merely reaching down his hand to him but he did not even look at him. He was looking at the Place de Grève, at the gibbet, at the gypsy girl. Leaning against the balustrade at the same spot where the archdeacon had been a moment before, he did not take his eyes off what was for him the only object in the world. He stood completely mute and motionless, except that a long stream of tears flowed from that eye which until then had shed only one.

Meanwhile the archdeacon was panting, his bald forehead was streaming with perspiration, blood oozed from beneath his fingernails and the skin of his knees was rubbed off against the wall. He heard his cassock, which had caught on the waterspout, rip and come apart at the seams with every movement he made. To crown his misfortune, the waterspout ended in a lead pipe which was gradually bending under the weight of his body. He realized that when his cassock tore in half, when his hands yielded to fatigue and when the lead pipe bent double, he would fall. Terror gripped him. From time to time he looked down at a narrow ledge about ten feet below him and begged God from the depths of his soul to allow him to finish his life on that space of two square feet, even if it should last for a hundred more years. Once he looked down at the square below him; when he raised his head his eyes were closed and his hair was standing on end.

The silence of the two men was frightful. While the archdeacon writhed in horrible agony a few feet away from him, Quasimodo continued to weep and stare at the Place de Grève.

The archdeacon, seeing that all his struggles only served to loosen the fragile support that was left to him, decided to remain motionless. He hung there, clutching the waterspout, scarcely breathing and making no movement except that convulsion of the belly which one experiences in dreams when one feels oneself falling. His eyes wore a sickly, astonished expression. Gradually, however, he began to lose hold: his fingers slipped along the waterspout, he felt his arms growing weaker and his body heavier and the lead pipe supporting him continued to turn slowly downward. Beneath his feet he saw the roof of Saint-Jean-le-Rond as small as a card bent in two. He glanced over the impassive carved figures of the tower, suspended, like himself, over the abyss but without fear for themselves or pity for him. Everything around him was of stone: the gaping monsters before his eyes, the pavement below him and, above his head, the weeping Quasi-modo.

Down in the square several groups of people were looking up and calmly wondering what kind of madman could be amusing himself in such a strange manner. Their voices reached the archdeacon faintly but clearly: "He'll break his neck up there if he's not careful!"

Quasimodo continued to weep.

Foaming with rage and terror, the archdeacon finally realized that all was useless, yet he mustered all his remaining strength for one last effort. He stiffened his muscles, pushed against the wall with his knees, hooked his hands into a crack between the stones and succeeded in raising himself about a foot. But his struggles caused the lead pipe to bend down suddenly and at the same time his cassock ripped in half. Then, feeling everything giving way and having nothing but his stiffened, weakened hands with which to support himself, he closed his eyes, let go of the waterspout and fell.

Quasimodo watched him fall.

A fall from such a height is seldom perpendicular. At first the archdeacon fell head downward with his hands stretched out in front of him, then he turned over several times. The wind carried him against the roof of a house. His body was terribly smashed but he was not yet dead. Quasimodo saw him clutching at the gable with his fingernails but the slope was too steep and he had no more strength left. He slid rapidly down the roof like a loose tile and rebounded on the pavement. There he lay still.

Quasimodo raised his eye to the gypsy girl dangling at the end of the rope. He saw her body quivering beneath her white dress in the last convulsive agonies of death. Then he looked down at the archdeacon, who was now only a shapeless mass lying at the foot of the tower. A sob burst from the depths of his chest and he cried out, "Oh! Everything I loved!"

CHAPTER THREE

The Marriage of Phoebus

TOWARD EVENING, WHEN THE JUDICIAL OFFICERS OF THE bishopric came to remove the mangled corpse of the archdeacon from the pavement of the square, Quasimodo had disappeared from Notre Dame.

There was much talk of the incident. No one had any doubt that the day had finally come when, according to their pact, Quasimodo—the devil—was to carry off Claude Frollo —the sorcerer. It was assumed that he had broken the body in taking the soul, as a monkey breaks the shell in order to get the nut. For this reason the archdeacon was not buried in consecrated ground.

Louis XI died the following year, in August, 1483.

As for Pierre Gringoire, he managed to save the goat and later achieved a certain degree of success as a writer of tragedies. It appears that, after having taken up astrology, philosophy, architecture, alchemy and every other sort of folly, he finally returned to tragedy, the greatest folly of them all. This was what he called "coming to a tragic end." Concerning his dramatic triumphs, we may read the following in the Ordinary's Accounts for the year 1488: "To Jehan Marchand and Pierre Gringoire, carpenter and playwright, the sum of one hundred livres for staging and composing the mystery play performed at the Châtelet for the entry of the legate, directing the cast, properly costuming them for their parts and constructing the necessary scaffolding."

Phoebus de Châteaupers also came to a tragic end: he was married.

CHAPTER FOUR

The Marriage of Quasimodo

WE HAVE JUST STATED THAT QUASIMODO DISAPPEARED FROM Notre Dame the day the archdeacon and La Esmeralda died. He was never seen again and no one ever knew what became of him.

The night following La Esmeralda's execution the hangman and his assistants took her body down from the gibbet and carried it, as was customary, to the vault at Montfaucon.

Sauval tells us that Montfaucon was the "oldest and most superb gibbet in the kingdom." Located several hundred feet outside the walls of Paris on a hill which made it visible for miles around, it was a strangely shaped edifice which looked something like a Celtic cromlech and which, like the cromlechs, was also the scene of human sacrifices.

Imagine a great oblong mass of masonry fifteen feet high, thirty feet wide and forty feet long, with a door, an outside ramp and a platform; on this platform, sixteen enormous pillars of rough-hewn stone, thirty feet high, spaced out at regular intervals around three of the four sides of the rectangular mass supporting them, with their tops connected by strong beams from which chains are hanging; skeletons at the ends of these chains; in the surrounding plain, a stone cross and two smaller gibbets, springing up like shoots from the great central stalk; in the sky above all this, a perpetual flight of carrion crows. This was Montfaucon.

By the end of the fifteenth century the formidable gibbet, which had been built in 1328, was already quite dilapidated. The beams were rotten, the chains were rusted, the pillars were green with moss, there were wide cracks between the stones and grass grew on that platform which no foot ever touched. Its outline against the sky was horrifying, especially at night when the moon shone on the white skulls or when the evening breeze shook the chains and the skeletons and made them rattle in the darkness. The presence of this gibbet gave a sinister character to the whole surrounding territory.

The mass of masonry which served as the base of the odious edifice was hollow. Its interior, closed off by a battered iron grating, was an enormous vault into which were thrown not only the human remains which were taken from the chains of Montfaucon, but also the bodies of all those executed at the other permanent gibbets of Paris. In that deep charnel-house, in which so many bodies and so many crimes moldered together, many of the great of the world—and many of the innocent also—came to lay down their bones.

As for Quasimodo's mysterious disappearance, here is all we have been able to discover: A year and a half or so after the events which terminate this story, when a party of men entered the vault of Montfaucon to take out the body of Olivier le Daim, who had been hanged two days before and to whom Charles VIII had granted the favor of being buried at Saint-Laurent in better company, among all the hideous remains they found two skeletons, one embracing the other. One of them, the skeleton of a woman, still had a few scraps of a dress which had once been white and around its neck hung a little silken bag, decorated with green beads, which was open and empty; it was apparently of so little value that the hangman had not thought it worth while to take it. The second skeleton, which held the first one tightly in its arms, was that of a man. They noticed that it had a twisted spine, a head sunk down between its shoulders and one leg shorter than the other. There was no rupture of the vertebrae at the neck, so it was clear that the man had not been hanged. He had apparently come there and died. When they tried to pull his skeleton away from the one he held in his arms it crumbled into dust.

• A BANTAM CLASSIC • A BANTAM CLASSIC • A BANTA

Bantam Classics bring you the world's greatest literature—books that have stood the test of time—at specially low prices. These beautifully designed books will be proud additions to your bookshelf. You'll want all these time-tested classics for your own reading pleasure.

☐	21137	**PERSUASION** Jane Austen	$2.95
☐	21051	**DAVID COPPERFIELD** Charles Dickens	$2.50
☐	21148	**DRACULA** Bram Stoker	$1.95
☐	21044	**FRANKENSTEIN** Mary Shelley	$1.50
☐	21171	**ANNA KARENINA** Leo Tolstoy	$2.95
☐	21035	**THE DEATH OF IVAN ILYICH** Leo Tolstoy	$1.95
☐	21163	**THE BROTHERS KARAMAZOV** Fyodor Dostoevsky	$2.95
☐	21175	**CRIME AND PUNISHMENT** Fyodor Dostoevsky	$2.50
☐	21136	**THE IDIOT** Fyodor Dostoevsky	$3.50
☐	21166	**CANDIDE** Voltaire	$2.25
☐	21130	**THE COUNT OF MONTE CRISTO** Alexandre Dumas	$2.95
☐	21118	**CYRANO DE BERGERAC** Edmond Rostand	$1.75
☐	21048	**SILAS MARNER** George Eliot	$1.75
☐	21089	**FATHERS AND SONS** Ivan Turgenev	$1.95
☐	21032	**THE HUNCHBACK OF NOTRE DAME** Victor Hugo	$1.95
☐	21101	**MADAME BOVARY** Gustave Flaubert	$2.50
☐	21059	**THE TURN OF THE SCREW AND OTHER SHORT FICTION** Henry James	$1.95

These books have been bestsellers for generations of readers. Bantam Classics now bring you the world's greatest literature in specially low-priced editions. From the American epic Moby Dick to Dostoevsky's towering works, you'll want all these time-tested classics for your own.

☐	21128	THE ADVENTURES OF TOM SAWYER	$1.75
☐	21079	THE ADVENTURES OF HUCKLEBERRY FINN	$1.75
☐	21091	A CONNECTICUT YANKEE IN KING ARTHUR'S COURT	$1.75
☐	21081	LIFE ON THE MISSISSIPPI	$1.75
☐	21150	PRINCE AND THE PAUPER	$1.95
☐	21158	PUDD'NHEAD WILSON	$1.95
☐	21005	THE CALL OF THE WILD/WHITE FANG Jack London	$1.75
☐	21103	THE LAST OF THE MOHICANS James Fenimore Cooper	$2.50
☐	21007	MOBY DICK Herman Melville	$1.95
☐	21011	RED BADGE OF COURAGE Stephen Crane	$1.50
☐	21009	SCARLETT LETTER Nathaniel Hawthorne	$1.50
☐	21119	UNCLE TOM'S CABIN Harriet Beecher Stowe	$2.75
☐	21139	WALDEN AND OTHER WRITINGS Thoreau	$1.95
☐	21094	BILLY BUDD Herman Melville	$1.95
☐	21087	DR. JEKYLL and MR. HYDE Robert Louis Stevenson	$1.95
☐	21099	TREASURE ISLAND Robert Louis Stevenson	$1.75
☐	21067	KIDNAPPED Robert Louis Stevenson	$1.50

Prices and availability subject to change without notice.

Bantam Classics bring you the world's greatest literature—books that have stood the test of time—at specially low prices. These beautifully designed books will be proud additions to your bookshelf. You'll want all these time-tested classics for your own reading pleasure.

Titles by Charles Dickens

☐	21123	**THE PICKWICK PAPERS** Charles Dickens	$4.95
☐	21108	**BLEAK HOUSE** Charles Dickens	$3.95
☐	21086	**NICHOLAS NICKLEBY** Charles Dickens	$4.50
☐	21051	**DAVID COPPERFIELD** Charles Dickens	$2.50
☐	21113	**GREAT EXPECTATIONS** Charles Dickens	$2.50
☐	21106	**A TALE OF TWO CITIES** Charles Dickens	$1.95
☐	21016	**HARD TIMES** Charles Dickens	$1.95

Titles by Thomas Hardy:

☐	21152	**JUDE THE OBSCURE**	$2.75
☐	21024	**THE MAYOR OF CASTERBRIDGE**	$1.95
☐	21080	**THE RETURN OF THE NATIVE**	$1.95
☐	21168	**TESS OF THE D'URBERVILLES**	$2.95
☐	21131	**FAR FROM THE MADDENING CROWD**	$2.75

☐	21059	**THE TURN OF THE SCREW AND OTHER SHORT FICTION** Henry James	$1.95
☐	21021	**WUTHERING HEIGHTS** Emily Bronte	$1.75
☐	21149	**LADY CHATTERLY'S LOVER** D. H. Lawrence	$2.75
☐	21159	**EMMA** Jane Austen	$1.95

Prices and availability subject to change without notice.

Buy them at your local bookstore or use this handy coupon for ordering:

These books have been bestsellers for generations of readers. Bantam Classics now bring you the world's greatest literature in specially low-priced editions. From the American epic Moby Dick to Dostoevsky's towering works, you'll want all these time-tested classics for your own.

☐	21138	**THE HOUSE OF MIRTH** Edward Wharton	$2.25
☐	21133	**THE DIVINE COMEDY: PURGATORIO** Dante (trans. by Allen Mandelbaum)	$2.50
☐	21041	**THE AENEID** Virgil (trans. by Allen Mandelbaum)	$2.95
☐	21005	**THE CALL OF THE WILD** and **WHITE FANG** Jack London	$1.75
☐	21166	**CANDIDE** Voltaire	$2.25
☐	21082	**THE CANTERBURY TALES** Geoffrey Chaucer	$2.95
☐	21130	**THE COUNT OF MONTE CRISTO** Alexander Dumas	$2.95
☐	21175	**CRIME AND PUNISHMENT** Fyodor Dostoevsky	$2.50
☐	21134	**THE SECRET AGENT** Joseph Conrad	$2.95
☐	21088	**HEART OF DARKNESS & THE SECRET SHARER** Joseph Conrad	$1.75
☐	21007	**MOBY DICK** Herman Melville	$1.95
☐	21021	**WUTHERING HEIGHTS** Emily Bronte	$1.75
☐	21117	**KIM** Rudyard Kipling	$2.25
☐	21115	**LITTLE WOMEN** Louisa May Alcott	$2.95
☐	21077	**CAPTAINS COURAGEOUS** Rudyard Kipling	$1.50
☐	21067	**KIDNAPPED** Robert Louis Stevenson	$1.50
☐	21079	**THE ADVENTURES OF HUCKLEBERRY FINN** Mark Twain	$1.75

Prices and availability subject to change without notice.

Buy them at your local bookstore or use this handy coupon for ordering:

Bantam Books, Inc., Dept. CL4, 414 East Golf Road, Des Plaines, III. 60016

Please send me the books I have checked above. I am enclosing $_____ (please add $1.25 to cover postage and handling). Send check or money order —no cash or C.O.D.'s please.

Mr/Mrs/Miss _____

Address_____

City_____ State/Zip_____

CL4—7/84

Please allow four to six weeks for delivery. This offer expires 1/85.